Full Surrogacy Now

Full Surrogacy Now

Feminism Against Family

Sophie Lewis

VERSO
London • New York

First published by Verso 2019
© Sophie Lewis 2019

1 3 5 7 9 10 8 6 4 2

Verso
UK: 6 Meard Street, London W1F 0EG
US: 20 Jay Street, Suite 1010, Brooklyn, NY 11201
versobooks.com

Verso is the imprint of New Left Books

ISBN-13: 978-1-78663-729-1
ISBN-13: 978-1-78663-732-1 (UK EBK)
ISBN-13: 978-1-78663-731-4 (US EBK)

British Library Cataloguing in Publication Data
A catalogue record for this book is available from the British Library

Library of Congress Cataloging-in-Publication Data
A catalog record for this book is available from the Library of Congress

Typeset in Sabon by MJ & N Gavan, Truro, Cornwall
Printed in the UK by CPI Group (UK) Ltd, Croydon, CR0 4YY

Contents

Acknowledgments

This book owes its existence to Rosie Warren. The other most obvious people to thank are Judy Thorne, whose years-long excitement about what I've been trying to pursue here was contagious; the brilliant editrix and comrade Madeline Lane-McKinley; Alyssa Battistoni, my longtime partner-in-Harawavianism; Michelle O'Brien, most passionate of readers; and Victoria Osterweil, my soul. In addition to these six women, the effort was made possible by the interest and encouragement of many—a collection of past and present friends who either read the whole thing and provided crucial comments, or simply at some point said something that happened to inspire self-belief—Natasha Lennard, Ryan Ruby, Tom Houseman, Johanna Isaacson, Sarah Leonard, Richard Woodall, Mathura Umachandran, Paul Jackson, Yuan Yang, Anna Sidwell, Hannah Schling, Nick Evans, Sophie Williams, Molly Huzzell, Kate Hardy, Dave Bell, Kyle Stone, Jonny Bunning, Gwyneth Lonergan, Het Phillips, Hannah Berry, Petra Davis, Marie Thompson, Simon DuCon, Giles Lane, Max Fox, P. E. Moskowitz, Indiana Seresin, Jonathan Kopp, Sarah Brovillette, Merve Emre, Wilson Sherwin, Billy La Cava, Nelle Ward, Zach Howe, David Haub, Jenny Turner, Joanna Biggs, Patrick Harrison, Joy Kristin Kalu, Elise Thorburn, Matt McMullen, Elizabeth Johnson, Joshua Clover and Anne Boyer. I am equally indebted, of course, to everyone who—without ever talking about surrogacy—handed me biscuits, cleaned for me, fed me, shared their scotch, bought me a pint, or picked up the pieces: you know who you are. Thank you to everyone who, in addition to Rosie, worked on this book at Verso—Duncan Ranslem, Ida Audeh, Lyn Rosen, Emily Janakiram and Maya Osbourne. Thanks are due to my PhD supervisors Erik Swyngedouw and Noel Castree at the University of Manchester, who were kind and patient, arguing with me about reproduction and surplus value, and played their part as midwives of *Cyborg Labour* (the predecessor to this book) really admirably. And, lastly, I'll state that I was blessed with the time of gracious and solidaritous scholars Sharmila Rudrappa, Michal Nahman, Charis Thompson, Cindi Katz, Kalindi Vora, Pamela Fuentes, Reecia Orzeck, Claudia Garriga Lopez, Becky Mansfield, Kathi Weeks, and Donna Haraway. Insofar as the name on the cover of this book refers to me alone, (as though I were) a singular entity, it does not keep faith with the argument of the pages that follow.

1

Introduction

It is a wonder we let fetuses inside us. Unlike almost all other animals, hundreds of thousands of humans die because of their pregnancies every year, making a mockery of UN millennium goals to stop the carnage. In the United States, almost 1,000 people die while doing childbirth each year and another 65,000 "nearly die." This situation is social, not simply "natural." Things are like this for political and economic reasons: we *made* them this way.

Pregnancy undoubtedly has its pleasures; natality is unique. That is why, even as others suffer deeply from their coerced participation in pregnancy, many people excluded from the experience for whatever reason—be they cis, trans, or nonbinary—feel deeply bereft. But even so, and even in full recognition of the sense of the sublime that people experience in gestating, it is remarkable that there isn't more consistent support for research into alleviating the *problem* of pregnancy.

The everyday "miracle" that transpires in pregnancy, the production of that number more than one and less than two, receives more idealizing lip-service than it does respect. Certainly, the creation of new proto-personhood in the uterus is a marvel artists have engaged for millennia (and psychoanalytic philosophers for almost a century). Most of us need no reminding that we are, each of us, the blinking, thinking, pulsating products of gestational work and its equally laborious aftermaths. Yet in 2017 a reader and thinker as compendious as Maggie Nelson can still state, semi-incredulously but with a strong case behind her, that philosophical writing about actually doing gestation constitutes an absence in culture.

What particularly fascinates me about the subject is pregnancy's morbidity, the little-discussed ways that, biophysically speaking, gestating is an unconscionably destructive business. The basic mechanics, according to evolutionary biologist Suzanne Sadedin, have evolved in our species in a manner that can only be described as a ghastly fluke. Scientists have discovered—by experimentally putting placental cells in mouse carcasses—that the active cells of pregnancy "rampage" (unless aggressively contained) through every tissue they touch. Kathy Acker was not citing these studies when she remarked that having cancer was like having a baby, but she was unconsciously channelling its findings. The same goes for Elena Ferrante's protagonist in *The Days of Abandonment*, who reports:

> I was like a lump of food that my children chewed without stopping; a cud made of a living material that continually amalgamated and softened its living substance to allow two greedy bloodsuckers to nourish themselves.[1]

The genes that are active in embryonic development are also implicated in cancer. And that is not the only reason why pregnancy among *Homo sapiens*—in Sadedin's account—perpetrates a kind of biological "bloodbath." It is the specific, functionally rare type of placenta we have to work with—the hemochorial placenta—which determines that the entity Chikako Takeshita calls "the motherfetus" tears itself apart inside.[2] Rather than simply interfacing with the gestator's biology through a limited filter, or contenting itself with freely proffered secretions, this placenta "digests" its way into its host's arteries, securing full access to most tissues. Mammals whose placentae *don't* "breach the walls of the womb" in this way can simply abort or reabsorb unwanted fetuses at any stage of pregnancy, Sadedin notes. For them, "life goes on almost as normal during pregnancy."[3] Conversely, a human *cannot* rip away a placenta in the event of a change of heart—or, say, a sudden drought or outbreak of war—without risk of lethal hemorrhage. Our embryo hugely enlarges and paralyzes the wider arterial system supplying it, while at the same time elevating (hormonally) the blood pressure and sugar supply. A 2018 study found that post-natal PTSD affects at least three to four percent of birth-givers in the UK (the US percentage is likely to be far higher—especially among black women).[4]

No wonder philosophers have asked whether gestators are

persons.[5] It seems impossible that a society would let such grisly things happen on a regular basis to entities endowed with legal standing. Given the biology of hemochorial placentation, the fact that so many of us endowed with "viable" wombs are walking around in a state of physical implantability—no Pill, no IUD—ought by rights to be regarded as the most extraordinary thing. To be sure, it has been relatively straightforward in many parts of the world to stop gestating *at the very beginning of the process*, simply because an unremarkable—even unnoticed—miscarriage occurred, or because the gestator has had access (through a knowledgeable friend) to abortifacients. In 2008, Aliza Shvarts self-inseminated with fresh sperm and then "self-aborted," over and over again, every month for nine months, by swallowing pills, as a kind of art project.[6] I'm curious what that perverse start–stop labor experiment was like. Shvarts's true, nondefensive thoughts on the matter are unfortunately obliterated by a wall of right-wing bellowing. Unsurprisingly, given that one would expect to feel good upon being extricated from a nonstop job one isn't willing to do, in general the experience of termination generates feelings of relief and cared-for-ness. As Erica Millar evidences in *Happy Abortions*, sustained negative emotions are extremely rare in connection with having an abortion.[7]

Gestational Fix

Pregnancy has long been substantially techno-fixed already, when it comes to those whose lives really "matter." Under capitalism and imperialism, safer (or, at least, medically supported) gestation has typically been the privilege of the upper classes. And the high-end care historically afforded to the rich when they gestate their own young has lately been supplemented by a "technology" that absorbs 100 percent of the damage from the consumer's point of view: the human labor of a "gestational surrogate." Surrogacy, as news media still report, began booming globally in 2011. Around 2016, the industry began suffering a series of setbacks: Thailand and Nepal banned surrogacy altogether for the foreseeable future, and other major hubs (India, Cambodia, and Mexico) legislated against all but "altruistic" heterosexual surrogacy arrangements. Nevertheless, there are still privately registered, profit-making "infertility clinics" on every continent, listing surrogates for hire who will remain, so they say, genetically entirely unrelated to the babies that customers carry away at the end of the process. For, just as the cannier commentators predicted, surrogacy bans do not halt but actually fuel the baby trade, rendering gestational workers far more vulnerable than before.[8]

Surrogacy bans uproot, isolate, and criminalize gestational workers, driving them underground and often into foreign lands, where they risk prosecution alongside their bosses and brokers, far away from their support networks. In July 2018, thirty-three pregnant Cambodians were detained and charged in Phnom Penh, together with their Chinese boss, for "human trafficking offences."[9] Separately, one Mumbai-based infertility specialist began recruiting surrogate workers from Kenya immediately after India's Supreme Court decision against commercial and homosexual surrogacy. Through in vitro fertilization, he implants the Kenyans with embryos belonging to his gay clients. Pregnant, these contractors are flown back to Nairobi after 24 weeks' monitoring in India. The babies are birthed in designated hospitals in Nairobi, where clients can pick them up. The doctor maintains that he has not broken Indian law, because he has not interacted with gay clients within that territory: all he has provided, technically, is IVF for Kenyan "health care" seekers. In other words, clinicians simply jump through legal loopholes by moving surrogate mothers across borders, exposing surrogate mothers to greater risks while expanding and diversifying their business partnerships worldwide.[10]

The trend toward commercial surrogacy does not constitute a qualitative transformation in the mode of biological reproduction that currently destroys (as those aforementioned mortality statistics show) so many adults' lives. In fact, capitalist biotech does nothing at all to solve the problem of pregnancy per se, because that is not the problem it is addressing. It is responding exclusively to demand for genetic parenthood, to which it applies the logic of outsourcing. While the development remains uneven and tentative, it is clear that what capitalism is proposing by alienating and globalizing gestational surrogacy in this way is, as usual, an option involving moving the problem around. Pregnancy work is not so much disappearing or getting easier as crashing through various regulatory barriers onto an open market. Let the poor do the dirty work, wherever they are cheapest (or most convenient) to enroll.

And no wonder, given that the ground for such a development was already being laid as early as the late nineteenth century, when large swathes of the colonial, upper-class, frequently women-led eugenics movement in Europe and North America argued that the best way to realize pregnancy's promise—namely, a thriving future "race" achieved through sexual "virtue" and white-supremacist "hygiene"—was for the state to economically discipline all sexual activity unconducive to that horizon.[11] As good social democrats, these "feminist" progressives wanted a nation-state that was duty-bound to feed, shelter, clothe, educate, and train the gestational laborers present within its territory, and (especially) the products of that gestational labor.[12] Since this was then, and remains now, a costly sounding proposition, a set of enduring ideas and policies were propagated around the turn of the century, according to which, as far as metropolitan proletarians were concerned, having babies spells financial irresponsibility and surefire ruin in and of itself—especially out of wedlock. The same discouragement applied, more or less, to non-white (Italian, Irish, Arab) immigrants on the eastern American seaboard. Lumpenproletarian populations in "the colonies" (notably India) faced more hands-on methods, including (famously) sterilization. Meanwhile, curiously, for families of the capitalist class, having babies represents a virtuous and vital investment guaranteeing their—and the very economy's—good fortunes.

"That there is even a relationship between material well-being and childbearing is a twentieth-century, middle-class, and to some extent white belief,"[13] historian Laura Briggs insists. Nevertheless, it's been but a series of logical steps from that hegemonic notion of reproductive meritocracy to the beginnings of the pregnancy "gig economy" we can glimpse today. In unprecedentedly literal ways, people make babies for others in exchange for the money required to underwrite *morally*, as well as materially, their own otherwise barely justifiable baby-having. It's not quite accurate, though, to say that the basic ideas of early eugenicist reproductive policy have resurfaced in late capitalism—or even to say that they've survived. Rather, as W. E. B. Du Bois lays out in *Black Reconstruction in America, 1860–1880*—or Dorothy Roberts in *Killing the Black Body: Race, Reproduction, and the Meaning of Liberty*—these interlocking logics of property and sub-humanity, privatization and punishment, form the template that organized capitalism in the first place and sustains it as a system.[14] Dominant liberal-democratic discourses that hype a world of postracial values and bootstrap universality only serve to render dispossessed populations the more responsible for their trespass of being alive and having kids while black. Stratification is self-reproducing and not designed to be resolved.

It is still useful to call out contemporary iterations of eugenic common sense for their face-value incoherence; still legitimate to point out (the hypocrisy!) that even as urban working-class and black motherhood continues to come under attack, the barriers to black and working-class women's access to contraception and abortion grow steadily more formidable. The positive "choice" to "freely invest" in having a baby is one that numerous laws are literally forcing many people to make, with dire and frequently fatal results. Obstetric care in India remains to this day among the most scant in the whole world—even though India exports and offers obstetric medical care to customers around the world—and the Indian clinic-factory is this book's chosen reference point for this reason. Such contradictions, we know, are part and parcel of capitalist geopolitical economy, which needs populations to extinguish in the process of making others thrive. It's not just *life* that is a sexually transmitted disease, as the old joke has it. Birth justice campaigners know, as indeed AIDS activists knew in the 1980s and 1990s, that it is death that sex spreads, simultaneously, in the context of for-profit health care.

However, this depressing state of affairs hasn't ever been the whole story. From Soviet mass holiday camps for pregnant comrades, to Germany's inventive (albeit doomed) "twilight sleep" methods—designed to completely erase the memory of labor pain—human history contains a plethora of ambitious ideologies and technological experiments for universally liberating and collectivizing childbirth. It's admittedly an ambivalent record. Irene Lusztig, director of a beautiful 2013 archival film on this subject, has understandably harsh words for the various early-twentieth-century rest-camps and schools of childbirth she discusses. But, she suggests, you have to hand it to them—even the most wrongheaded of textbooks written a century ago at least stated the problem to be solved in uncompromising terms: "Birth injuries are so common that Nature must intend for women to be used up in the process of reproduction, just as a salmon die after spawning."[15] *Well if that's what Nature intends,* the early utopian midwives and medical reformers featured in *The Motherhood Archives* responded: *then Nature is an ass.* Why accept *Nature* as natural?[16] If *this* is what childbirth is "naturally" like, they reasoned, looking about them in the maternity wards of Europe and America, then it quite obviously needs to be denatured, remade.[17] Easier said than done. Pioneering norms of fertility care based on something like cyborg self-determination have turned out to be a moving target. The exceptionality and care-worthiness of gestation remains something that has to be forcibly *naturalized*, spliced in against the grain of a "Nature" whose fundamental indifference to death, injury, and suffering does not, paradoxically, come naturally to most of us.

Moreover, many of these efforts to emancipate humanity from gestational "Nature" have claimed the name of "Nature" for *their* cause, too. For instance, the turn to so-called "natural childbirth"— which earned such fiery contempt from Shulamith Firestone in 1970 for being bourgeois—more accurately stands for a regimen full of carefully stylized gestational labor hacks and artifices, a suite of mental and physical conditioning that may be billed as "intuitive" but which nevertheless take time and skill to master. Natural childbirth has never gone entirely out of fashion and is still extremely popular among diverse social classes.[18] And while particular subdoctrines of natural childbirth continue to come under well-justified fire wherever they stray into mystification, the broader free-birthing movement's foundational critique of just-in-time capitalist obstetrics and its colonial-patriarchal history—whereby midwives, witches, and their indigenous knowledges were expelled from the gestational workplace—is hard to fault.[19]

Likewise, I have absolutely no quarrel with the trans-inclusive autonomist midwives and radical doulas, the ones lobbying for their work to become a guaranteed form of free health care.[20] I have no quarrel with "full-spectrum" birth-work that supports people of all genders through abortion, miscarriage, fertility treatments, labor, and postpartum, often operating outside of biomedical establishments, spreading bottom-up mutual aid, disseminating methods geared toward achieving minimally (that is, sufficiently) medicated, maximally pleasurable reproduction.[21] Quite the contrary: power to them. With their carefully refined systems of education, training, and traditional lay science, they are, in their own way, creating a nature worth fighting for.[22] It can hardly be an accident that, as anyone who spends time in midwifery networks will realize, so many of them are anti-authoritarian communists.[23]

Few people consciously want babies to be commodities. Yet baby commodities are a definite part of what gestational labor produces today. Given the variety of organizing principles that can apply to the baby assembly line, it is ahistorical (at best) to claim that what we produce when we're pregnant is simply life, new life, love, or "synthetic value": the value of human knitted-togetherness.[24] Such claims are unsatisfying, in the first instance, because they fail to account for gestators who do not bond with what's inside them. And they can't fully grasp altruistic surrogacy, where the goal is explicitly to *not* generate a bond between gestator and baby in the course of the labor (even if some surrogates do attach and sometimes propose a less exclusive, open adoption–style parenting model after they've given birth). The related, philosophically widespread, claim that social bonds are grounded biologically in pregnancy—what some call the "nine-month head-start"[25] to a relationship—is ultimately incomplete. The better question is surely: a head-start to what? What type of social bonds are grounded by which approach to pregnancy?

Clearly, if I am gestating a fetus, I may feel that I am in relationship with that (fetal) part of my body. That "relationship" may even ground the sociality that emerges around me and the infant if and when it is born, assuming that we continue to cohabit. But I may also conceptualize the work in a completely different way—grounding an alternate social world. I may never so much as *see* (or wish to see) my living product; am I not still grounding a bond with the world through that birth? For that matter, people around me may fantasize that they are in a relationship with the interior of my bump, and they will even be "right" insofar as the leaky contamination and synchronization of bodies, hormonally and epigenetically, takes place in many (as yet insufficiently understood) ways. We simply cannot generalize about "the social" without knowing the specifics of the labor itself. And, regardless of the "ground" the gestational relationship provides, the fabric of the *social* is something we ultimately weave by taking up where gestation left off, encountering one another as the strangers we always are, adopting one another skin-to-skin, forming loving and abusive attachments, and striving at comradeship. To say otherwise is to naturalize and thus, ironically, to *devalue* that ideological shibboleth "the mother-fetus bond." What if we reimagined pregnancy, and not just its prescribed aftermath, as work under capitalism—that is, as something to be struggled in and against toward a utopian horizon free of work and free of value?

Despite the sense of an absence in culture, of course, I am far from the first to engage with surrogacy and pregnancy in the framework of gestational labor. One key predecessor is Mary O'Brien, a Scottish midwife, philosopher, Marxist-Hegelian feminist, and extraordinarily gifted rhetorician, who took up the subject of pregnancy in the frame of "gestational labor" in 1981. Unfortunately, like many of those who have taken gestational work seriously, she never (as far as I know) addressed the questions of miscarriage and abortion at all. This is more than an innocent lacuna in this field of theory, because ignoring withdrawals, mutations, and failures of gestational labor cannot but undermine the central thesis that gestating advances history and creates synthetic value (O'Brien's term), since it makes that thesis unfalsifiable. Perhaps this is partly why the book in which O'Brien pioneers the account in question, *The Politics of Reproduction,* runs into all kinds of other pitfalls.

Trans-exclusionary, romantically gynocentric, race-insensitive, it is apparently unacquainted with historic forms of coerced surrogacy *or* traditions of polymaternalism and consequently does not manage to theorize a place in history for those materially marked as "women" who can't or don't gestate.

The peculiar effect of *The Politics of Reproduction* is to enshrine, in excitingly revolutionary language, a depressingly conventional sense of biology as destiny. In short, there are many good reasons to redo O'Brien's inquiry into the political and productive labor of gestation.

Pregnancy and the Handmaid Dystopia

Armed policing of productive wombs; inseminations carried out through state-sanctioned ritual rape; newborns systematically expropriated by the gentry: the most widely known "pregnancy dystopia" of our times is Margaret Atwood's novel *The Handmaid's Tale*.[26] In Gilead, Atwood's fictional setting, human sexuation is neatly dimorphic and cisgendered—but that is apparently not what's meant to be dystopian about it. It's the "surrogacy." With its vision of forced surrogacy, the *Tale* is many people's favorite sci-fi account of a totalitarian American regime, and by far the most popular analogy for the Trump regime among academics and op-eds alike. This is unsurprising: *The Handmaid's Tale* neatly reproduces a wishful scenario at least as old as feminism itself. Cisgender womanhood, united without regard to class, race, or colonialism, can blame all its woes on evil religious fundamentalists with guns.

A reminder of the basics: drastic infertility has struck. A cult has staged a coup, and its paramilitaries are controlling, as chattel, the few fertile people remaining (who are, by definition, women), since the new government has taken the view that babymaking must be intensively husbanded. These Handmaids, formerly American citizens, are being brutally indoctrinated, disciplined, and forced into private gestational service for the property-owning couples of the new society. Downplaying, however, the class dynamics of fascism, Atwood's narrative centers on what is often framed as "universal" agony: the separation of a mother from her daughter, on the one hand, and a human being's coerced use as a breeder, on the other. Two excellent demands could actually readily be extrapolated from this, namely, the first two axioms of the Reproductive Justice movement's credo: the right not to be pregnant and the right to parent one's children in a safe environment. It is regrettable that the progressive fans of *The Handmaid's Tale* have on the whole been inspired to shout mostly about the former while omitting to campaign around the latter.

Yet it is also understandable, since affluent white contemporary feminists like me are none too often made aware of the racist-misogynist formation Asha Nadkarni calls "eugenic feminism,"[27] which is our legacy. As cleansers and uplifters of the modern human race, many pioneers of female suffrage throughout the nineteenth century cultivated a productive maternity among white elites on both sides of the Atlantic while simultaneously suppressing an imaginary hyperfecundity (that is, excess production of babies) among subaltern classes, which they perceived as threatening. Eugenic feminism's heart beats still in campaigns of the kind endorsed by Barbara Bush, targeting "overpopulation" through uncontroversial social policy goods like "education for women" (because, it is implied, it is the poor women's kids who are the problem, and which could only be the result of a lack of education). Unabashed Euro-American neofascists might be the only ones willing to frame the declining "domestic" birth rate in rich nations in terms of "white genocide" explicitly, but close cousins of their xenophobic anxieties pop up often in mainstream discussions of the sacrifices (of liberalism) that might have to be made in order to curtail the crowding of earth.

Supposedly nonracist, universalist concerns about quality of life slip, easily, into competitive latter-day-imperial worries about being overtaken, overrun. Somehow, with the exception of a few self-important millenarians fond of trumpeting their intention to voluntarily go extinct, the phenomenon of the "objectively" crowded earth (not good for *any* of us!) is always imagined "out there." And it is this anxious fantasy that is literalized in Atwood's sterility apocalypse. Just as birth rates really are plummeting among citizens in many parts of the Global North—areas prone to complaining about the very "migrant crisis" that is saving them from demographic decline—the biological "necessity" that is supposed to justify "sacrifices" in Gilead is the flip-side of the coin of overcrowding. Other nations may be succeeding at reproducing themselves, but a catastrophic fertility crisis has struck *at home*. The fictional world of Gilead provides a space in which modern-day xenophobic and eugenic feminisms can covertly indulge the logic of a First World national natalist imperative. Meanwhile, the novel's memoiristic conceit conveniently serves to distance its author from what Rebekah Sheldon has called its "wolfish premise that all survival comes coupled to harm,"[28] and justifies the limiting of Atwood's ecological vision to one nation-state.

Atwood's cautionary version of America remains populated by men of different ranks but, above all, it distinguishes itself through subdivision of its subjugated sex-class into castes: not only Handmaids (indentured surrogate gestators) but Marthas (cooks and cleaners to the gentry), Jezebels (illicit sexual services), Unwomen (deportees doing hard labor in the colonies), and "Econowives." The latter lowly class of multitaskers, and thus the question of class as a whole, were disappeared from the 2017 series, along with all trace of white supremacy. This decision did not escape the notice of critics who had long recognized, even in Atwood's original premise, a de-raced slave narrative. Borrowing the historical experience of forced surrogacy from the American plantation, Atwood had, they said, clearly adapted its emotiveness for the purposes of a color-blind—white—feminism.[29] At least the original novel had referred to Gilead's eugenic purging of the tacitly African "Children of Ham," thereby demonstrating some recognition of the racial character of reproductive stratification as elaborated through the Middle Passage. In 2017, Hulu series director Bruce Miller took blithe erasure of black women's historic connection with surrogacy to the next level. Announcing that he had "simplified" the story, Miller presented an image of a society with no race, class, or history: a society in which "fertility trumps all."[30] His interpretation of Gilead, he said, is "diverse" and "postracist"; there, the value of this thing "fertility" is somehow completely abstract. Remarkably, he and his cast went on to publicly disavow even the word "feminist."

Nevertheless, the alarum "We are living in *The Handmaid's Tale*" became the refrain of an infinite number of "women against Trump" tweets and opinion pieces on the state of reproductive health care and institutional sexism. The mere existence of (commercial) gestational surrogates anywhere on earth was referenced in these breathless announcements as "proof" that Atwood's "prediction" had "come true." Eventually, a striking revelation did provide a portion of plausible grist to this mill, in the form of far-right Republican US Congressman Trent Franks. A former oilman, religious zealot, millionaire, and founder of the hard-line anti-abortion Arizona Family Research Institute, Franks resigned from office in December 2017, admitting that he had tried to pressure "two previous female subordinates" into bearing a baby for him. Unrelatedly, Mr. Franks and his wife had previously commissioned a self-advertising gestational carrier for twins via in vitro fertilization and embryo transfer (the average going rate for this being, in America, about $50,000). The proposition before the "subordinates" in his office, on the other hand, clearly involved achieving conception through sexual intercourse with Trent Franks, with a view to eventually handing the baby over in exchange for $5 million.[31] As one legal commentator translated: "that isn't really a surrogacy arrangement. It's more like an affair, where the man expects the mistress to give up rights to the child conceived from the situation."[32]

Even so, we are not yet living in *The Handmaid's Tale*. People's eagerness to assert that we are betokens nothing so much as wishful thinking. What do I mean by this? That, inasmuch as it promises that a "universal" (trans-erasive) feminist solidarity would automatically flourish in the worst of all possible worlds, the dystopia functions as a kind of utopia: a vision of the vast majority of women *finally* seeing the light and counting themselves as feminists because society has started systematically treating them all—not just black women—like chattel. My point is not that religious fundamentalisms don't do real violence. They do, although I'm not sure this is unequivocally conveyed in the serialization, which takes lots of stylized pleasure in its chastity cos-play; its drawn-out torture scenes; the erotics of master/slave relationships; the mournful visual delight of wimples, veils, and cloaks assembling in rows and circles, commuting to and from their own ritual rapes in twos or single file. My point is that the pleasures of an extremist misogyny *defined as womb-farming* risk concealing from us what are simply slower and less photogenic forms of violence, such as race, class, and binary gender itself. Again, religious stalwarts *are* implicated in producing and reproducing these ills—but so are liberals and atheists, much though they prefer not to be reminded of it.

In 2017, Hillary Clinton–supporting Atwood fans' reveries about indignant exodus north from Trump's America complemented their other tendency: to point the finger of blame for social misery always away from themselves, at a sinister (male, Republican) other within. It is unsurprising, too, that the deluge of attention Atwood's novel has garnered since 1985 overlaps (broadly speaking) with a resurgence of right-wing governance in the United States and of the corresponding meme among US progressives: "Let's move to Canada." What with its tacit positioning of Canada as the progressive sanctuary to which refugees from Gilead can flee, Anglo-American liberalism discovered in the Great Canadian Feminist Novel about America the perfect no-place in which it can play out its own (anti-totalitarian and anti-patriarchal but not anti-racist or anti-imperial or pro-trans) version of women's struggle.[33] In the mood created by *The Handmaid's Tale*, fans can instrumentalize commercial gestational surrogates fleetingly as mascots for reproductive rights and quintessential victims of patriarchy, without ever feeling the need to engage a critique of capital. Politics would be much less challenging for liberal feminists—much easier for all of us, I dare say—if we *were* living in *The Handmaid's Tale*.

Surely, though, the fact that a personal encounter with this particular text has been the moment of feminist coming-to-consciousness for thousands of people is not to be sniffed at. Indeed it should not, but nor should one overrate the political participation the book directly inspires. This is not to discount the inevitable role of people's desires, and erotic drives, within revolutionary action, but rather to suggest that the desires activated by the *Tale* are perhaps more libertarian than they are liberatory, more morally reproachful than political, more conservative than communist.

The hundreds of enthusiastically "crafted" Handmaid caps, capes, pins, necklaces, T-shirts, candles, and totes listed on the Etsy marketplace were not, I realize, prerequisite purchases for attendance at various events protesting Donald Trump's inauguration in feminism's name. They did, however, perhaps suggest something a little discouraging about the boutique crafts-shopping demographic organizers had in mind. Oblivious to such potential objections, *The Boston Globe* proclaimed a "new look for women's rights protests" when, following International Women's Day and the attendant Women's March in Washington, DC, activists dressed in the bloodred robes and blinkered white bonnets of Gilead's breeder caste to disrupt the anti-abortion proceedings of the Texas Senate. If the protesters were suggesting—by their attire—something like "We are all reproductive slaves," they weren't clear who they were speaking as (or about). Most of them did not call out, as Reproductive Justice protests tend to do, the heavily racialized character of prosecutions for illegal abortion; the routine incarceration, deportation, and detention of the pregnant; or hospital-bed shackling during labor.[34] Clearly the aim the protesters had in mind was in itself perfectly laudable: they were out scuppering attempts by legislators to reduce access to abortion, a vital form of care relevant to most of the population. However, by distancing themselves from Reproductive Justice precedents for this kind of protest and from a corresponding working-class consciousness, they substantially limited their power. Since the same can be said of the literary story they were referencing, these shortcomings are arguably inevitable.

The reproductive dispensation we face under capitalism is fortunately and unfortunately far more mundane than that of *The Handmaid's Tale*. And, thankfully, other pregnancy dystopias possess greater explanatory power for our times and greater relevance for a nongynocentric, transfeminist left seeking to parse the meaning of surrogacy. Octavia Butler's "Bloodchild," for instance, overflows with potent, volatile, and ambivalent political implications.[35] This short story in Butler's much broader oeuvre on xenogenesis (the production of difference) vividly captures the perversity and alienness of gestational labor, particularly as it is husbanded within a horrifyingly violent and hierarchical social system governed ever so softly and intimately—through consent.

Yet the conflation of real-world gestation work with forced and coerced impregnations in fiction comes from an unreflexive horror at the idea of gestational surrogacy.[36] It is a horror that greets, perhaps understandably, its commercial "neoliberal" form more than any other; abhorring above all else the scenario in which marginalized, often racialized proletarians (who aren't encouraged to reproduce themselves) are encouraged by the market to behave as self-managing contractors of their own bodily organs in the perpetuation of rich people's existence, the realization of their dreams. Despite or perhaps because of the wage incentives in play, this horror is sufficient to justify its comparison with a situation of literal human ownership.

But is gestational surrogacy *intrinsically* the apogee of alienation, a violation that can only ever be arranged in different—feudal, neoliberal, settler-colonial—flavors? I argue in this book that we must resist this kind of reasoning and unlearn gestation-exceptionalism in our thinking about labor militancy. If entering into a situation of pregnancy-as-work were in and of itself tantamount to entering a state of slavery, where would this leave the immense amount of thinking over the past century that has positioned "social reproduction" as work—work that is often alienated and waged, but market disciplined rather than enslaved? "Our uterus is the wheel," Wages for Housework said, "that keeps capitalism moving."[37] Or, if the specific idea that *making babies for others* is slavery, then the former garment workers in Bangalore who wanted to start their own gestational surrogacy co-operative[38] have to be accounted for somehow or else excluded from the analysis. We've already seen how, in order to paint the neat picture of surrogacy-as-dystopia that First World feminists so often seem to want to paint, actually existing gestational workers have to be ignored almost by definition.

That includes inhabitants of the "internal colonies," for commercial surrogacy is by no means the only "antithesis of motherhood."

Historically, motherhood in the United States was elaborated as an institution of married white womanhood. Thus, black enslaved women could make no claim of kinship or property to the fruits of their gestational labors. Indeed, they were not even publicly recognized as women, let alone mothers or Americans. Other eugenic and patriarchal laws dispossessed unwed proletarians of babies they made as well. Then, and now, surrogacy consists above all of human gestational labor pure and simple, a fact that tends to disappear from view in the various dystopian nightmares-cum-fantasies about humans and breeding, which emphasize either an elaborate and terrifying form of technology, or a ritual of sexual domination (whether by centipede-alien, as in "Bloodchild," or at a zealot's gunpoint, as in *The Handmaid's Tale*). We urgently need such reminders, because in today's debates, and indeed whenever surrogacy appears in our newsfeeds, the same anxious assumption always rings out: we've entered a brave new world of degraded, artificial life. In actuality, as Angela Davis patiently explained two decades ago, this isn't really the case. Rather, new technologies have rendered the old news of the "fragmentation of maternity"—for good or (usually) for ill—"more obvious"³⁹; they have made new types of contract-for-hire possible.

The racial and class dynamics of US society continue to trouble the commonplace certainty (*mater semper certa est*) that gestation produces the status of motherhood for the gestator. But this also raises the question of whether it *should*: whether motherhood and pregnancy are viable cornerstones of a liveable world. When everybody is announcing calamity and dystopia, it is very important to notice that, with surrogacy as with so much else, *plus ça change, plus c'est la même chose*. But equally, and far more excitingly, there is this: the more things stay the same with surrogacy, the more people force them to change.

Terms of Engagement

What is commercial gestational surrogacy, in concrete terms? It is a means by which capitalism is harnessing pregnancy more effectively for private gain, using—yes—newly developed technical apparatuses, but also well-worn "technologies" of one-way emotional and fleshly service—well-beaten channels of unequal trade. Surrogacy is a logistics of manufacture and distribution where the commodity is biogenetic progeny, backed by "science" and legal contract. It's a booming, ever-shifting frontier whose yearly turnover per annum is unknown but certainly not negligible: "a $2bn industry"[40] was the standard estimate quoted in 2017. One freelance international broker alone, Rudy Rupak, who set up the medical tourism outfit PlanetHospital, described himself as "an uncle to about 750 kids around the globe" before he was convicted for fraud in 2014. It is safe to say that several thousand babies every year are seeing the light of day and immediately swapping hands in a fast-changing number of legislatures that may or may not (at the time of printing) include California, Ukraine, Russia, Israel, Guatemala, Iran, Mexico, Cambodia, Thailand, India, Laos, and Kenya.

Even outside of academia, with its publishing time constraints, scholars stand little chance of capturing changes in the landscape of commercial surrogacy as they happen. "With Cambodia closing its doors to surrogacy," supplies one blog tentatively, "Laos will possibly become the next destination for these reproductive services,"[41] at least for a few months, until Laotian legislators too crack down. In a breakthrough for the far-right Israeli homophobia lobby, it was announced that the enormous industry in Israel tailoring its surrogacy services specifically to gay men would now be shut down from summer 2018 on, sparking mass protests.[42] By contrast, one legislature poised to legalize compensated third-party gestation for clients of all sexual orientations in 2019 is the state of New York, which numbers among just four states in the United States to still ban *any* surrogacy arrangement more than three decades after "Baby M" became the focus of debate. The government of the United Kingdom, too, is now undertaking a three-year inquiry into its rules determining parentage, as a consequence of which "laws could be reformed to remove automatic rights" from the person who gestates or genetically donates toward a baby—that is, from the individuals one shrill article in *The Telegraph* pre-emptively calls "the parents" (specifically, "birth parents").[43]

The basics: a commercial gestational surrogate receives a fee, the disbursement of which (across the trimesters) varies by country. The surrogate's capacity to undertake a pregnancy is essentially leased to one or more infertile individuals, who subsequently own a stake in the means of production, namely, the surrogate's reproductive biology. This grounds a corresponding claim upon the hoped-for product, living progeny, which more often than not denotes genetic progeny, although donor gametes are also used. Assuming the pregnancy has gone smoothly, the surrogate is contractually bound to relinquish all parental claims soon after the delivery, which proceeds, in a disproportionate number of cases, by caesarean section.

Commercial or not, gestational surrogacy is the practice of arranging a pregnancy in order to construct and deliver a baby that is "someone else's." So then, if that is what this book is about, this is a book about an impossibility. An impossibility, how so? I mean something which all the best parents on earth (particularly "adoptive" ones) already know, namely, that bearing an infant "for someone else" is always a fantasy, a shaky construction, in that infants don't belong to anyone, ever. Obviously, infants *do* belong to the people who care for them in a sense, but they aren't property. Nor is the genetic code that goes into designing them as important as many people like to think; in fact, as some biologists provocatively summarize the matter: "DNA is not self-reproducing ... it makes nothing ... and organisms are not determined by it."[44] In other words, the substance of parents gets scrambled. Their source code doesn't "live on" in kids after they die any more than that of nonparents. Haraway extrapolates from this that "there is never any reproduction of the individual" in our species, since "neither parent is continued in the child, who is a randomly reassembled genetic package," and, thus, for us, "literal reproduction is a contradiction in terms."[45] There is only degenerative and regenerative co-production. Labor (such as gestational labor) and nature (including genome, epigenome, microbiome, and so on) can only alchemize the world together by transforming one another. We are all, at root, responsible, and especially for the stew that is epigenetics. We are the makers of one another. And we could learn collectively to act like it. It is *those* truths that I wish to call *real* surrogacy, *full* surrogacy.

Such a move is inspired by utopian traditions—those of various socialist biologists, queer and transfeminist scientists, antiracists, and communists—that have speculated about what babymaking beyond blood, private coupledom, and the gene fetish might one day be. These traditions remain utopian because surrogacy today can be everything from severely banal to disturbingly ghoulish. Nightmarish mishaps within the transnational choreography of surrogacy have repeatedly occurred, and although they were so far, in each case, eventually resolved, they have prompted lurid mass condemnation of a sector that creates babies only to consign them to the limbo of statelessness, the helplessness of orphanhood, the predations of traffickers, the acquisitiveness of other random child-starved couples, and other calamities. Amid significantly less fanfare, surrogates have died from postpartum complications.

That covers what's "ghoulish" in the picture. As far as "banal" goes, notwithstanding the myriad news stories about sensational individual cases, the unconventional gestational provenance of many newborn babies who have been collected from fertility clinics (from "host" uteruses) passes overwhelmingly under the radar. Being a "surrobaby" goes unremarked upon on birth certificates and is frequently not disclosed in the children's social milieus. There is a gap, an aporia, between the familiarity of millions of primetime television viewers with surrogacy, where surrogacy is an extravagant possibility happening "out there" to other people, and the fact that "surro-babies" pass among us in their thousands, invisibly. The everyday flow of surrogacy among populations remains unknown to many, since it barely troubles the surface of the spectacle that is the conventional nuclear family.

At the same time, there are countless books in existence on the topic, the vast majority of which are bioethical in focus, which is to say they set out to question surrogacy by discussing the saleability either of wombs or of "life itself" from a moral and humanitarian standpoint. Others present thoughtful and granular studies of the sales already taking place by focusing variously on things like the role of religious faith in surrogacy[46]; its patterns of racial stratification and (thwarted) migration[47]; the role of shared metaphors in establishing motherhood[48]; the specificity of these in LGBTQ kinmaking ontologies[49]; the neocolonial aspects of the industry (a "transnational reproductive caste system"[50]); discourse norms on online surrogacy forums[51]; prehistories of "pro-natal technologies in an anti-natal state"[52] (i.e., the significance of sterilization policy previously endured by groups now recruited to gestate for others); and other localized features of the market, such as the boom among US "military wives" who make use of their high-end medical insurance packages to gestate, as boutique freelancers, while their husbands are away on deployments.[53]

What is the point of *this* book? *Full Surrogacy Now* is not a book primarily derived from case studies. Nor, as you've seen, does it argue that there is something somehow desirable about the "surrogacy" situation such as it is. It presents brief histories of reproductive justice, anti-surrogacy, and saleswomanship at one particular clinic—but its main distinction, or so I hope, is that it is theoretically immoderate, utopian, and partisan regarding the people who work in today's surrogacy dormitories. The aim is to use bourgeois reproduction today (stratified, commodified, cis-normative, neocolonial) to squint toward a horizon of gestational communism. Throughout, I assume that the power to get to something approaching such a horizon belongs primarily to those who are currently workers—workers who probably dream about not being workers—specifically, those making and unmaking babies.

Although I do not call for a reduction[54] in baby-making, this book seeks to land a blow against bourgeois society's voracious appetite for private, legitimate babies ("at least, *healthy white* [ones]," as Barbara Katz Rothman specifies, presumably using the word "healthy," here, with irony—to signify absence of disability).[55] The regime of quasi-compulsory "motherhood," while vindicating itself in reference to an undifferentiated passing-on of "life itself," is heavily implicated in the structures that stratify human beings in terms of their biopolitical value in present societies. If, as Laura Mamo finds in her survey of pregnancies in the queer community in the age of technoscience, the new dictum is "If you can achieve pregnancy, you must procreate,"[56] it is a dictum that, like so many "universal" things, disciplines everybody but really only applies to a few (the ruling class). And, while the questions of LGBTQ and migrant struggle are sometimes separated from class conflict, any understanding of this system of "economic" reproductive stratification will be incomplete without an account of the cissexist, anti-queer, and xenophobic logics that police deviations from the image of a legitimate family united in one "healthy" household.[57] Drug users, abortion seekers, sexually active single women, black mothers, femmes who defend themselves against men, sex workers, and undocumented migrants are the most frequently incarcerated violators of this parenting norm. They have not been shielded by the fact that the Family today is now no longer necessarily heterosexual, with states increasingly making concessions to the "homonormative" household through policy on gay marriage.[58]

Full Surrogacy Now is animated by hatred for capitalism's incentivization of propertarian, dyadic modes of doing family and its purposive starvation of queerer, more comradely modes.[59] Patriarchy clearly has much to do with that. But some readers will probably have noticed by now that the terms "women" and "female" appear only infrequently in this text. The reason for that is simple: I feel there's no call for them. The formulation "pregnant people" is just as good as the alternative "pregnant women, men, and non-binary people," and it is more precise than "expectant mothers" or "pregnant women." Precision is important, I firmly believe, because there can be no utopian thought on reproduction that does not involve uncoupling gestation from the gender binary. Besides, trans people have always been part of gestational and nongestational reproduction, not to mention reproductive justice struggle. Standing fast on this is a political duty, not least because trans people are once again coming under attack. In 2017, when anti-trans feminists in the United Kingdom produced a leaflet to protest Gender Recognition legislation, they used—as their avatar of a "biological woman" whose welfare the mere existence of trans women supposedly puts at risk—a naked human figure in chains with a heavily pregnant belly.[60]

The "EMERGENCY" the leafleteers were flagging was not even, as with *The Handmaid's Tale* role-players, a threat to abortion services in Britain or even Ireland. Rather, the activists were mobilizing around the threat of category implosion supposedly posed by the UK government's consultation on how to make the Gender Recognition Act better for trans people. They were consciousness-raising about the ontological threat posed by figures like the woman with a penis—and the pregnant man—to "womanhood" as a sex-class. Their message? That pregnancy's identification with womanhood needs to be upheld in language at all costs. Rather than adapt their materialism to the diverse reality of existing women, they prefer to deny and expel those who do not fit. At the time of writing, well over forty years have passed since the lesbian radical Gayle Rubin published "The Traffic in Women," in which she argued that the prevalent system of biological kinship is in itself a "sex/gender system"; that (patriarchal) understandings of pregnancy *produce* women rather than vice versa.[61] Further: a constantly growing body of work in the natural sciences is gradually debunking the dyadic model of human sexuation on which cultural notions of maleness and femaleness and, by extension, manhood and womanhood have been built.[62] Nevertheless, sadly, it seems that definition is one many people will go to their graves defending.

Some otherwise trans-affirming (and infinitely more reasonable) scholars have expressed the worry that dispensing with the term "woman" in the context of reproduction might "constitute a form of erasure that is *also* incompatible with the principles of reproductive justice."[63] I am unpersuaded by this concern. It is not that I do not understand the momentous history of the mass repression and murder of the witches and midwives, the dispossession of their knowledge, as a class history.[64] Quite the reverse: I know it is *for them*, and thanks to them, that I—and other feminist cyborgs—pursue the cause of gender abolition. As far as this book goes, I am curious to see if the not-yet-thinkable movement that is gender abolition can be advanced through the application of a kind of methodological pig-headedness in precisely those conceptual areas—procreation being top of the list—that are most overdetermined with gendered meaning. That, at any rate, is the hunch informing my experimental stance, which can be paraphrased as follows: gestation is work and, as such, has no inherent or immoveable gender.

To date, the gender of gestating has been ambiguous. I am not talking about pregnancy's deepening of one's voice, its carpeting of one's legs in bristly hair, or even about the ancient Greek belief that it was the direct analogue of men's duty to die in battle if called upon. I am not even thinking of the heterogeneous gender identity of those who gestate. Rather, in a context where political economists are talking constantly of "the feminization of labor," it seems to me that the economic gendering of the work itself is not as clear-cut as it would appear. The feminization-of-labor thesis, which presumes what "femininity" is and then describes global trends toward emotional labor and job precarity—sorry, flexibility—in those terms, is not applicable here. The waged baby-making workplaces of the twenty-first century just don't fit well into that model. Commercial gestational surrogates are not "flexible." They are supposed to be unemotional, committed, pure *techne*, uncreative muscle. Dreams of artificial wombs may have been largely abandoned in the 1960s, but ever since the perfection of IVF techniques enabled a body to gestate entirely foreign material, living humans have become the sexless "technology" component of the euphemism Assisted Reproductive Technology.[65]

If feminists want to denaturalize the gender of reproductive work more generally, we have to stop (re-)imposing gender on gestation and gestators in particular. As physician and abortion provider Cheryl Chastine professes:

> We can't advocate that each pregnant person be able to effect the best decision for themselves while simultaneously insisting that people who aren't cisgender should go along silently with language in which they don't exist.[66]

While quoting Chastine approvingly, Loretta Ross and Rickie Solinger seem to be obliquely apologizing, in the preface to their recent book, for the fact that theirs is only an "inconsistent" and "ragged beginning" to the project of using trans-inclusive obstetric terminology.[67] Like Ross and Solinger, I want everyone to develop "acute attentiveness to the politics of language in this domain," but unlike them, I have felt no need to use the phrase "women and girls" at any point. It's important to make the effort because "while acknowledgment that not all women are mothers is fairly commonplace, the fact that not all pregnant or potentially pregnant persons are mothers or women has yet to transform our language and conceptual frames substantively."[68] Whereas Erica Millar asks doubtfully, for instance, "Is it possible or desirable to envisage gender neutral subjects of experiences, such as pregnancy, that are so firmly attached to gendered subjects?"[69] the truth is that the tides of history, and more specifically progressive health care providers, have long since overtaken her on that one. The answer is yes. Chastine reports: "Never once have I felt that any of my cisgender patients was harmed, confused, or distressed by my talking about 'pregnant people.'"[70] If *Happy Abortions* can so powerfully show that pregnant people "are not automatically mothers,"[71] cannot its author see that neither therefore are they automatically *women?*

While I'm at it, let me include here a remark on positionality. Like most feminized survivors of the capitalist higher education system, I am superficially acquainted with selling sex and have been solicited (without success) for egg "donation." I have never gestated nor worked as a surrogate. I understand that some—obviously not all—people who *have* gestated for money cite a genuine investment in making babies as part of their motivation. Enrollees talk, not only to their managers but anonymously and to each other, about acute empathy for involuntary childlessness, pleasure in some aspects of being pregnant, and enthusiasm about helping other adults into a situation where they are able to experience the intensity of neonatal nurture. In this sense, I am sympathetic to them and to the likely disappointment they will face, since "nothing so effectively stifles our lives as the transformation into work of the activities and relations that satisfy our desires."[72] I believe there's been too scant attention to the question of what that "stifling" feels like in the context of a job that never stops, dominates your mood, hijacks your blood vessels and sugar supply, while slowly exploding your anatomy from the inside out.

Admittedly, I could find out for myself. I possess what might or might not be a "viable" uterus. I could perhaps one day shed my inexperience on this front and report back. But since other less dangerous and more appealing forms of revenue are—at least for now—available to me, if I do, it will likely be because I've blithely decided to do "participatory" fieldwork (and the insights I'd garner in this manner would likely be highly circumscribed). I suspect there's no way of wholly mitigating the hubris involved in writing normatively in favor of a self-theorizing, self-emancipating surrogacy from my remote perch outside of surrogates' class standpoint. Instead I'll say this: I am trying to stand behind any proletarian's contrivance to accommodate herself as bearably and as profitably as possible to the discipline of work—just as I would expect a little acceptance in turn, of my accommodation to the transformation into work of the activities that satisfy my desire (in this case) to read, think, and write.

Gestational Commune

"Full surrogacy now," "another surrogacy is possible": to the extent that these interchangeable sentiments imply a revolutionary program (as I'd like them to) I'd propose it be animated by the following invitations. Let's bring about the conditions of possibility for open-source, fully collaborative gestation. Let's prefigure a way of manufacturing one another noncompetitively. Let's hold one another hospitably, explode notions of hereditary parentage, and multiply real, loving solidarities. Let us build a care commune based on comradeship, a world sustained by kith and kind more than by kin. Where pregnancy is concerned, let every pregnancy be for everyone. Let us overthrow, in short, the "family."[73]

It is admittedly quite hard to imagine the book by me that would do full justice to that remit. Happily, the ideas I've just glossed over aren't new or original and will continue to be refined and concretized for years and years after this. Writing is, of course, an archetypal example of distributed, omni-surrogated creative labor. While the name on the cover of this book is mine, the thoughts that gestated its unfinished contents, like the labors that gestated (all the way into adulthood) the thinkers of those ongoing thoughts, are many. Mario Biagioli puts it well in his essay comparing gestational surrogacy with intellectual plagiarism: "authorship can only be coauthorship."[74] This said, the fiction of individualized authorship (as it pertains to far more things than books and babies) has been naturalized around the world with depressing success. The impact of generations of cultural enforcement of sex/gender-normative, marriage-based models of procreation and heredity is hard to exaggerate. It is probably the case that everybody is marked to some extent, and that includes the vast numbers scarred by the racialized state gatekeeping of the reproductive resources required to participate. (Meanwhile, the most privileged among us don't see or even consciously know about this gatekeeping, even as they are pleased with its effects.)

Wanting a mode of gestation that itself contributes to family abolition makes my little book a clear descendant of disparate elements of the Second Wave, but a disloyal, monstrous, chimerical daughter indeed. (No wonder that the text I revere most is that errant, homeless one, the Cyborg Manifesto.[75]) There would obviously be no *Full Surrogacy Now* without *Xenogenesis, The Dialectic of Sex, The Second Sex, Of Woman Born, Woman on the Edge of Time,* "Bloodchild," and *The Politics of Reproduction.* The stars by which one navigates in that bright constellation are mostly well-known: Simone de Beauvoir and Octavia Butler see pregnancy as terrifying, colonizing, imprisoning; Mary O'Brien and Adrienne Rich, on the other hand, very much do not. In their different genres, Shulamith Firestone and Marge Piercy both articulate postcapitalist, postgender (and apparently postracial) futures in which procreation would mostly be accomplished outside of human bodies, in machines— incubators or "brooders"—and democratically planned.[76] Firestone, as part of her proposal that anti-capitalists immediately adopt a demand for free gestational automation for all who might want it, observes that those of us who have wombs "have no special reproductive *obligation* to the species."[77] While disagreeing neither with this nor with the infamous Firestonian point that it is "barbaric ... like shitting a pumpkin,"[78] Piercy's fictional narrator, Connie Ramos, expresses far more ambivalence about humanity's loss of gestational labor as an experience: "she [Connie] hated them, the bland bottle-born monsters of the future, born without pain ... without the stigmata of race and sex."[79]

Despite my debt, and despite that particular family of feminism's popular association with the biological, it still feels to me as though their assay into the question of gestational labor qua labor was rather limited. That most were "bad" on race is often said, but is no less true for all that, and it isn't a subsidiary gripe: it's surely a major part of why a sense does not emerge—still hasn't—of pregnancy as a contingent material process shaped by structural antagonisms. In particular, too few of the speculative ectogenesis texts grappled at all with the relationship between social reproduction and repro-duction of capital—the unequal distribution of technology, and the limits of (the desirability of) automation. My complaint here is not about priggishly demanding to know what the process is, exactly, for reaching the brooder-utopia of Mattapoisett, or the post-Oedipal world *The Di ᵗᵉ⁻ᵗᵒᵗ of Sex* describes, as destinations. (That said, I do think it is important to ask, for example, what the operations might be by which race and sex are technologically dissolved; or where the rare-earth minerals presumably required for the enormous full-time placenta-computers should come from.[80]) Rather, I'm talking about a sense I have that *The Dialectic of Sex*, and even *Woman on the Edge of Time* are insufficiently ambitious in their approach to the labor of gestation.

I'll wager that there is a babymaking to be aimed for that will be defined neither by the alienated misery of the status quo nor the silver absolutism of their techno-fix. Apart from anything else, it seems relevant to me that, despite the many good reasons I've already enumerated to liberate humanity from the *necessity* of gestating to reproduce the species, our desires for gestating—perverse creatures that we are—may well persist. "Full surrogacy now," as I see it, is an expression of solidarity with the evolving desires of gestational workers, *from the point of view of a struggle against work*. It names a struggle that, by redistributing the burden of that labor, dissolves the distinction between reproducers and nonreproducers, mothers and nonmothers, altogether. In the hope and belief of one day seeing the world that that struggle brings into being, this book asks, how does the contemporary phenomenon we call "surrogacy" contradict itself? How might these contradictions threaten broader projects of capital, opening up opportunities for new fights? Throughout, I endeavour to pit a critical-utopian gaze against the reality of commercial gestation. The other slogan for this method could be: Surrogacy against Surrogacy. Or even: *Surrogates* against Surrogacy™.

Unabashedly interested in family abolition, I want us to look to waged gestational assistance specifically insofar as it illuminates the possibility of its immanent destruction by something completely different. In other words, I'd like to see a surrogacy worthy of the name; a real surrogacy; surrogacy solidarity. *That is* the reason for flagging this one particular multisited project of capitalist reproduction; not the fact that it is intensive, or unique. I want others to help me read surrogacy against the grain and thereby begin to reclaim the productive web of queer care (real surrogacy) that Surrogacy™ is privately channelling, monetizing, and, basically, stealing from us.

I'll wager there is no technological "fix" for the violent predicament human gestators are in. Technologies for ex utero babymaking *might* be a good idea, and the same goes for more ambitious research and development in the field of abortion and contraception. But, fundamentally, the whole world deserves to reap the benefits of already available techniques currently monopolized by capitalism's elites. It is the political struggle for access and control—the commoning or communization of reprotech—that matters most. It is certainly going to be up to us (since technocrats wouldn't do it for us, or hand it over to us if they did) to orchestrate intensive scientific inquiry into ways to tweak bodily biology to better privilege, protect, support, and empower those with uteruses who find themselves put to work by a placenta.

Far from a cop-out, saying there is no miracle fix for gestation—except seizing the means of reproduction—should light a fire under our desires to abolish the (obstetric) present state of things. Beyond the centuries-long circular debate about whether our pregnancies are "natural" or "pathological," there is, I know, a gestational commune —and I want to live in it.

2

"But Aren't You Against It?"

In 1986, Mary Beth Whitehead was a lower-middle-class married white woman with three children, living in New Jersey. Having allowed her own ovum to be inseminated with a commissioning father's sperm the year before, Whitehead gestated a fetus to term in her womb that year and gave birth vaginally. Some days later, she changed her mind about having relinquished the baby (known as "Baby M" in the court proceedings thereafter) to the upper-middle-class couple who had contracted her to do so; but a succession of judges upheld the $10,000 surrogacy contract and denied her appeal. The case of Baby M immediately launched surrogacy into public infamy. In response to the drawn-out litigation and Supreme Court appeal that ensued, enormous crowds demonstrated up and down the east coast, and the Coalition Against Surrogacy was born. Four years later, that same coalition failed to mobilize at all for the sake of Anna Johnson. Johnson was an African American nurse and single mother from Santa Ana on food stamps who found herself in a situation similar to Mary Beth Whitehead's—even her payment was for the same amount—except for one thing. None of the genetic material used in Anna Johnson's IVF and embryo-transfer procedure was Anna Johnson's: half belonged to the Filipina-American commissioning mother and half to the white commissioning father.

The lack of interest in the latter case belonged not only to the east coast feminist campaigners but to the public more broadly. Johnson's trial was much shorter than Whitehead's, and the case itself—involving what some were calling a black "welfare queen"[1] and a nonblack baby—struck most people as much less tricky. The judge who decided against Johnson's custodial rights analogized her to a "home" and a "wet-nurse" and used a quite strikingly passive formulation in describing her role in the creation of the infant: "a baby boy was delivered from Anna Johnson on September 19, 1990."[2] Yet it was as though the activists who had agitated so vociferously about the classist logics deployed against Whitehead in severing her from Baby M, and who had championed Whitehead's right to be a mother, were suddenly content to concur with this assessment: that Johnson had neither a social (because no husband) nor a biological (because no genetic) stake in the child she had borne. It is for this reason that Johnson became the inspiration for the "Black Surrogate" in legal philosopher Anita Allen's landmark essay of the same name.[3] As Allen perceived, the adjudication of the case— *Calverts v. Johnson*—illustrated the cultural stratification built into US racial capitalism to date, whereby "Blacks are not supposed to have white children. Blacks are not supposed to want to have white children of their own."[4]

Both surrogates claimed parenting rights and were denied those rights, but Whitehead alone became the milestone and universal talking point. After all, delegitimizing Johnson's desire to parent, in the context of her racial heritage, her "broken" household, and her proletarian condition, was hardly necessary. Reframing the historic rise of surrogacy in the United States, Allen's essay puts the matter succinctly: "Before the American civil war, virtually all Black southern mothers were … surrogate mothers. Slave women knowingly gave birth to children with the understanding that those children would be owned by others."[5] One consequence of this is that the very logic of surrogation, which requires the presence of a preexisting maternity with social weight, does not map onto all bodies identically. In order to legitimate the expropriation of the baby Whitehead had borne, it proved necessary to diminish the ontological privileges and moral challenges carried by her whiteness. While Whitehead was painted by the commissioning parents' defense as "a high school dropout and former sex-worker,"[6] Johnson was already those things in the eyes of the law. So when one sets out to evaluate ethical opposition to surrogacy, or to assess the rationales behind anti-surrogacy feminisms, it is vital to ask: *which surrogacy* is even in question here? *Whose surrogacy* is visible as such?

~

From its origins in relative proximity between the parties in the 1980s—Anna Johnson shared a workplace with her commissioning mother; Mary Beth Whitehead lived a short drive away from hers— commercial surrogacy has become characterized by elaborate nonliability clauses, middlemen, and long distances. Enthusiastic appraisals of the industry do exist: Oprah Winfrey, for instance, literally beamed at a surrogacy clinician who came on the Oprah Show in 2006—Dr. Nayna Patel—summing up her view as follows: "Women helping women! I love it!"[7] Knowing even only a *little* more about the industry than Winfrey did when she passed that glowing judgment, however, one would have to be callous indeed to want to celebrate. Complaints against the industry have been widely and convincingly documented, and (crucially) these have been voiced by those employed in it.

Payment-related abuses—deception, wage stealing, and money skimming—are evidently rife in many locales.[8] Adequate medical care for postpartum surrogates (certainly in India, Romania, Mexico, and Guatemala) is horrifyingly absent. Lack of informed consent appears depressingly endemic outside of the United States: workplace ethnographies from Bucharest to Bangalore have found that "most surrogates do not understand what surrogacy really entails."[9] Often, multiple attempts are required to achieve implantation, while the long-term effects of the hefty hormone cocktails administered each time (in order to "synchronize" the surrogate's and egg-donor's bodies) are unknown. At the end of the process, parturition itself is typically taken entirely out of the worker's hands. The birth is premature (eight months is standard), nonconsultative, heavily sedated, rushed, invasive, long to recover from, and retroactively traumatic.

C-sections conform to the temporal logic of logistics: shaving five weeks or so off production time, delivering the baby just-in-time for collection. It is sometimes alleged that couples *prefer* caesareans because they deem their baby's contact with the surrogate's vaginal canal to be too intimate.[10] Meanwhile, the repercussions of this "choice" in *her* life are significant: she risks years of infection, pain, and scarring. What's more, she becomes "locked" into the method as an employee. Any vaginal births after a C-section are medically unsafe. Conveniently, then, if she re-enrolls successfully, a C-section it will have to be, once more. "Oh, you get the money," says Revati, Amulya Malladi's fictional character in the 2016 surrogacy novella *A House for Happy Mothers*, of this ever-deepening circuit of abdominal laceration.[11] But your body has paid the price.

Although such bet-hedging strategies are in many places explicitly illegal, consumers sometimes contract two different surrogates at different clinics simultaneously as a form of "security": should both embryo transfers prove successful, the procedure is then to abort one of them and put the other surrogate summarily out of a job. Alternatively, clinicians themselves may feel tempted to insert multiple embryos to better the odds of implantation and speed up production timelines for impatient clients. Consequently, embryonic quadruplets or quintuplets often implant, most of which then have to be (sometimes nonconsensually) killed—culled, "reduced"— in utero. Some surrogate gestators find this experience intensely traumatic.

Much to my chagrin, some surrogacy abolitionists will probably continue to mistake me for a "neoliberal" advocate of the industry[12] on the basis of the argument I've laid out against criminalizing it— perhaps imagining that I believe it somehow "queers" the family. And it is easy to see why my partial defense of the marketization of this previously relatively noncommercial realm of human activity could be misinterpreted as a defense of markets per se as a mediating principle of human relationships. In reality, what I believe is this: in order to become ethically acceptable by any noncapitalist standard, surrogacy will have to change beyond recognition. The path to freedom for humanity is a flight from market dependency, and one name for this path is "full surrogacy." It cannot simply be legislated for, by decreeing, for instance, that all trade in a particular sector must be cooperatively run. Unfortunately, in the absence of a broader revolutionary process of transformation of the economy, no number of worker-owned surrogacy cooperatives would be enough to break free from the matrix of human dependency on markets. Cooperatives would, however, secure for surrogates much better working conditions and rights and concretely improve people's lives.

They could also provide a place from which to leverage challenges to surrogacy capitalists while formulating political visions that link up with countless other struggles and thereby gesture—*beyond* cooperativization—toward the commune.

Were I a surrogate worker, my minimum immediate-term demands would probably include those suggested by Sharmila Rudrappa: that workers "have the right to choose how they get pregnant, the right to opt out of medical interventions, the right to refuse surgeries and the right to maintain contact with the babies they birthed."[13]

It's true: I am not thinking of children here. Like Madeline Lane-McKinley, author of "The Idea of Children," I take children's liberation very seriously.[14] But there is no evidence that a childhood spent out of proximity from the womb one originated from correlates with unhappiness. In fact, surrobabies are probably disproportionately among the luckier ones. Adult emotional suffering in the wake of relinquishment is not infrequently reported in surrogacy,[15] especially in the context of transnational commissioning parents reneging on pledges to stay in touch. Kathi Weeks has pointed out how clients are generally quick to "excise" their surrogate "from the family photos."[16] It's no wonder, really: the transaction is set up to be a naturalizing one, designed to be self-erasing at will—*your kids, 100% certified, your way*. Contracts encrypt the purchaser's mandate to "disappear" the unsightly prosthesis from the happy natal scene, as though she was never there. The effect on the surrogate of being treated as a temporary helpmeet rather than as kin, or as kith, is unpredictable. There *is* a real possibility—though it is a possibility, and not the certainty that anti-surrogacy activists make it out to be—that the job leaves her rocked by an interpersonal sense of betrayal, loss, violation, and abandonment.

Other more diffuse reasons explain why the majority of surrogates are likely to have a bad time. The hypermedicalization of pregnancy in the private medical sector is completely unlike anything proletarian women in the Global South are likely to have experienced before in the context of their prior, unpaid pregnancies. Workers are actively encouraged to infer from this that the surrogacy process itself really is somehow "medical," mystical, and beyond their nonexpert ken. It is quite normal for workers not to be aware, for example, that the sonograms performed for the peace of mind of the high-paying customers—or the injections of vitamins, say—have nothing *technically* to do with surrogate pregnancy. Clinicians have admitted to considering this ignorance convenient, both in terms of the compliance it encourages and because such outward signs of virtuous nonlitigiousness[17] can be explicitly marketed as perks of the local culture, a spiel in which ordinary patriarchy is euphemized as "tradition." *Our women*, doctors can proclaim, don't drink, don't smoke, don't have sex, don't do sports ... and they *really feel for* anybody, anywhere in the world, who can't have a child by natural means.

Patronizingly constructed as docile, hyperaccommodating paragons of responsible womanhood, it can hardly be surprising that surrogates describe getting wildly bored. Resentful of the stigma they face in their communities, on the one hand, and of the intense surveillance at their workplaces, on the other, they complain of melancholia, stir-craziness, and sorely missing their friends and offspring in between visits.[18]

Anti-surrogacy

All of this clearly demands redress, but it is not the major source of the hostility from the surrogacy-abolitionist onlookers. *Their* problem—as they make it known—is more abstract, more fundamental, than these aspects and harks back to the elisions noted in the preceding discussion of the Handmaid utopia, notably, the elision between exploitation and rape. Given the authoritarian and carceral state logics that are justified through that very elision, for example, when anti-traffickers rescue sex-trade "victims" from their jobs and communities but not from their poverty,[19] the surrogacy-critical among us must be almost as wary of the forces ranged against commercial surrogacy as we are wary of those profiting from it. Many of these anti-surrogacy forces evince surprisingly little interest in listening to surrogates who do not advocate for a legal ban on the industry, and they seem to pay but scant attention to the idea that surrogates may have something to say about their situations. World ecologist Daniela Danna, for example, suggests that a surrogate is a victim of "false consciousness" who has "enslaved herself ... with her own hands"[20] by creating a baby destined for separation from its "mother."

For many people—among them influential bioethicists, feminists, liberals, radicals, and conservatives—the line of inquiry, *How might surrogacy be redeemed?* sounds no different than a call to unionize a torture chamber or turn a nuclear war base into a cooperative. The well-networked lobbying campaign Stop Surrogacy Now, for instance, argues that "womb rental" inflicts a kind of degradation and alienation upon women and children that is *qualitatively unique.* Book-length arguments to this effect are regularly published; for instance, Renate Klein's self-explanatory book titled *Surrogacy: A Human Rights Violation* calls on its readers to join Stop Surrogacy Now without delay.[21] The campaign touts a list of demands diametrically opposed to those formulated in this book: a criminal ban; a halt to all discourses and "technological" interventions that "denaturalize" mother–baby bonds; an end to babies parting ways with their gestators no matter the circumstances; and an indefinite moratorium on framing gestational labor as work.

Even adoption is anathema, here, because the multiplication of parental figures in a baby's life is deemed a potential source of confusion. As such, anti-surrogacy militates against the separation of babies from bodies in the maternity ward *tout court*, taking the radical line that there is no determining whether meaningful consent thresholds for such separations are being met in any given instance. This same logic, which holds that no one but the biological "owner" of a child must have rights to it, has driven the campaign against "named person legislation" in Scotland (whereby "each child and young person is appointed a named person other than the Child's parents" to be accountable for their well-being).[22] Unsurprisingly, in this context, it has become common among anti-surrogacy activists to take a (tacitly or explicitly) anti-gay-parenting stance. In other words, in a context where much neoliberal discourse "positions commercial surrogacy as a means to gay male reproductive citizenship," as Charlotte Kroløkke and Michael Petersen contend, the anti-surrogacy lobby is, if nothing else, consistent, positioning itself as a rejection of even altruistic surrogacy, because "the child should not be disentangled from its gestational mother (a disentanglement that leads to the baby becoming 'a thing')."[23]

Petitions are in no danger of running out of signatories willing to characterize surrogacy transactions as baby-milling, baby-googling, baby-selling, baby-brokering, baby-farming, or indeed any combination of "baby" with a verb from the sphere of exchange. Like outcries about "test-tube babies" in the 1980s, such characterizations function precisely by not spelling out the meat of their denunciation, which is merely implied. I am sympathetic to the impulse, in that the advancing frontier of commodification elicits, in so many of us, a form of recoil that feels almost beyond words. I think I get it. We refuse the concept that the most precious things should be for sale, as though that will change the reality that—exploitatively, yet consensually—they are.

Still, I believe I have given the abolitionist anti-surrogacy case more than fair consideration. The most relevant data for anyone considering whether or not to acknowledge commercial gestation as a "free" industry—in the sense that proletarians are free under capitalism—do not bear that case out. The following facts are undeniable: the class profile of recruits tends to be assessed as relatively low-income but aspirationally middle-class; the pay on the whole tends to be evaluated as okay; and, at the end, whatever the outcome, an overwhelming majority of "alumna" sign up to do the whole thing again. One 2007–2014 study concluded: "surrogate mothers did not perceive themselves as victims, or as people brutalized in their employment in markets in life."[24] A low bar, but an important finding nonetheless when we are contemplating "saving" people from their work, as opposed to banding together with them, such that them (freeing themselves) becomes indistinguishable from us (freeing ourselves).

In the past decade, the press has given voice to a fresh wave of anti-surrogacy feminism. These articles have borrowed heavily from the 1980s feminist playbook, characterizing today's transnational commercial surrogacy as "dehumanizing," "womb trafficking," and "pimping." Julie Bindel wrote of the "misery and pain [for] women who will end up being viewed as nothing but a vessel," while Suzanne Moore referred to commercial surrogacy as "a repulsive trade ... a twisted version of slavery." These are tropes that were first deployed in 1984–1989, around the time of Baby M. The major actor then was the Feminist International Network of Resistance to Reproductive and Genetic Engineering (FINRRAGE), a loosely structured international women's network with branches, at its apogee, in thirty-seven countries across several continents, albeit always led and based in the United States, United Kingdom, and Australia. At FINRRAGE's inauguration, members declared: "We, women ... declare that the female body ... is being exploited and dissected as raw material for the technological production of human beings." The "new reproductive technologies," this manifesto insisted, represented "a declaration of war."[25]

One major FINRRAGE propaganda effort combines a list of the names and affiliations of "criminal" US doctors and brokers with a heavily stylized catalogue of sorrows intended to indict surrogacy as a self-evident "crime."[26] Written by Gena Corea, the essay, "Junk Liberty," is a kind of dirge created out of the names and stories of specific American surrogates whom Corea is positioning as survivors or martyrs: Alejandra Muñoz, Laurie Yates, Nancy Barrass, Mary Beth Whitehead, Patty Foster, and Elizabeth Kane. The tactic implies, but fails to demonstrate, that all these women support the criminalization of surrogacy and the FINRRAGE line. Certainly, the famous figurehead Elizabeth Kane did support a ban; her 1988 book *Birth Mother* inveighed against the pain of a life dashed by her experience of surrogacy's callousness.[27] But the desires and views of the first generation of former working-class surrogates in the United States are clearly not the determining factor for the pamphlet's political program. "Junk Liberty" is punctuated by its author's personal avowals of grief, mourning, and "white rage"[28] on behalf of its subjects. But it is ultimately unclear what evidence would *not* bolster Corea's conclusion, since "it is the 'happy surrogates,' the 'Stepford surrogates,' I worry about," as she says.[29] Explicitly, Corea repeats, "the cases which are alleged to be smooth and happy are the ones I worry about *most*."[30] Choice and desire are discredited in favor of the immutable and certain standard of women's dignity. "She"—the mythical happy surrogate—"hears herself described as ... an incubator, a kind of hatchery, a rented property" and "protests none of this."[31] Luckily, it is implied, FINRRAGE is close at hand to help her learn how to protest.

As signalled by the title of the decisive panel at the 1984 conference in Groningen where FINRRAGE was founded, the network's impetus and underlying anxiety was a fear of the so-called "Death of the Female." FINRRAGE's six creators and leaders—Corea, Robyn Rowland, Jalna Hanmer, Renate Klein, and Janice Raymond— perceived a world-historic takeover of the "female" sex's sole distinguishing power, the ability to bear children. They foresaw this coup, when it eventually transpired, as leading to women's social redundancy and "replacement" by mechanical methods for continuing the species. Their method for preventing this fate hinged on consciousness-raising, which they achieved in part by inserting terminological coinages into legal and policy circles in the hopes of their being more widely take up: for example, "women used in systems of surrogacy" (WUSS) as a replacement for the word "surrogates." Klein warned that, in the future, feminists would be fighting for "a woman's right to bear our own natural children"[32] ("own natural children" being a locution she had no interest in challenging).

There is sometimes nothing particularly more complex or edifying than disgust and paranoia driving the fundamentalist stance against surrogacy, but this can be difficult to spot since it is typically dressed up as righteous feminist rage and as pity, or even framed in the socialist language of "solidarity." This is true especially among groups calling themselves RadFems, even though their politics can more accurately be described, not as "radical" or "feminist," but rather as "ontologically oriented."[33] Perceiving the limits of groups like FINRRAGE becomes easier through the lens of *Daring to Be Bad*, Alice Echols's history of women's liberation in the United States, which convincingly demonstrates that the most revanchist, bitter, and reactionary of the many streams of "radical" feminism was the one that ultimately triumphed and thrived—including in moneyed institutions—throughout the 1980s. Echols calls this resentful residue of mid-1970s New Left defeat "cultural feminism."[34]

More recently, in the wake of the complications brought by queer theory to the categories "family," "child," "woman," and "motherhood," some of the most prominent postmodern theorists of reproduction have brought up FINRRAGE's legacy with a tone of awkward, apolitical embarrassment and regret, suggesting that "it is [now] crucial to avoid the denunciatory rhetoric ... associated with the so-called 'FINRRAGE position'."[35] This, however, is missing the point. As Michelle Stanworth noted as early as 1987: "the problem with this analysis is not that it is too radical."[36] Rather, in the words of two Dutch onlookers at the time, the problem was that they proposed "the same political strategy"[37] as porn-abolitionists Catherine MacKinnon and Andrea Dworkin, without any of Dworkin and MacKinnon's trans-inclusive redeeming features.[38] Surrogacy, possibly even more than porn, was to them the "'ideal' issue for stating both the legitimacy and the 'truth' of cultural feminism."[39] Under the appalled eyes of the transnational women's movement, in FINRRAGE, "natural motherhood" (universalized motherhood) was being restored to the place it held at the apogee of eugenics—defended as the beating heart of feminism—with surrogacy as its "negative mirror image."[40]

An indication of just how (non)radical we should understand cultural feminism to be is provided by FINRRAGE's language of "medicalized abuse," which is perfectly aligned with mainstream policy statements on surrogacy today. In 2015 and 2016, the European Parliament and The Hague each provisionally resolved that surrogacy should be proscribed without exception on the grounds that it "violates women's dignity and human rights" and makes their bodies "*marchandises.*"[41] The right-wing Bharatiya Janata Party declared a "revolution for women" after several of its party stalwarts helped achieve a Supreme Court ruling banning a practice that renders India "a baby factory."[42] These legislative crackdowns are not so much feminist as—borrowing from Sara Farris—*femonationalist*:

they represent patriarchal-nationalist responses to perceived abuses of the nation's women by nefarious outsiders.[43] Their playbook is lifted straight from the big multinational anti-trafficking and anti-prostitution campaigns, which is to say, they emulate the mechanisms of an institutional feminist-humanitarianism that greases the wheels of imperial wars and justifies a heavy-handed "rescue industry."[44]

Academics like me have unsurprisingly been schooled on all of this by the writings of outcasts from the university and refugees from the normative family: the militant queer, trans, and sex worker literatures of many nations. What this originally "low" (now canonized) theory tells us is that most prominent white feminists, no matter how queer they are at home, no matter how critical of the family as the primary site of patriarchal and queerphobic abuse, are remarkably prone to forgetting this antipathy when it comes to legislating lives in sufficiently "other" (proletarian) neighborhoods and, in particular, the Global South.

It could be speculated that anti-surrogacy reforms are primarily attempts by states to spare themselves the geopolitical headache of infant statelessness. But there is overwhelming evidence that FINRRAGE is also "taken seriously because basically it's saying the same thing as the Catholic Church."[45] Today, signatories to the EU lobby group No Maternity Traffic are almost exclusively faith-based, pro-life, and right-wing. Stop Surrogacy Now, an umbrella petition geared toward the International Criminal Court, includes pro-life groups like the US-based Center for Bioethics and Culture (on which, more later). In France, the right-wing "family values" organization La Manif pour tous ("The Protest for Everyone"), fresh from its legislative defeat in outlawing same-sex marriage in 2014, remobilized on the issue of "la gestation pour autrui" (gestation for others) the following year. Activists publicly paraded plastic baby dolls in shopping carts, picketing judiciaries associated with softening French anti-surrogacy legislation.

It seems a little too tidy to say that all the above is simply bad-faith co-option of what was originally a completely separate (and legitimate) feminist beef with the genuinely patriarchal medical complex; a little too charitable to say, ruefully, with Briggs, that "feminists did not get to own this critique [of surrogacy] once they had elaborated it."[46] RadFem and the right are close cousins. The particular Manichaean radical feminism of FINRRAGE was never univocally pro-queer or anti-establishment to begin with, so it is no great surprise that it has been taken up over the years by right-wing actors in power.

Politicians tend to do knee-jerk, mediagenic things in response to popular horror at the specter of the "womb farm."[47] Mass sympathy with surrogates seems to translate inexorably, in capitalist democracies, into a welter of paternalistic fantasies of criminalization, rehabilitation, and rescue. For feminists, participation in this cycle is a reliable route to forgetfulness. In souls that once cultivated suspicion toward "family values," particularly the romanticization of babies and motherhood, there is suddenly a revanchist anxiety about protecting against this one sector of the family's technological mediation. There is fretting about what "these technologies" will do to "the children"; excess villainization of bioengineers; and hefty amounts of pity toward the impoverished girls "selling themselves."

The analogy between surrogacy and sex work, I will argue, unlocks a critical step in the project outlined in this book. It is admittedly an analogy that surrogates themselves, as a group, are explicitly ambivalent about. Gestation and sexual services have only so much in common as work processes, and in a hostile political climate, the association between the two only makes both more difficult for workers, at least from some workers' point of view. It is admittedly also hard to imagine how exactly either form of work would persist in any postcapitalist moment. All we really know is that their articulation *as work* in the first instance will be key to abolishing them (as work) in the long run. It seems clear that surrogates and their allies have much to learn from sex workers' struggle for recognition and decriminalization.

As with sex work, the question of being for or against surrogacy is largely irrelevant. The question is, why is it assumed that one should be more against surrogacy than against other risky jobs. Kalindi Vora juxtaposes the labor struggle facing Indian surrogates with that of Indian call center agents and information technology programmers, all of whom she sees as gendered service workers producing commodities that flow toward the Global North.[48] This isn't complacency: it is the attitude of the most involved and active campaigners. Obviously, we do not take garment workers fighting for their dignity to be advocates of textiles, clothing, or fashion. Then consider the following statement, impossible to imagine under capitalism: "if and when surrogate mothers are treated as full human beings, with respect for their emotional, physical, and intellectual well-being, their sense of self, dignity, and body intact, then I am an advocate of commercial transnational surrogacy."[49] While we wait for that day (don't hold your breath), in Nigeria, campaigners are arguing that increasing the acceptability of surrogacy will likely play a crucial role in resolving the abuses of *actual* baby factories.[50] In India, attempts are underway to hash out a system of "fair trade surrogacy" founded on "openness and transparency on three fronts: in the structure of payments, in the medical process, and in the relationships forged."[51]

Practical reforms of this type, needless to say, are not anti-surrogacy; nor, despite the positive conditionality embedded in transitional demands, are they pro-surrogacy. They are treatments of contract gestation attuned to the many forms of pain and unfreedom that, in different ways and to dramatically different degrees, touch every confrontation between capital and the living human body. More than that, they are perspectives attuned to stratification, that is, to the ways that systemic misery is itself actively *sustained* by the immiserated body's stolen labors. Vora, in her book *Life Support*, summarizes a key example:

> the reproductive work of women has served not only to perpetuate families in the predominantly white middle class but also to perpetuate a discourse of white middle-class families as needing more care than working-class families and other families of color.[52]

While anti-surrogacy discourse does sometimes appreciate this, it often seeks only to arrest and criminalize the most egregious among the suite of services that keep society's hierarchy of care-needs afloat, rather than unmake its basis in thought, economy, and language.

This project, in contrast, seeks to render such a vampiric, zero-sum definition of need literally unthinkable. It stands for the levelling up and interpenetration of all of what are currently called "families" until they dissolve into a classless commune on the basis of the best available care for all. To move in that direction, I think we have to read the oldness, the not-newness, of surrogacy against the grain, retheorizing gestation from the standpoint of a plural womb and a world beyond propertarian kinship and work alienation. This implies a multigender feminism in which the labor of gestation is not policed by well-meaning ethicists but, rather, ongoingly revolutionized by struggles seeking to ease, aid, and redistribute it.

Today's industrial gestation already depends—dishonestly—on that solidarity gestators possess, which it simultaneously represses. The bodily generosity of surrogacy laborers is amazing. And we should rejoice, because it is completely ordinary: it is the same regenerative mesh that glues together life and limb for the "motherless" the world over. The potential of this mesh to transform and remake reality remains as yet unknown. Abolitionist anti-surrogacy, which is uninterested in finding out, is in that sense an anti-utopianism. Stop surrogacy now? On the contrary, to borrow from what Gandhi said when asked what he thought of "western civilisation": I think "surrogacy" would be a very good idea.

Compared to What?

Pregnancy is not something society as a whole tends to question. Surrogacy, on the other hand, is hotly contested. Yet we can readily perceive that all that really separates the two is the possibility of a wage. Take, for instance, the wording of this proposal for a "professional model of surrogate motherhood" that explicitly argues against waged or salaried pregnancy: "intended parents are allowed to reimburse pregnancy-related expenses, but are not permitted to pay anything beyond that."[53] Presumably the *surrogacy* is that surplus, that element "beyond" pregnancy. Taken in the aggregate, surrogate pregnancy is no more nor less medicalized than pregnancy that takes place within a marriage (at least, as it is experienced by people with full access to state-of-the-art health care). It is no more nor less "technological." It is substantially the same thing. This, as I hope I've already begun to show, doesn't let surrogacy off the hook; rather, it puts gestational labor *on* the hook. It serves to point out that we're collectively too busy, worrying about what surrogacy being pregnancy makes surrogacy, to think about what that very same realization makes pregnancy.

In *Against Love: A Polemic*, Laura Kipnis wrote in passing: "Clearly the answer to the much-debated question 'Does divorce harm children?' should be 'Compared to what?'"[54] This, I believe, is a good way to ground thinking about commercial gestational surrogacy. The question occupying thousands and thousands of bioethical publications every year—"Does surrogacy harm people?"—is not a question we can answer without first determining what harms we regard as "natural" and thus invisible preconditions of exploited labor. Unlike most legal scholars and activists in the Stop Surrogacy Now campaign, I am interested neither in defending against disruptions to the prevailing mode of reproduction per se, nor in applauding Surrogacy™ simply on the grounds that it *is* a disruption.

Abolitionist anti-surrogacy campaigners do not ask "compared to what." They draw dollar signs on belly bumps and talk about "breeding machines" and "meat" as though that were already an argument that is self-evident and fully formed. It isn't: for one thing, people produce lots of things through their wombs that aren't living babies, and IVF and surrogacy's rates of live baby production, calculated per exorbitantly expensive attempt, are minuscule. We should take issue for that reason, among others, with the fact that, as Laura Briggs says, across these literatures "the important stories are those that result in pregnancy and birth."[55] Dion Farquhar is unsparing about the exaggerations in play: "According to the feminist antireproductive technology narrative, a phallocratic conspiracy of woman-hating, womb-envying 'pharmacrats' foist their high-priced, risky, invasive, and low-success-rate reproductive technologies on the class of 'natural' women."[56] Note that:

> pharmacrat and technodoc are derogatory words coined by the
> Coalition Against Surrogacy ... to describe the medics, lawyers and
> businessmen who control and profit from the reproductive technol-
> ogy industry.[57]

As Farquhar rightly sees, the frustrating implication of this vocabulary
—borne of the FINRRAGE tradition's failure to even consider
asking "compared to what?"—is that with pharmacrats and technodocs "off women's backs," everything about reproduction would
more or less be just fine. Never mind the injuries; the maternal
mortality rate; domestic partner violence; or the 38 percent of low-
income mothers and mothers of color who develop postpartum
depression.

As we've already seen, brave new world narratives about the
"new reproductive technologies" are easier on the collective palate:
scarier, and thus, in a weird way, more consolatory. When it comes
to this kind of millenarian alarm, as Marilyn Strathern once sighed
ruefully, "There will be no shortage of good copy."[58] It is a remarkable characteristic of baby-related topics as they are understood in
cultural and liberal feminisms that they possess no exact analogy
in the other abolitionisms: it's not as though Dworkin was simply
anti-commercial when it came to sex, believing that the realm of
sexual politics would be benign if only pimps and pornographers
would vanish. Yet that is exactly what the most absolutist anti-
surrogacy firebrands (who also happen to be white) think about
babymaking: that it is automatically lovely—a "spiritual experience
for women"[59]—as long as it is unpaid and consensual. Puzzlingly,
they have developed no "rape culture" equivalent concept for the
culture that naturalizes violence in the everyday gestational work
environment (such as obstetric harm culture and gestational injury
culture). In the Swedish Women's Lobby "No to Surrogacy" campaign touchstone *Being and Being Bought,* for example, pregnancy
is described as normal, "beautiful," and, defined above all by a
woman's love of her own body. As long as it is outside of a surrogacy
context, pregnancy is treated as a matter of maternal-fetal bonding,
a "universal human emotion."[60]

Juliette Zipper and Selma Sevenhuijsen wrote a powerful, queer feminist alterfamilial takedown of this kind of reasoning in 1987, in which they laid out their view that the rigid moral idea of "the mother-child bond" is itself the problem.

> Commercialization is posed as the problem that has to be solved in the context of surrogacy. But underneath this critique of commercialization lingers a condemnation of the woman who gives away her child, or worse still, consciously and rationally decides to get pregnant and to abandon her child. The discourses around surrogacy ... are [thus] inspired not just by anxieties about the development of technology, but also by fears about ... a world where the mother-child bond is more transient and more fragile.[61]

The authors here powerfully critique the role of soi-disant radical feminisms in policing the "bond" as though it were sacrosanct. They point to the banality of "surrogacy" in the anti-capitalist squatter communes of Amsterdam and specifically to a friend of theirs who arranged to make a baby specifically for other friends lacking the ability. Since "women help each other in this way more frequently than is known," they argue, there is plenty of exciting scope for embracing a left feminist ethics in which mother-child bonds can more easily be discontinued, handed over, and multiplied.[62] Thirty years later, we hear all too few echoes of this call in feminist theory. Preciado subjects the commonplace "certainty that maternity is a natural bond" to a passingly brief attack, couched in the language of nihilist queer theory.[63] In the more direct formula of biological anthropologist Sarah Blaffer Hrdy, the question remains: "If women instinctively love their babies, why have so many women across cultures and through history directly or indirectly contributed to their deaths?"[64]

By refusing to define motherlove as a nonfungible, indissoluble intergenerational bond and by exploring alternatives, Zipper and Sevenhuijsen's on-the-ground engagement of early anti-surrogacy dogma struck a note that is too rarely heard in contemporary debates. The dogged opposition, on the other hand, keeps its messaging constant. Jennifer Lahl, the director of the Stop Surrogacy Now and anti-stem-cell research organization, The Center for Bioethics and Culture, dedicates her memes and films exclusively to reinforcing the anxieties, the fears, and the "myth" that keep maternity "natural." Her social media feed consists of legal op-eds about the coming-true of *The Handmaid's Tale*, teasers for CBC's *Eggsploitation* (a 2010 documentary about egg donation), and melancholic headless shots of white women with price-tags, or simply the word "USED," photoshopped onto their bellies.[65] "The fertility industry sees this woman as a commodity," CBC ominously explains to its Facebook followers in its caption. "'Like' if you see what we see—a woman with dignity."

The humanist idealization of "fetal motherhood" rests on the conviction that gestation is not work but the very pinnacle of wholeness and self-realization. It goes hand-in-hand with an even more dubious correlate: that surrogacy is contamination (a kind of forced cyborgicity), fragmentation ("the body in bits"), and abjection (victimization by brothel, tech cabal, or industrial farm). So far so FINRRAGE; but what's interesting to me is that the problem CBC bumps up against in the world, the phenomenon it cannot accept, is, simply, the tragedy of worldly contingency. Sometimes people can't become mothers; sometimes mothers die; sometimes they don't love their babies; sometimes they abort them, abuse them, abandon them, divorce their co-parent, or even kill. If none of these things happened, the world of Jennifer Lahl would be as it should be.

In a promotional video for the anti-surrogacy feature *Breeders: A Subclass of Women?* (2015), Lahl proclaims that, in life, "what happens, what *should* happen, is that mothers, women, and children bond and connect."[66] It's easy to infer that what Lahl is denouncing is the pain of separation (never mind that this seems somewhat inconsistent coming from someone given to sharing platforms with advocates for separating undocumented migrants from their children at the US border). The problem is: she hasn't thought through her identification of this pain with surrogacy. Couldn't there be more (rather than less) opportunity for bonding and connecting between mothers, women, and children, in a surrogacy context? In any case, Lahl's elaboration on her statement runs right into intense logical trouble. Her spiel becomes more and more obviously confused about what exactly it is she is campaigning against, as Lahl proves completely unable to name the social force—capitalism, property, technology, cis-heterosexuality, patriarchy, the family?—that prevents bonding and connecting from taking place, in *any* context. Lahl doubles down, opting simply to refer to the bad thing she is defending motherhood against as a vague, undefined "it."

> No matter how you slice it, no matter how much you think "if we don't pay women," or "if we *do* pay women," or "if we do it for family members," or "if we do it for strangers": it doesn't go well. And there's no guarantee that it will go well.

That what will go well? At this point, the risks of surrogacy, pregnancy, foster care, extended families, and adoption have all become indistinguishable.

The main person *Breeders* puts a spotlight on is Jessica Kern, a woman who, just like Baby M, was conceived and birthed in the mid-1980s via a "traditional" contract: that is, one in which the surrogate gestator is also the embryo's genetic parent. As an adult "surrobaby," Kern is the author of a sensational weblog about her life's plight, The Other Side of Surrogacy, and acts as a spokesperson for several anti-surrogacy groups, as well as a mascot for activists with agendas regarding foster care or adoption protocols. (It is worth noting that even in the documentary itself, and certainly in public life, Lahl noticeably prefers to ventriloquize Kern rather than quote the paranoid tone of the blog.) "Jessica feels very strongly," Lahl testifies grimly, "against the reality that her birth mother was basically paid $10,000 to hand her over. She refers to herself as a product."[67] In the dramatic pause that follows this revelation about Kern's self-perception, it is apparently understood that viewers will not require an explanation as to why that is bad. Thinking of oneself as a product, as far as Lahl is concerned, excludes thinking of oneself as a person.

Lahl is not the only one who is inordinately fond of citing Kern's dehumanization in her diatribes against surrogacy. At the 2014 Festival of Dangerous Ideas, Kajsa Ekman stated: "when you know [as Kern does] the only reason you exist is a big fat paycheck, it doesn't feel that nice."[68] Peculiar as it undoubtedly is to look at the most preplanned and purposeful instances of human procreation (assisted reproduction) and then to say that the human results stem "only" from a transfer of money, it is perhaps not the oddest thing about that argument. A self-declared Marxist feminist, Ekman does not seem to know Marxism's number one tenet: that if there's one quasi-universal under capitalism, it's existing because of a paycheck.[69] As this book goes to press, a new salvo, edited by Ekman together with Renate Klein and the antipornography campaigner Melissa Tankard-Reist, is due to be released under the title *Broken Bonds*. Its blurb declares that "love is not to be bought."[70]

I bring up these examples of anti-surrogacy discourse not because they are egregious but to evidence the symbiosis I've posited between these feminist exceptionalisms around sex work and surrogacy. Looking at these mainstays of the argument allows us to uncover the image of human labor-power that lurks behind all that energetic repudiation, an image that is limited and limiting in a far wider set of political contexts than just surrogacy. Consider the radio interview Ekman gave to Meghan Murphy at Feminist Current, about her view that "prostitution is a lie, it's overly simplistic to say it's just a job." Attempting to demolish the view that sex work is work, Ekman sarcastically proposes: "Let all the women lie there and do nothing and just look at their watches—then see how much the men like it!"[71]

Weirdly, Murphy's "Marxist" guest is not defending the prerogative to do nothing while at work and simply look at one's watch: quite the contrary. Nor does she seem to realize that she is undermining her own point by indicating, rightly, that few sex workers could actually get away with being so lazy, or stay afloat that way, or avoid getting fired for it. (The concept of "The Right to Be Lazy" never did enjoy so positive a reception among feminists as it received among queer communists.) Furthermore, given that surrogacy is the other big bugbear of Ekman's oeuvre, it can hardly be a coincidence that her description of a nonjob is something that sounds suspiciously like the later stages of a surrogate's work in a surrogacy dormitory. Rather than let her bait us into justifying the skill and laboriousness of either occupation, however, the correct response to Ekman is this: we can affirm our nondesire to work even if we don't work hard. *Even* when it comes to making fetuses that will die if we stop working.

Far from being "overly simplistic," a historical materialist account of commercial sex (such as Melissa Gira Grant's) will go to great lengths to do justice to the overlap workers experience between it and "free" unpaid heterosexual lovemaking, with its comparable pressures to feign nonboredom, manage power-laden transactions, and regulate enjoyment. In contrast, in the minds of the figures I've treated in this section, it is the necessity of performing orgasm convincingly—the necessity of lying—that "proves" that something other than work must be the substance of sex work. An exactly analogous contradictoriness haunts their anti-surrogacy position: they are disquieted by the aspects of doing pregnancy that don't simply "come naturally" or feel spiritual, while simultaneously condemning anyone who does simply feel okay with whatever extent of effort, alienation, and separation has been arranged. In denial about the existence of gestational nonparenting and nongestational parenting, they refuse to see the naturalization already operative in everyday biogenetics.

Anti-anti-surrogacy

It seems to me odd and arbitrary to choose the moment of formalization of the labor relation to voice denunciations of womb work—to wait, in other words, until some gestators are paid. The desire to stop surrogacy might have made some sense a century or two ago as a class struggle intervention: *Stop the ruling classes stealing babies to solve their infertility crises, while farming out care of their bastards! Stop slave-owners' appropriation of slaves' gestational products!* But Stop Surrogacy Now and similar campaigns, founded circa 2013, really pick their moment: objecting loudly to the market's desecration of a symbolically pure productive organ just as womb-workers are starting (some of them) to get paid. Stung at the unconscious level by what payments for sex and pregnancy potentially reveal about sex and pregnancy, these voices want to abolish the commodification without abolishing the work.

The everyday appropriation of indentured gestational labor went on in wealthy households throughout early modernity and colonialism.[72] And in many parts of the world it goes on still.[73] This is why the decision of the Bharatiya Janata Party to make surrogacy in India purely "altruistic" should be of concern to those who understand how Indian class society works. Commercial surrogacy was certainly no panacea for working-class women but, as Sharmila Rudrappa avers, "the ban can potentially be far worse [because] 'altruistic' surrogate mothers might be in deeply dependent, long-standing relationships with intended parents and unable to refuse when asked to provide their biological reproductive services for free."[74] Unpaid quasi-feudal arrangements for womb-use appear in the Old Testament and, as Jennifer Lahl would say, they didn't go well— "traditional" though they were.

What infertility clinics don't mention when they invoke biblical surrogacies are basic facts about those stories. Hagar the slave bore a baby on behalf of her master's wife Sara, and not only did she not get paid, she ended up getting banished *and* having the child foisted back onto her to boot.[75] Clinicians gesture vaguely toward Hagar as a way of legitimizing surrogacy; but going slightly deeper, as I have sought to do, serves to reiterate Angela Davis's point that surrogacy was not lately invented.[76] Thanks to emergent biotechnology, it has been *adapted* as a form of independent revenue for people with viable uteruses in disparate legislatures.

The central source of anti-surrogacy, as I've presented it, is the reluctance to consider that bonding in utero might be a kind of work— for gestational parents and not just surrogates—and that, on the other hand, the commercially tainted adoptive care of a child (such as that undertaken by commissioning parents) might be just as authentic and good (or bad) as any other form of parental love. I am compelled to quote Paul B. Preciado once again: in this discourse, "sex work and the work of reproduction [are] considered to be disinterested, the origins of the supposed dignity of the female subject, who would feel completely degraded by the commodification of sexual services."[77] Preciado implies this worldview is now defunct, and I think he is being overly optimistic. Cultural feminists are far from alone in "contin[uing] to believe that keeping sex work and reproduction free services (read: pauperized or politically obligatory services) is equivalent to preserving the essential dignity of ... the entire human population."[78]

Nine times out of ten, you can bet that the reason someone is declaring so vehemently against one specific microbranch of the contemporary economy is because it is a branch of productive labor that involves *wombs* or *orifices* as well as frontal lobes and hands. The fixation on "the inside of a woman's body" should tip us off: many surrogate-exclusionary radical-feminists—not only Lahl, Bindel, Ekman, and Murphy—follow the lead of veteran sex-worker exclusionary radical feminists and transexclusionary radical feminists Sheila Jeffreys and Janice Raymond in explicitly linking the violence of surrogacy not only with sex work but with transfeminine identity. In rhetoric heavily loaded with prurient anatomical imagery involving "holes" and "vessels," this camp paints a diabolical picture in which gender-affirming surgery, commercial sex, and procreative "artificiality" are inseparable facets of a conspiracy of erasure of "the Female."

Female erasure is a warmed-over metaphysical concept invented by the paranoid, ultra-pessimist residues of the defeated Second Wave. It hasn't yet run out of steam: the 2017 anthology *Female Erasure* collects forty-eight such cultural-feminist screeds, proposing a return to "language referring to females as a distinct biological class" and supposedly exposes (among other things) the "profits of an emerging medical transgenderism industry."[79] When talking about its most prominent proponent, Janice Raymond, it is key to note that she is the author not only of a rash of online jeremiads against "legalized prostitution" but of the 1978 transphobic propaganda fountainhead *The Transsexual Empire*, which (as Susan Stryker and Stephen Whittle put it) "seriously advances the claim that male medical doctors are involved in a conspiracy to create a race of artificial women."[80] More to the point, this fantasy is nearly identical to that expressed in the title of the 1987 book on surrogacy, *Man-Made Women*, also co-authored by Raymond. In these texts, the lines between surrogacy, technology, sex work, and transsexuality blur and even disappear; all four phenomena, incommensurable though they are, are parsed here in the same ontologically oriented Manichaean language, as encroaching threats, sick perversions, cultural appropriations of women's culture, false idols, rape personified, and specters of "slavery."

These nightmare visions are animated by a foreboding that cis women will devolve en masse into *man-made women*, this category that is supposed to encompass everything from sex robots to postoperative trans women and, yes, clinically supervised pregnancy. Depressingly, a fresh generation of YouTube-proficient RadFems—some of them avowed anticapitalists—is preventing this heuristic from dying out. The talking points involved are often revivals of FINRRAGE's—the ire has been triggered by self-consciously laboring, cyborg, hacked, "whored out," self-styled and modified femininities. "In bed with churchmen" was one phrase used, in 1989, to describe the Faustian alliances being forged between ostensibly leftist women opposed to reprotech, and antifeminist faith groups.[81] The phrase is perhaps even redundant insofar as Raymond began adulthood as a Catholic nun. But her worldview, which regards the bodies of sex workers and gestational laborers as literally reified—rendered machinery or meat—by the act of leasing relationships that stem uniquely from a woman's immortal soul, is obviously not shared by all Catholics. They are, unfortunately, shared by some members of the left, insofar as they appear in a genre of ostensibly secular yet deeply apocalyptic reportage—the columns seem to write themselves—arguing that "some things should not be for sale"[82] (with the passive implication that other things *should*).

It would be foolish to argue that there was no value whatsoever in the body of feminism that coalesced in the mid-1980s specifically to repudiate capitalist "infertility solutions.[83] Despite being co-founded by Janice Raymond, the short-lived network FINRRAGE enabled many socialist feminists to work together to analyze gendered prejudice within science and to question the deeply exploitative recruitment practices and employment norms suffered by test subjects and gestational workers in the course of biomedical profiteering.

Some members of FINRRAGE (although, again, unfortunately not those in control of the network) also began to articulate a family-critical anti-contractarianism—an insistence that kinship ties should not be treated as property—that might have led them away from their perception of surrogacy as the problem.[84] My approach in this volume is definitely educated by these things, but it ultimately cleaves to traditions that clashed with and superseded FINRRAGE: queer and cyborg feminisms, autonomist and social reproduction marxisms, and the Reproductive Justice movement. These, to my mind, have been the intellectual players in the field of reproductive politics who have always put the "compared to what?" question at the center of their approach—call it dialectics, call it utopianism. Without loss of radicality, they manage to avoid the technophobia, colonial prescriptivism, and class-flattening cissexism that plagued FINRRAGE's truncated style of abolitionism.

Instead of seeking to do away with waged pregnancy work, neo-anti-surrogacy all across the political spectrum would do well to learn from the recent demise of sex worker–exclusionary feminism. Admittedly it has taken sex workers' unions and prostitutes' collectives decades of tireless advocating for their trade's decriminalization —but Amnesty International announced its support for the cause in 2015. As Amnesty's report recognized, a raft of excellent critiques of the corporate feminist NGO-led rescue industry has irrecoverably proved how mainstream assertions of "women's rights" are systematically used, not to lend support to the struggles of people making a living in informal economies, but on the contrary to advance missions that patronize, criminalize, and materially harm sex workers around the world in the name of anti-trafficking.[85]

The radical sex workers' critique of "anti-trafficking" initiatives contends that feminist humanitarianism is an increasingly hegemonic development monolith, which promotes carceral solutions to the "problem" of informal economies and even legitimizes military campaigns in the name of downtrodden women. I want to propose—noting that Janice Raymond's high-profile career segued from anti-surrogacy into anti-trafficking in the 1990s—that contemporary anti-surrogacy is extensively animated by these same structures of neoimperialist humanitarian feminism. For revolutionaries engaged in this area, it will be vital to aggressively defend the point that hatred of a particular form of work in no way justifies attacks on those workers' self-organization—quite the opposite. We would do better to concentrate on what sex workers and surrogacy workers have actually called for (free housing, medical care, police abolition, freedom of movement, and so on).

In the same way that many militant sex workers sometimes invite their allies to understand the ways in which we, under capitalism, are all "whores," surrogacy politics aren't just a concern for an infinitesimal, niche sliver of the proletariat. The broader radical tradition I've gestured toward (from Allen and Davis to Briggs and Vora) is indispensable in that it allows us to revive an expanded sense of the term "surrogacy," making the relevance clearer still. Narrating capital's evolving history then becomes a matter of revealing a web of surrogacy relations at the heart of empire, reaching into every intimate abode. Social reproduction theory becomes a matter populated by a whole raft of "surrogates": provisioners, test subjects, helps, and tech supports. "Surrogate," more than "reproductive" or "feminized," might be a word that proves useful for that field in bringing together the millions of precarious and/or migrant workers laboring today as cleaners, nannies, butlers, assistants, cooks, and sexual assistants in First World homes, whose service is figured as dirtied by commerce, in contrast to the supposedly "free" or "natural" love-acts of an angelic white bourgeois femininity it in fact makes possible. Surrogacy, in its current connotation, is the lie and the truth of their situation. It speaks of the millions of living bodies secretly crouching inside the automatons, and behind the customer-service machine interfaces, of what Kalindi Vora has called "surrogate humanity."[86]

Who will remake, redirect, expropriate, or indeed "stop" all *that* surrogacy now (or ever)? The answer is obvious: the surrogates themselves. Their agency, like everyone's, is severely constrained, which is why they will need vast numbers of us to step up and become surrogates in turn for surrogates' interests; surrogates upon surrogates; actors who can't even remember if they were doing care *on someone else's behalf* or their own, nor tell the difference.

3

The World's (Other) Oldest Profession

In the *National Geographic* documentary film *In the Womb*, an authoritative male voice-over explains pregnancy in terms of an "odyssey" accomplished by the future "baby girl"; he calls it a "journey" of which the gestator is "most likely unaware." It depicts a stand-alone fetus's traversal and transcendence of maternal body-territory, painting a picture of a self-valorization process reminiscent of prevalent procapitalist narratives about capital itself. It seems that culture is more than capable of imbuing the lie of autonomous value-creation with the full force of scientific authority. Sophisticated graphic animations accompany *In the Womb*'s narration of "natural reality"; one sequence depicts the embryonic ball of cells at two weeks, folding in on itself to create a tube that will eventually become a fetal torso, morphing like a melted marshmallow in outer space. The impression throughout is of miraculous growth autonomy. Throughout these microscopic interior sequences, it is as though the mother's body *isn't there*. To ensure the point is rammed home, the viewer being educated about the biology of "becoming" (not *making*) a human is repeatedly treated to underwater footage of the adult gestator at various stages of her pregnancy, kicking around in a swimming pool, oblivious to the "drama unfolding inside her." *National Geographic* strips the maternal subject's consciousness while paying incessant tributes to the will to self-determination of the baby-to-be. "The mother provides the shelter and the basics: food, water and oxygen," we are told. "But the real star of the show is the fetus herself."

Many people would agree abstractly that pregnancy should not be work, should not be alienated labor. Unfortunately, there is far less agreement about how deep the problem of pregnancy-work-alienation already extends. It was once suggested, with bitter sarcasm, that "the quickest way to "disalienate" work is to do it for free."[1] In penning these lines, Silvia Federici and Nicole Cox succinctly conveyed the wisdom that a reproducer-led revolution will always struggle to gain traction in a world that persists in telling the pro-work, pro-"life" lies that throw those at the margins of society under the bus of hegemonic Motherhood. Foremost among these lies, as surrogate gestators know too well, is the lie of natural femininity more generally. Many women collude in and even spearhead the lie, which says that generating the continuity of life is itself simply *life* and *love*—or, rather, magic. Oddly, a version of the lie even comes from self-described "radical feminist" locations, and examining this phenomenon can tell us something about the stakes of "value" debates—specifically, the need to antagonize and transcend value—in formulating our politics.

Given that one of women's liberation's major accomplishments has been the insistence that daily invisible acts of reproduction (childbearing and childrearing) and social reproduction (feeding, loving, and otherwise replenishing the workforce) constitute concrete labor, it is odd, to say the least, that numerous "RadFems" with mass platforms still feel so comfortable attempting to humiliate some workers for allegedly not producing value. It's a tactic they learn from orthodox Marxism—which widely still continues to fail to recognize reproductive work that is appropriated rather than exploited as work—and it is a deep error. In the first place, to quote Alyssa Battistoni: "the problem with exploitation is not that it robs the worker of the value she has produced";[2] and by the same token, appropriation is a problem even when that which is appropriated isn't value producing. Charlotte Shane, writing as a sex worker rather than a gestational surrogate, has noticed that the soi-disant feminists here "evince the same attitude a lot of the men hiring us do: it's the easiest money one could ever make. You need only be a body to do it."[3] For those who revere a clean, sovereign conception of work, in other words, there's something implicitly foul—"femme," Julie Bindel calls it—about "only" being a body.[4]

In my experience one should strive not to make a habit of stooping to refute Julie Bindel, but actually, when it is performed for clinical firms, the work that commercial surrogates do creates value—a technicality that may or may not matter for the purposes of strategizing the struggle of surrogates. Like many forms of alienated labor—commercial boxing, say, or radio-hosting—gestational labor power is (consensually) plugged into a hi-tech extraction apparatus that starts it up and cuts it off, in these cases. Needless to say, it is the pregnancy itself that creates the value, even if techniques such as IVF and C-section are required to capture that value in an efficient enough manner to be competitive. When a commercial surrogate miscarries, that value is lost—and clinicians will attempt to deny her the vast majority of her wage. Destroying capitalist value can certainly be of strategic value in the context of collective disputes. Non-value-producing gestators, leveraging their social and cultural status as reproducers of life, can play a powerful role in defending and amplifying the power of value-producing gestators who destroy their product, particularly in the context of a dual strategy geared toward a world freed from the value-form.

Noncommercial pregnancy is a capitalist hinterland. Commercial surrogacy is capitalist industry. In unpaid gestation (as in other spheres of reproductive labor such as sex and dating), a feminized person's body is typically being further feminized: it is working very, very hard at having the appearance of not working at all. In commercial surrogacy, in contrast, the work surrogates do is visible. But, in both cases, the crucial point is that it is *work*. Just look at the factory temporality that emerges wherever production gathers any speed. In one clinic in Bangalore, a majority of the workers are scheduled for caesarean delivery between weeks thirty-six and thirty-eight of their pregnancy, a regimen that subsumes the organic temporality of their labor into capitalist time. Sharmila Rudrappa recounts that these surgeries allowed doctors to "better organize their workdays":

> the surrogacy agency could calculate how many beds it had available in its dormitory, how many more new clients it could take on, and how many new mothers could be housed for new babies to be borne all over again ... By scheduling the births, the doctors and

surrogacy agencies did not have to house the babies in neonatal units, coordinate care, and make crucial life or death decisions, if it came to that, for intended parents who had not yet arrived ... The intended parents, too, saw advantages to receiving the babies on schedule. They could coordinate work and family care obligations, hire nannies to care for the babies when they returned home, and otherwise plan their lives around the scheduled caesarians performed on the surrogate mothers.[5]

Economists have rightly cautioned that "it is difficult to see how the market prices of reproductive products could be regulated by the productivity of the people involved in producing them."[6] But the dynamics described by Rudrappa are clear signs that markets are attempting and (to some extent) succeeding at "equalizing" gestation as a productive process.[7]

Marxists have not generated much by way of theoretic resources on gestation-as-production as it has emerged into historic view. One of the first historical-materialist salvos on the topic argued that "surrogacy is the quintessence of capitalist patriarchy's estranged construction of motherhood,"[8] twice implying that it might be a form of commodified labor power but overall proving unwilling to explore the consequences of that. In her essay "Marxism and Surrogacy," Kelly Oliver admitted that she remained unsure:

> if a friend has a baby for you, even if you don't pay her, isn't she still, in some sense, estranged from her labor? Although I am perplexed by this question and not convinced that the answer is yes, I'm also unwilling to admit that the answer is no.[9]

I applaud Oliver's puzzlement. Clearly, to find our way out of this impasse, we need to establish that we want a world in which the baby need not become the friend's property, while recognizing that we do not yet inhabit such a world. The degree of estrangement experienced by Kelly Oliver's friend would depend, in this case, on the degree of distance society has achieved regarding the capitalist family.

A rejoinder essay by another Marxist, Marvin Glass, reiterated the *Handmaid's Tale*-esque understanding of surrogacy already prevalent in the 1990s. In "Reproduction for Money," Glass speculated that Karl Marx's ideas "would have led him to predict that paid surrogacy would be 'forced labor.'" The contracted gestator's activity, he averred, is "not spontaneous activity ... it belongs to another; it is the loss of self."[10] Confusingly, Glass also notes, two pages later, that surrogacy "is not a well-paid job" when you calculate the pay as an hourly rate.[11] It seems possible that this latter comment, some version of which tends to appear quite frequently in surrogacy discourse, is only meant as a kind a joke, a punch line, an unintentional ridiculing of the thought of social reproduction militants. If I am correct in this ungenerous reading, we have to conclude that Glass's analysis ultimately does little to challenge the tendency, in most Marxism and even much Marxist feminism, for "children to appear spontaneously or perhaps magically."[12] In the tacit imaginary of those who pen these quips, as Mary O'Brien saw, reproductive labor "does not produce value, does not produce needs and therefore does not make history nor make men."[13]

Funnily enough, there is no shortage of published arguments inveighing against theorizing gestation as work (a specter, perhaps, haunting the social sciences). Some commentators even copy the perverse point often repeated by the telegenic surrogacy CEO, Dr. Patel, when promoting her surrogacy business: since what her employees do is somehow so much more, it's better to call it "priceless," they say. It should never be discussed as fungible or transferrable (even though that's exactly what is happening) because, well, we're talking about babies. One academic author, somewhat in this vein, makes much of the fact that surrogates in Mumbai are "inducted into the work through a complex and multifaceted network of kin relations ... a complex affective matrix" that frequently results in their calling bosses and managers "sister" or "auntie."[14] These terms of affection are then taken to suggest that parties "do not have an employer–employee relationship," have "no experience of formalised labor or of unionisation,"[15] and would never venture to undertake an appeal, in the case of breach of contract.[16] It's a mystery to me where this knowledge comes from. In Amrita Pande's six-year study of a similar Indian clinic, she found that "the stigma of surrogacy starts getting diluted, and women, especially the repeat surrogates, start negotiating higher payments and more support from their families and start demanding less interference by brokers."[17] It never even occurs to thoughtful ethnographers like Pande to interpret these commonplace workplace speech conventions (which she also documents openly) as evidence that relations in the surrogacy dormitory/clinic aren't capitalist. A boss is still a boss when you call her "Susan" or "auntie."

Research-optimized, guideline-conforming, vitamin-saturated, clinically supervised, the responsible gestator has an immense amount of work to do in order to be competitive (not to mention escape punishment). In this sense, besides sex work, an illuminating analogy for the capitalist discipline of the surrogate dormitory is the twenty-first-century classroom which, as Malcolm Harris explains, extends its tentacles ever deeper into the hours of a child's day. In *Kids These Days,* Harris convincingly challenges the standard idea that contemporary children's long hours in schools and, after hours, doing homework, isn't work.[18] Just as this school work reproduces, models, and trains children for office work, the work-intensive "vigilante" approach to pregnancy we see in surrogacy is by no means special to the sphere of assisted reproduction, where it did not originate. In both spheres, schematically speaking, the placentated person fulfils a duty to optimize herself, which is the same duty the product of her labor will face, in school, a few years down the line. It is in this sense that calls for mothers and children to join together in a struggle against patriarchal exploitation (voiced for instance by Shulamith Firestone in 1970) still make so much sense. It was O'Brien who predicted that, in a society liberated from patriarchy and capitalism, "children will be different."[19] The two groups are inseparable: as Harris notes in the context of his incitement toward a twenty-first-century kids' strike, the system "could never survive a mom strike."[20]

Why Call It Work?

Surrogate pregnancy "is much better work than a laborer, a construction worker, or a maid"; so said the star clinician Nayna Patel to the English BBC World talk-show host Stephen Sackur on a 2013 edition of HARDtalk.[21] Many viewers possess first-hand experience of performing nonsurrogated pregnancy to help weigh Patel's claim. She herself has gestated two of her own children, decades ago, unwaged and off-camera. I am not, however, interested in pursuing the question of which jobs are better or worse than surrogacy. I'm interested in giving weight to the comparison itself. My sense is that Dr. Patel's ontological claim about gestation ("it's a job") might be exploitable by the other side in class struggle.

Nayna Patel, doyenne of the Akanksha Infertility Clinic (formerly Akanksha Surrogate Hospital) in Anand, India, remains at the time of writing the most visible individual surrogacy specialist in the world: famous, above all, for describing herself as "absolutely a feminist." Although she seems, in this video clip, to be hailing gestation as productive work, the doctor (or, as one Israeli newspaper has termed it, "pregnancy producer")[22] actually has it both ways. While insisting that her employees do "much *better* work than" other menial workers do, Patel refuses to frame gestational labor as creative or saleable. She even directly muddies her claim that pregnancy is a "job" in that same interview, immediately afterwards, when she claims that producing a child for a childless couple is a "priceless"[23] act that could "*NEVER*" be rendered commercial.[24] While ostensibly normalizing surrogacy as a choice of job, she paradoxically promotes a set of more conventional forms of gainful employment that a person can do at the same time as gestating: embroidery, machine-sewing, computing, candle-craft, and beauty treatments. She would rather see "my surrogates" doing "something *else,*" she says.[25] In short, a tension arises in the clinic dormitory, between surrogacy-as-means and surrogacy-as-end-in-itself; surrogacy as work and surrogacy as back-to-work program; surrogacy as a job like any other, and surrogacy as training and career development for low-income Indian women.

For the last decade or so, a wealth of coverage about Patel has been more or less constantly aired. And in this coverage, a ghoulish fascination with "race" is evident, most obviously in the treatment of foreign "tourists" to the exclusion of all others, in these representations. This is not because race-making, or the ways in which labor itself is racialized, is of concern to the BBC. Rather, western reporters have tended to sensationalize—somewhat pruriently and with misplaced pity—the "otherness" of the birth-ontology to which Patel plays midwife; they choose for instance to dwell on her exclaiming about the skin tone of a newly glimpsed newborn: "Pure white! Even when the egg is Indian, you can always tell when it is British … *European*." Mention is never made of any caste-inflected electoral tensions in the area, for example, far less the labor struggles intersecting with the clinic and the feminist movement sweeping through streets throughout India. Rather, we get a sense that pure whiteness is being immaculately delivered, single-handed, by a circumspect lady alchemist. Domestic (Indian) commissioning parents are, as far as I can see, *never* represented in the Anglo-American reportage on the Akanksha.

No doubt "crossracial reproductive tourism" (Laura Harrison's term for it) is the most mediagenic aspect of Patel's business.[26] It strikes me, however, that this term lends itself a little too easily to the same mystification it seeks to describe, in that the model of kinship creation parents are buying into relies precisely on there being *no substantive "crossing"* whatsoever. The interpretation of gestational genetics upon which Surrogacy™ is founded is one in which identity emerges from a caesarean section already (pun intended) cut and dried. The idea that "you can always tell" is Patel's public message. Scratch the surface of the enterprise, however, and you realize that the Indian gestators she employs have often wandered drastically offmessage, describing their personal conceptualization of the genetic stranger inside them as their "own sweat and blood" behind Patel's back. That brown gestators are capable of manufacturing white babies through application of their own sweat and blood is, apparently, uncongenial information for marketing purposes.[27] We shall return to the problems and nuances of reading this laboring biology as "subversive"—because suppressed by surrogacy capitalists— at the end of this book.

So What Will These Females Do?

In 2017, Vice News reporter Gianna Toboni dramatically described her visit to Patel's clinic as "the most heartbreaking experience I ever had."[28] Toboni did not *see* workers at work; what she saw at the Akanksha was a place where babies were sold, a place of organ-harvesting, a traffickers' brothel. Unsurprisingly, her reportage fed seamlessly into calls inside and outside India for a ban on commercial surrogacy and, as we've seen, such calls do not constitute informed solidarity. A recent multilateral study concluded that workers unanimously "did not support the ban on international surrogacy."[29] In parsing the Bharatiya Janata Party's announcement in late 2016 that it would rescue Indian women from the "baby factories" set up in their land by unpatriotic repro-pimps, Rudrappa shows that it is perhaps not so much commercial surrogacy but rather the proposed *ban* on commercial surrogacy that tells us more "about how the Indian state perceives working-class women's bodies and reproductive labor"—that is, it views them as *res extensa*.[30] If the Indian state will indeed now allow only unpaid surrogacy between citizen couples and their "female" kinfolk, then, as Rudrappa says, "by positing altruistic surrogacy as a superior alternative," it has renaturalized feminine labor and "effectively deregulated surrogacy, potentially allowing deeper exploitation of women."[31]

Unsurprisingly, Vice's orientalist feature on the ignominy of Dr. Patel's little commercial dominion also served various rich nations as the negative foil for their self-congratulating and self-exceptionalizing discourses in favor of elite surrogacy. Take for instance the dominant discourse in Norway, spurred by the gay chief of police Øystein Mæland's publicly lauded employment of a California surrogate. Celebrations of Mæland actually *emphasized* the colonial exploitation prevalent in surrogacy economies in the Global South the better to celebrate "the agency of surrogate mother-workers as reproductive entrepreneurs," meaning the ethical consumer alternatives on offer (at five times the cost) in California.[32] As a sharp group of authors in *GLQ* have shown, the American surrogate could be construed in Norway as "a modern woman" *because* the Indian surrogate "is construed as a victim." As for "the *children* of the Indian surrogate": they "become the victims of a victim."[33] In a constitutive contrast to the homonationalist Gay Pride generated by the police commander's choice of international parenthood labor market ("good surrogacy"), there was a negative nationalism—a great public show of approval—when Norwegian crown princess Mette-Marit travelled to New Delhi to "rescue" a different gay couple's newborn twins from the "back alley" in which the babies were imagined as having been stranded following India's gay-parent-excluding law reform ("bad surrogacy").[34]

Back in the medical-tech and Hindu-nationalist stronghold of Gujarat, Dr. Patel vacillates with regard to the issue of surrogacy for same-sex parents. In 2014, she did enable two Gujarati-American women to pay her for some rounds of IVF, stating publicly that, although lesbian, they "belonged to conservative Gujarati families"[35]—an implicit mitigating factor. When it comes to the workers, however, be they Californian or Indian, in Patel's domain of business they "ha[ve] to be imagined as a mother (and not as a worker or as extended family) in order to produce identification and sympathy."[36] The parallels surrogacy shares with sex work in this sense raise their conspicuous head once more, in terms of moral toleration being made conditional upon an impossible and contradictory set of requirements. A "deserving" surrogate or sex worker must have children of her own, not have children of her own, want children of her own (and not feel entitled to them), display humility, accept full self-responsibility, surrender to rescue, and (perhaps above all) be heterosexual as well as asexual—maintaining a perfect absence of desire.

In a TIME segment, Patel's customers were acutely impressed by her visit to a "slum."[37] As though touring a factory dormitory or model village, at one point she helpfully translated for the camera, in real time, what one of the women (no doubt spontaneously met, and without prior instruction) was saying: "Because Dr. Patel selected me for surrogacy, now everything is great." Patel framed her visit as tangible evidence that her business is "a boon to society." With one European commissioning father seated beside her in a shack owned by a former surrogate, Patel spoke English, explaining for his benefit (and ours as viewers) that "This is a *good* house as far as this area is concerned." Patel continued:

> There are so many NGOs who start criticising [me], but why don't they come and *help* such people? They should come here to the slum every day and help the people, if they want to help! They also blame the surrogate—that she is trying to "sell her body." They compare it to prostitution: "*the poor surrogates, they don't know anything and they're being exploited and their body is being used like a machine …*" [here the commissioning father interrupts her inaudibly]—yeah, they should not be ashamed of what they do, they should be *proud* of what they are doing. We have come out in the open. Rather than get scared of the society and do it behind the closed doors, not letting anyone know, hush-hush, we have come out in the open and said: yes! We do surrogacy! These are the surrogates: they are carrying babies for foreigner couples. She could not have earned this kind of money, if you're talking about 300,000–400,000 rupees, even if she works 24 by 7 throughout her life. In the beginning, they start for money. Even in the end, money is a criterion, all said and done; the world is like that, you know. *But she has that feeling!* That positive attitude in her that says "I'm going to be of some use to someone."

Seconds after she has apparently repudiated the whorephobic under-pinnings of anti-surrogacy moralism and stigma, Patel props up the equally problematic principle that women ought to be eternally seeking opportunities to "be of some use." The philanthropic and capitalist impulses in this speech feed into each other figuratively in a self-undermining loop or Ouroboros—a hallmark of postfem-inism. Patel takes it as given that she is "helping" by providing such opportunities and implies that she visits the village every day. But even cursory research quickly reveals the key elements of this narrative to be straightforwardly misleading. For example, the real pay usually reported by Patel's employees is Rs. 200,000 and this, according to a recruiter, might realistically only "keep her going for … three years."[38]

That Gujarati participants in Patel's ventures should appear outwardly every bit as uncoerced and as willing as Californian surrogates —and moreover, downright enthusiastic and grateful for the opportunity—is crucial for the Akanksha brand. Take it from Patel: they have been empowered to capitalize on their hitherto uncapitalized-upon uterine resources and be of use to someone. Of course, if this were more than a question of appearances, recruitment agents would not be necessary. But Patel *denies* that she employs such agents, claiming that surrogates and their husbands come to her by word-of-mouth referrals.[39] She has built from nothing, she says, an invaluable network of trust: "a *community* of 2,000 surrogate mothers in Anand."[40] But these words—"community" and "word-of-mouth" —are clearly stretching the truth. In 2014, Vice spoke (through an interpreter) to a woman in an outer Anand slum who alleged she brokered surrogate labor for Patel directly, on commission.[41] The documentary *Ma Na Sapna* begins unabashedly with this same "scout," who goes by "Madhu."[42] The findings of two local groups, Sama and the Human Rights Law Network, document the widespread practice of such people skimming off the (usually illiterate) surrogates' fee.[43]

Wombs in Labor confirms this picture by documenting the centrality of two live-in agents, viewed by surrogates as a cruel and haughty moralizer and a "crocodile eating up their savings," respectively. (Both double as hostel matrons.)[44] Of the latter, pseudonymously called "Vimla" (also a midwife at a different hospital), Pande writes:

> Nurses joke about her and refer to her as the "greedy broker." The doctor refuses to acknowledge Vimla's role in the surrogacy process and emphasizes she is not paid a "cut" by the clinic. Vimla, however, tells the story differently: "Doctor-Madam pays me a cut."

In fact, Pande found that the cut amounted at one point to 50 percent of the surrogate's wage. Surrogates at the time also reported to Pande that "Vimla" took huge additional referral fees out of their pay.[45] The boss's only on-record comment directly responding to this line of inquiry is "I do not encourage that."[46]

Patel alleged on BBC Radio that she turns down 67 percent of candidates who want to "serve" as surrogates at the clinic.[47] Indian women, she declares by way of explanation, come from a culture in which childlessness is so much feared, pitied, and abhorred that "when they learn that a woman is not having a womb, *they will do anything* to let that couple have a child."[48] This preposterous insinuation tallies neither with her own admission that "in the beginning, they start for money," nor with the evident need for brokering practices—not to mention the heaps of evidence that surrogates coming to the Akanksha do not even understand the mechanics of gestational surrogacy. In Mumbai at a different clinic, a worker explained: "We sign the contract but nobody reads it to us. And if there's a literate person in the room, they ask them to wait outside."[49] Even if the Akanksha does not go to those lengths to impede its employees from learning their loss of rights, the language with which it clarifies the task required of its recruits is euphemistic: *imagine that a child has come to stay at your house for a while.* Whore-stigma clearly shrouds the work that surrogates do, regardless of Patel's claims that "we have come out in the open."

What we see here is the valorization of two quite different attitudes in parallel. In public, Patel lionizes the grandmother's lack of shame; in her everyday manner, however, she rewards the unobtrusiveness of what Pande has dubbed "the perfect mother-worker": a mythical volunteer so angelic and so compassionate that she is willing to incur stigma upon herself worse than the stigma of childlessness in order to free someone—a stranger—from the latter.[50] Patel, in conjuring this Victorian fantasy, invites us all to believe in a proletarian who is not particular about her fee. At the same time, Patel proposes to be the workers' champion when it comes to their income, claiming to have "fought with IT [Income Tax] officials who wanted to deduct TDS [Tax Deducted at Source] from their earnings."[51] She insists that savings accounts be in women's names, imposing financial independence coaching on them, and patronizingly threatening their husbands: "I don't want any trouble."[52] Patel's anti-poverty, then, is not so much ungenuine as circumscribed by her overriding personal class interests. Her feminism is not so much "fake" as loyal to her class position and prejudiced against working-class men. Nor are her piety and her work ethic exceptional: they are simply inscribed with the affective contradictions of a society that incites many women to better themselves while still being premised on a gendered division of labor whereby "women's work" (unstinting, unseen) is socially required to manifest a total lack of desire for compensation.

Masterfully squaring this circle, Patel marries a protective baronial "feminism" with neoliberal bootstrap individualism. Deployments of the former can serve to smooth the way for the latter; and the combination of both secures the functioning of the Akanksha as a social enterprise. While the métier mediating all of this is indeed iconoclastic —literally dripping with viscera—the underlying thread of Patel's praxis is highly reminiscent of the nineteenth-century women-led eugenics movement's faith in personal striving, *noblesse oblige*, and god. For instance, in *Ma Na Sapna* (2013) she defends her dealings by appealing to a true enough dilemma. "In India there is no provision by the government to provide housing, food, and medical help to poor people, OK?" It is the *answer* she implicitly provides that we should question: "They cannot earn big money ... So ... what will these females do?" Well, some of the things they will do is exactly what Patel has found out. There is an apparent appeal for indulgence here, but there is also a heavy dose of capitalist-realist blackmail. The Akanksha is a branch of the Sat Kaival Hospital Private Limited Corporation, which is registered to four people: Dr. Patel herself (the founder), her husband Hitesh, her son Niket, and her daughter Mitali—all of them directors, all of them making millions.

In this clip, Patel is asking us, rhetorically: how could the Akanksha bringing jobs to town not be a good thing (crocodile brokers notwithstanding)? Actually, though: if the "females" of whom Patel is speaking cannot earn big money elsewhere in Anand, it turns out they cannot do so at the Akanksha, either. As the recruiter Madhu told the director of *Ma Na Sapna* in plain terms: "We tell Dr. Nayna to increase the payment, but she isn't doing it." Pivoting and contradicting her comparison of them to construction workers or maids, Patel tacitly justifies her denial of wage increases by framing surrogates as idle poor only *transitioning into* dignified work: "You came here illiterate but you won't leave that way."[53] The Akanksha, you see, is all about betterment, service, piety, and sisterhood. Dreaming big and loving what you do. But there is also this: doing what you're told, being of use, knowing your place, and working nonstop.

Skills trainings are indeed supplied. Yet, at the Akanksha (as we shall see in Chapter 4) the transmogrification of workers' fortunes— their self-liberation through service—mysteriously fails to happen. Medically dangerous "second surrogacies" are rife and even third and fourth cycles: "evidence," scholars have said, "of the clinic's failure to transform the lives of the surrogates."[54] Exploiting the idea that there is essentially "no alternative" to surrogacy for low-income Indian women, Patel mystifies their toil, even going so far at times as to flip the morally incumbent charitable relation on its head. The surrogates, in these moments, become smart decision-makers making a charitable gift to the rich. While appearing to grant low-income women newfound agency, this inversion primarily imposes bourgeois morality on them as a form of control, without however materially turning them into bourgeois subjects. Their economic need is painted as social enthusiasm for participation in the economy. Surrogacy isn't a job after all but a win–win investment, not so much a source of wealth as an internship.

I hope it has become clear by now why it is important to "call it work." The boss has provided an "in" by referring to herself as a feminist and describing the work she controls as "much better work." Refusing to back off that terrain—indeed, cleaving to it even as the boss tries to distance herself—looks to be a strong strategy for leverage.

Notwithstanding her flirting with a "labor" account of pregnancy, and notwithstanding her puff-chested invective against the phrase "wombs-for-rent," Nayna Patel's political economy doesn't break with the hegemonic account of surrogacy as a free gift of nature. This idea, which relies on a concept of (certain) human beings as empty space[55] available for leasing, is based on the *National Geographic* understanding of gestation as the unfolding of "life itself." It's a self-serving narrative, because bioclinical capitalists like Patel reap an immediate profit at the point where the commodity a commercial surrogate has produced changes hands, and it clearly seems more congenial to them to imagine themselves as indispensable agents and experts who help some random unfortunate set up a kind of anatomical Airbnb. Nobody has figured out yet how to automate the core labor, whether by developing ectogenic machines of a high enough calibre—along the lines of the Brooder in the imaginary town of Mattapoisett visited by Connie Ramos—or by *literally* renting out a disembodied womb (which would have to be grown and donated by a human being, then sustained in a kind of incubator), or by renting the uterine real-estate of a corpse on life support.

It will probably surprise no one to learn that capitalist governments do not recognize gestation as a productive form of employment, neither counting it in their employment statistics nor factoring it into labor law. This includes governments that "actively promote their reproductive tourism sector."[56] Amrita Pande reports that the bond between a gestator and her child tends not to be explained but is, rather, "*assumed* to be fundamentally different from the bond between a worker and his or her product."[57] Well-meaning leftists tend to trust their intuition that "the so-called 'surrogate mother' business" is "*obviously* exploitative."[58] Indeed, our wariness of anti-maternalism on the one hand and biological determinism on the other serve as powerful enough reasons to avoid "studying pregnancy, birthing and breastfeeding as material processes."[59] All too rarely do we spell out why it is that we find it possible to analyze other obviously exploitative industries qua industries, but not this one. It is time to shake up these tendencies and to update our politics with the knowledge that, as Michelle Murphy forcefully phrases it,

> the conceptual distinction of production-as-economic and reproduction-as-living was a forceful ruse that facilitated the demarcation of racial, sexual and colonial difference as "natural," legitimizing acts of violence and oppression.[60]

Even the professionally pregnant are far from being positioned as experts on life's production and distribution. In fact, where "life itself" is explicitly in play, politics risks disappearing into a vortex of the arcane. Nathan Stormer has posited that the dominant aesthetic within visualizations of gestation—where individuated human embryos are depicted as marshmallows ballooning as though in space—is a sublime one. We are enjoined to "look in wonder" rather than crediting ourselves or our comrades-in-labor for this "normal miracle."[61] The genesis of children is a matter of life's autonomous agency, or so the story goes. Life is probably, as such, "the ultimate commodity fetish."[62] Arising *sui generis*, it moves through earthly artisans like a holy spirit. Mere ordinary reproducers require expert tutoring in its productivities. We, the feminine substratum, albeit *wondrously* endowed, are "at once too feeble and too fertile" to know what we are doing, being "equally susceptible to excess production and to perilous passivity."[63] Confronted with a subject as sublime and enigmatic as that, who among us could be so pragmatic as to privilege the role of lowly, perhaps syndicalist, *gestators*?

I want to try. The term "gestational labor" is, in the first instance, a maneuvre intended to counteract "capital's capacity," advanced through pedagogical texts such as *In the Womb*, "to disguise itself as progenitor."[64] World-weary left-leaning readers may feel that to insist on labor as the source of worldly value is an overfamiliar point. Such a hunch, though, is not borne out by Tsipy Ivry's research, which asked whether the assumption that pregnancy is an active process has become embedded in prevalent twenty-first-century discourses. She concludes that, no, "the invisibility of women's procreative labor" in narratives of how children come into the world remains oppressive.[65] In sympathy with scholars like Ivry, affirming "gestational labor" defies the still-active ideologies that construct the womb as the passive object of efficient and expert harvesting, a space of waste, surplusness, or emptiness that is being profitably occupied.

Today's archetypal surrogated pregnancy is a site of labor; it is also, to paraphrase Margrit Shildrick and Deborah Steinberg, a "radically schismatic" site of "estranged bodily supplementarity."[66] But this schismatic structure of gestation—where disposability generates the surplus—extends Melissa Wright's observations about the cheapening of gendered labor in Mexican "maquiladoras" (export factories): "she creates extraordinary value with her extraordinarily low-value body."[67]

Who's Afraid of Gestational Labor?

In her study of surrogacy in the United States, *Labor of Love*, Heather Jacobson affirms: "As a group, surrogates are skilled at pregnancy and birth—and they speak about pregnancy and birth as skills ... a skill set that could be honed and practiced."[68] The sociological information contained in *Labor of Love* is valuable, both differing from and paralleling findings from cheaper parts of the market such as Russia, Central America, and the Indian subcontinent, where workers also hone their "craft" of pregnancy. But Jacobson insists on pregnancy and birth being work for a particular and (to my mind) noncongenial reason: she thinks work is an inherently good thing. This is a moral perspective widely echoed in popular condemnations of celebrity consumers of surrogacy. It inflects the common reproach levelled against so-called "vanity surrogacies," where there is no underlying fertility impediment motivating a female-bodied commissioning parent (who can therefore be deemed lazy). And this is particularly clear wherever the client is not dissimulating her glee and relief that she is not herself gestating, such as the case of Alex Kuczynski, the 2008 client of a commercial surrogate Cathy Hilling, who memorably described herself as an "Easy-Bake Oven." (The *New York Times*'s readership "loathed" Kucyznski for "skiing and white-water rafting in the ninth month of Hilling's pregnancy.")[69] Even Dr. Patel, despite the profits she might conceivably make if the culture of duty that still surrounds bourgeois women and childbirth were to shift, refuses to defend the right *not* to do gestational work and proclaims that she only serves deserving couples who would gestate their own baby if they could.

Anti-work feminists have been quick to identify this liability in their theorizing: in a "work society," as Kathi Weeks tells us, identifying something as work can all too easily be mistaken for moral praise.[70] I hope by now it is obvious that I'm with Kathi Weeks, not Heather Jacobson. Work is alienated labor, and it seems safe to say that—despite local concessions afforded by the welfare state—the vast majority of human gestation is at least somewhat alienated in a world in which people of all classes are equally free to starve. To say, with Amrita Pande, that "'gestational services' need to be added to the list of care work"[71] confers a kind of political legitimacy upon that alienation, if only the legitimacy of recognition. Looking at surrogacy as productive care labor is not a solution to all problems, but it opens up the realization that pregnancy workers can bargain, commit sabotage, and go on strike.

Approaches to being pregnant have varied massively across time and space and have included both communal forms of gynecology aimed at redistributing its burden and top-down exercise drills rolled out in mandatory classes on the basis that "the time to train for an athletic feat is before the event."[72] Though not under circumstances of their choosing, and not unilaterally, gestators have and make history: they "intervene in these processes and condition them according to their historically constituted needs."[73] While there is clearly a case for considering pregnancy a kind of ecosystem service or *animal* labor, it is also—simply—work. Kathryn Russell itemizes the basis for this definition succinctly: it features a unity of conception and execution, expends physiological energy, involves an interchange between a human being and nature, is planned, and utilizes instruments of (re)production.[74]

Treating the literal making of people in economic terms is likely to bring down on my head a harsher version of the left criticisms levelled at the Wages for Housework Campaign throughout the seventies: most pressingly, that I think gender oppression is entirely reducible to a division of labor and, hence, that it can be entirely surmounted through reproducers' insurrection. To address the last of my imagined critics first: I make no attempt in this book to address the question of gender directly and no claim about the sufficiency of an anti-work heuristic, unsupplemented by a theory of violence, for the purposes of revolutionary feminism's ultimate victory. What I address is not gender, but the development of procreation's professionalization. I'm simply talking about a form of work, gestating, that doesn't fit particularly well into the trend that many are referring to as "feminization."

I am not motivated by the goal of giving better recognition to this particular branch of reproductive labor, as though I could thereby effect some kind of compensation for the way it has historically been enclosed, monstered, and put on a pedestal by patriarchy. The aim is not to praise gestation as an essential use-value. As laid out, I am not pro-life and, frankly, the fact that gestation "makes an economic contribution" or "makes the world go round" is nothing much to be proud of, given the state of the world. (I'm more impressed by contributions gestating might make to this world's destruction.) No, making the labor of social reproduction visible—again, we Marxist feminists cannot stress this enough—is very much not an end in itself.[75] I'd even venture to say that seriously seeking to price the totality of reproductive labors (communicating, housekeeping, parenting, fucking, emoting, and so on) in order to secure monetary rewards for each of them conjures a world that is even worse than the alternative.

There is unfortunately a tendency to literalistically misapprehend the Wages For Housework Campaign provocation in that way—despite Federici's clarifications on the subject in the pamphlet Wages *Against* Housework.[76] This oft-touted critique worries that a bureaucratic reign of resentful accountancy will take hold, instead of the momentum of utopia, and it is motivated by a worthy concern. But, as the many-gendered autonomists of the struggle against housework have so often repeated to their critics: it's not us choosing to be economistic about gestation, it's capitalism. If we must cop to a kind of countereconomism regarding "what they call love," it is a needful demystification strategy. Unlike the Gender Equality policymakers of the UN, we aren't literally totting up a *bill* when we utter our stick-'em-up, claiming the wages due for centuries of babymaking "in cash, retroactive and immediately." We are demanding *everything*. That—not some pragmatic state-implemented basic income program for families—is the point of "serving notice" to the expropriators. "Wages for all gestation-work" is not a petition, and it does not describe an exciting destination. (Who'd get that excited about *wages* anyway?) It describes a process of assault on wage society. It's a noir joke, a provocation, an insurgent orientation intended to expose the ludicrousness of treating work as the basis for receiving greater or smaller amounts of the means of survival. It points somewhere beyond the horizon.

The immanent possibility of the gestational strike is probably, in the end, the most important reason for treating surrogacy as work. I am not talking about the "motherhood strikes" of the bourgeoisie. Those are the covert strikes carried out by the very mothers who get idealized in celebrations of maternity—namely, white members of the upper classes—who have, ironically, managed throughout the history of capitalism to reject and outsource the work of private mothering to a not insignificant extent. Undeniably, even bourgeois women have historically suffered and died from the problem of pregnancy. With surrogacy, however, *pre*partum labor is now included in the list of tasks to be delegated to nannies. Stratification has only deepened over time. The most affluent white "helicopter moms" hover nonstop but do less and less of the cleaning, cooking, and even birthing required to sustain their kids' basic functions, even as Euro-America's image of mothering remains tied to a quintessential whiteness—think of Jennifer Lawrence's blond, blue-eyed incarnation of the barefoot Mother Earth in the horror film *Mother!*[77]

It's with this fragile white symbol of maternal power and entitlement in mind that most of the culture seems to pay tribute to the notion of the motherhood strike (however watered down) on Mother's Day. But it was always working-class communities, first, who advanced the notion that reproductive laborers may refuse—in the face of unacceptable conditions—to do some of the habitual household tasks that sustain the lives of others. Festive days often distort this legacy when, instead of calling the beneficiaries and shirkers of reproductive labor to account, initiatives termed "motherhood strikes" are actually just cases of capitalist women dumping even more of their housework duties than usual onto the "help."

Though the "motherhood strike" is not an altogether unheard-of proposition in liberal democracy, there is a powerful injunction against ever thinking about abortion in these terms. When your job is exerting the capacity (gruelling, yet partly unconscious and uncontrolled) to manufacture another viable human, especially one who will be the child of other people far away, the stakes of anti-work refusal are likely to seem unfeasibly high. Downing tools, when your job is entirely within the limits of your own body, involves attacking a part of your own body—the baby—with murderous intent. Attempting abortion means trashing the living property; and, most likely, dashing someone's short-term dreams and hopes for the pregnancy. Yet gestators of oppressed classes *do* decide to abort their pregnancies, sometimes because other ways of bargaining over a distribution of labor have failed. To avert the need for this, obviously, the capacity of other people to be comradely, to treat the workers as kith (if not as kin and kind), becomes key.

What is abortion, if not the refusal to work up an embryo into someone's kin? For instance, enslaved women at various times have used a multitude of tactics to refuse the work of pregnancy and resist participating in the reproduction of slavery—ranging from herbalist birth control and abortifacient medicine to infanticide.[78] It should not surprise us then, to learn that workers in the formal industry, too, are threatening such tactics.

The following story is a mix of fact and fiction.

Outside Mumbai, a worker in a surrogacy house is being refused permission to travel back to her village to visit a dying relative. She is already regarded as difficult on account of standing up to the clinic in the name of a friend who was being denied part of her payment. Her job, she felt at the time, had been "almost compromised." Yet for the time being, alongside twenty-eight of her peers, she is still growing a fetus. Its genetic design and implantation via IVF-ET (in vitro fertilization followed by embryo transfer) was curated several months ago by the private clinicians in residence, on commission for "intending parents" from Europe, at significant cost to them. Now, she has heard, her grandmother is on her deathbed and wants to see her. But the pregnancy is nearing its third trimester, and the manager of the dorm denies her leave, invoking the contract she signed prior to beginning hormonal treatment to synchronize her cycle with that of the egg donor.

What do they mean, *she can't go*? She hasn't even been paid for the second trimester yet. Is that normal? Hard to say. It was a standard 2013-era Indian surrogacy contract, of which she had not been given a copy to keep, and which, in any case, she had not been able to understand—not least because it was written mostly in English (which she doesn't speak) and included no explanation for phrases like "transvaginal ultrasound" or "comply with clients' request for a caesarean section." Wait a minute, was her husband given a copy? It seems unlikely. The Non-Resident Indian ethnographer, who has been secretly visiting some of the surrogates after clinic hours, and bringing them sweets to share while she interviews them, has confided that—in her four years of fieldwork—she has never actually *met* a surrogate in possession of a copy of her contract. Anyway. The point is: the worker urgently wants to visit her family. But, unlike her friends and former colleagues in the garment factories, she can hardly bargain with her boss by going on strike.

Or can she? It occurs to her that she can "threaten to 'drop' the baby." And so, she takes the plunge and marches into the clinical office adjacent to the dormitory block. She demands to speak to the doctor who denied her, and—at the top of her voice, so that the others in the dormitory can hear her—she threatens to drop the baby. Lo and behold, "they finally let her leave for a few weeks." Since then, more surrogates have begun to follow suit ... suddenly, there's talk in the dorm of the rate American surrogates are paid; of demand for surrogacy far outstripping supply; of taking up that local farm-workers' representative on her offer of guidance in setting up a union—a fighting union, she said—and hammering out a set of demands.[79]

This lightly reimagined testimony captures a particularly visceral example of the moral blackmail to which all workers—but care and service workers in particular—are subjected. Nurses, midwives, and teachers (among others) face special social opprobrium for taking industrial action that puts other human lives directly at risk. Their chutzpah denaturalizes the violence required to keep webs of love flowing. But while striking nurses face imputations of personal responsibility for the harm (real or imagined) caused to patients during their missed shifts, surrogates have no "shift" as such. They have a nine-month, 24/7, piecework commission with a bioethical burden of responsibility attached to it that renders them very vulnerable to imputations of heartlessness in the event of their insubordination. Even so, the confrontation above, documented in the interview notes of a film crew, resulted (in real life) in a moment of victorious surrogate power.

Alternative tactics of resistance do exist. In her three-woman play about surrogacy, Satinder Chohan dramatizes a temporary slow-down deployed by a surrogate named Aditi.[80] Also based on real-life events—this time in Gujarat—Aditi refuses her confinement in the factory bedroom, refuses the expediency of the scheduled caesarean section, and runs away from the clinic in order to birth the surro-baby by herself in a shed. Chohan's production shows, effectively, that surrogates can sometimes rebel against unfair contracts by threatening something other than death—for instance, seizing the prerogative to flee, in defiance of the severe restrictions on their mobility. Once again, while there is only one way for gestational surrogates to literally *halt* their work, and that is by contriving a way to discontinue giving life to the fetus, by threatening to merely *steal* the fetal biocapital, surrogates have some hope, as Chohan intimates, of obtaining greater leverage by other means.

Unsurprisingly, since she is the boss of the outfit, it is not anti-work solidarity but a prowork sentiment—full of praise for the dignity of "service"—which undergirds Patel's appeals to destigmatize surrogacy and integrate it into the regulatory apparatus of global bioethics. Nevertheless, the proposals she is supporting—that international markets recognize surrogacy-as-work—would, if successful, represent a significant shift, even if cloaked in conservative rhetoric, and offer opportunities for grassroots movements to escalate surrogate workers' political prospects. Catherine Waldby and Melinda Cooper fully bring out the nuances of this in *Clinical Labor*.[81] The regime of bioethics has hitherto, they show, specifically sought to govern reproductive capacities for the express purpose of insisting that reproductive services should *not* be treated as work. While the determinations of the change remain an open horizon, there is no doubt that the proposed modification in international bioethical regulatory protocol is alarming bioconservative sensibilities (be they avowedly feminist or anti-feminist).

Historically, the bioethical proscription on baby commerce was based, first, on the masculine image of labor power's productivity at the core of classical political economy and, second, on the protective consensus that "women's labor is not a commodity"[82] (against mountains of evidence to the contrary). The elision of prescription and description in this latter claim is, I think, the basis of bioethicists' strange, yearning fixation on dystopia; what leads them to shudder pleasurably at the thought of handmaids in Gilead "out there" while completely failing to recognize the abyssal and systemic violence of the capitalist present. Uncomfortably for them, we are increasingly living in an age of social reproduction's primacy, where the ambiguously gendered productivities of clinical labor, unpaid labor, affective labor, and sex work are becoming hard to ignore. The traditional assumptions of bioethics are collapsing around us. As Alys Weinbaum trenchantly writes, "surrogacy as commodified labor power is the exceptional case that compels the redefinition of all forms of biological reproduction."[83]

Despite their declarations of deep respect for women's pregnancies, in the fevered imaginations of SERFs (surrogacy-exclusionary RadFems, a coinage I hereby propose), uteruses can only ever be put to use by bodies other than those of which they are part. The problem here is that they tend not to have heard of Bini Adamczak's term "circlusion," which designates "the antonym of penetration," designating "the same physical process, but from the opposite perspective"[84]—the perspective of the O, ring, chamber, aperture, or tube. Like mouths and throat cavities, vulvas, groins, anuses, and rectums, for SWERFs (sex worker exclusionary RadFems), uteruses—for SERFs—are irreducibly passive and cannot circlude. Circluding is the enfolding, sucking, holding, and—yes—*gestating* component of what is otherwise often referred to as poking, ploughing, seeding, fingering, or fucking. Failure to fully appreciate the ubiquitous reality of circlusion results in a thoroughgoing analytic femmephobia and means that, unlike the voice-boxes of call-center workers, the muscles of athletes, or the eyeballs of those on the smartphone-assembly line, it is assumed that the "inside of a woman's body"[85] cannot work: it can only be defiled, exposed, and ceded. In Laura Agustín's paraphrase: "the insertion of money" into relationships involving the inside of the body "signifies that no women can ever consent, even when they say they do." *Men consume, women are consumed*, it must ever be thus.[86]

Cross-referencing anti-trafficking/anti-prostitution and anti-surrogacy—these seemingly distinct policy arenas—is useful because it reveals the callousness at the heart of bioethicists' abstract deliberations; their ability to redefine sex and reproduction ("not for sale") as emotions (everybody's own personal prerogative) when it suits their aims. Take for instance the ruling, in that California court in 1990, that contract gestators "are not selling a baby; they are selling pain and suffering."[87] In handing down these words, the judge was awarding custody of a baby to the Calverts and denying the black gestator Anna Johnson's claim. "I see no problem," he said, "with someone getting paid for her pain and suffering." A revealing insight, given the racial dynamics in play, but one that still gives an unsatisfactory account of what is happening in surrogacy.

Surrogates *are* selling a baby, in a sense: I'm with the "anti-traffickers" and surrogacy abolitionists on this if nothing else. Generally speaking, they're right: even if their "emotional" duties of self-severance are complete, surrogates are not paid in full until live progeny has swapped hands. Where I diverge is in inferring that, therefore, they are selling the labor power that produces a baby, labor which then evanesces in that baby's still-moving, still-growing flesh. And this is where, for many, I become a messenger who needs to be shot. To philosopher Luna Dolezal, for example, my observations are horrifying. "Pregnancy *cannot* be likened to other forms of 'work' or 'labor,'" she states, categorically, "and any container or production metaphors are necessarily inadequate."[88]

Inadequate to what task, though? A production metaphor for pregnancy is no more inadequate to the task of making sense of gestating, in and against capitalist history, than is the "worker" metaphor for describing a human being. When surrogates' concrete labor is commodified, it congeals in the form of a creature whom specific individuals wish to regard as their talisman against mortality. As I discuss in Chapter 5, the child's nonfungibility—its quality of being "mine"—is paradoxically what makes it expressible as a quantity of abstract labor.

4

Dr. Patel Leans In

In 2009, pivotal minutes of Patel's daily business could be witnessed in the opening scene of the docudrama *Google Baby*.¹ Patel's moving image, broadcast on HBO, displays total confidence about allowing a film crew to train its camera not only on her, but on the face of a surrogate worker midpartum. Beforehand, she is completing a hurried call at her desk. She then stands and promptly makes another, failing to connect it. She steps briskly away from her cramped office, slips into different sandals, and dons operating scrubs that are tied at the back in a flash by a young attendant (one of many) who also takes the mobile phone. In the next room, a surgical team stands around the readied body of a pregnant woman, prone and partially covered in green cloth. Placing herself between her exposed thighs, a now-masked Patel claps the dust from her surgical gloves and utters praise in one breath to both Krishna ("Jaya Bhagavan") and "Mother Mary: bless her and bless the baby." The surrogate opens her eyes and forces a smile. She is visibly anesthetized. Immediately, final incisions are made: presumably an episiotomy, cutting the flesh between vagina and anus. Besides the co-surgeon, another clinician is positioned at the other end of the table, touching the forehead of the employee undergoing the cutting. The film pans to him reaching under the cover in order to vigorously push down in sharp bursts on the woman's upper belly, propelling the baby through the vaginal canal. During this, she makes no sound. This is not a caesarean section, yet the control of the surgeon over the birthing process is total.

At that exact moment, somewhat comically, the mobile phone rings. Patel switches to Gujarati to mutter to a second man "don't answer that call" (the subtitles translate), and then, immediately, "Jaya Sri Krishna" again (this is not subtitled)—because the baby has popped out. She lifts the urinating newborn into the air by the feet in a swift, visibly familiar, motion—and, while an aide is cutting the umbilical cord, she laughs about the tiny, still copiously spouting penis, mock-grandly announcing in English: "urine *passed!*" The ambience the camera now captures is both bustling and casual: many things have become inaudible; the baby is screaming while being cleaned in the background. But the person out of whom the baby has just been pressed is, we notice, discreetly sobbing. Subtitles indicate that the words Nayna and others are peremptorily addressing to her (in both languages) are "*You're fine? Is anything wrong? Then why are you crying? You're happy? Good*"—to which the response is simply dazed silence. The postpartum worker receives another injection.

"*Google Baby*'s rendering of transnational surrogacy," Asha Nadkarni writes, "would seem to be a revaluation of the pathological fecundity of the subaltern Indian woman ... turning it from a problem into a solution."[2] Patel herself might even agree with this assessment. A hawk-eyed spotter of a gap in the market, mistress of an ingenious logistics solution, she effects a redistribution of fertility worldwide. Inside or outside of the operating theatre, Patel's very favorite thing to quote is the glowing endorsement Oprah bestowed upon in 2006: *women helping women*. And, with Oprah as her role model, it follows naturally that Patel also emulates the head of Facebook and author of *Lean In*—Sheryl Sandberg—both in proclaiming herself "absolutely a feminist" and cheerfully describing her daily labor as "never-ending."[3] It is striking (given Patel's field) how, while the most obvious task that shares this daily quality is pregnancy, Patel pointedly does not make the link. Or perhaps it isn't, since leaning in—as critically explored by Dawn Foster—consists of the art of outsourcing and then re-invisibilizing social reproduction; identifying with the culture of the environment in which one's success will be defined, no matter the cost; and, above all, giving the impression of not having a life (let alone lives) to reproduce.[4]

Here is one continuous shot of Patel in the BBC Four documentary *House of Surrogates*.[5] She is finishing up a prayer session and striding out of her home past her servants, who are serving the family lunch, and toward her chauffeured car. To the hurrying camera crew following her, she is explaining diffidently the template of her usual working day:

> Full day. I am in the clinic, seeing my patients, delivering babies, doing IVF, laparoscopic surgeries. Afternoons, I remit to my email consultations, Skype, surrogacy work, any problems, anything to solve. Evenings, again, I see my patients, and I typically work twelve to fourteen hours a day. When you do something different in society that is challenging, and when you want to come up in a world which is ruled by men, you know, as a female, you want to fight that out. It is still difficult [for a woman] all over the world.

The glaring issue here is that, true to the in-built gap between the letter of *Lean In* and its on-the-ground realities—the same gap which allows the ideology to position itself as paradoxically both "feminist" and "postfeminist"—what Patel has shown is significantly different from what she has asserted. For one thing, the host of domestic servants responsible for her nutrition do not appear in her account. The work that goes into reproducing *her* is cheerfully invisibilized: a fitting irony for the commercial obstetrician who gives hundreds of women a nine-month pseudoholiday from their existence as wives and mothers in order to capitalize on their pregnancies.

While "women helping women" and holding hands across international borders is the Akanksha corporation's official credo, an attentive onlooker will readily glimpse Patel's nationalist streak. She speaks often of her pride in India and has dropped hints to Gujarati politics commentators since 2012 about intentions to run for election on the Bharatiya Janata Party ticket for the district of Anand—a move which, if successful, shall enable her to lobby internationally for more procapitalist surrogacy legislation.[6] She has always served foreign and domestic clienteles at different rates and is enthusiastically dedicated to holding devotional ceremonies in which the surrogates are honored as the "mothers" who made India's national economy "the cradle of the world." The theorist Banu Subramanian has even advanced the hypothesis that "the gestational surrogate of the new clinic is best understood as a figure of

Hindu bionationalism than as an avatar of technoscience."[7] What remains more intractable, for Subramanian, is the mystery of how, "in a country where Hinduism is deeply entrenched in the politics of purity and pollution … so intimate a practice of gestational surrogacy *isn't* centred around the primacy of caste."

It is true that caste keeps a surprisingly low profile in surrogacy mediations in India. It is partly a function of the export-facing character of the enterprise. The disposability inscribed upon low-caste lives has, however, been part and parcel of the muted perception of recent deaths such as that of the Indian surrogate Premila Vaghela and underage Indian egg donor Sushma Pandey.[8] And part of the answer for the disappearance of norms of caste endogamy in commercial surrogacy is provided in Amrita Pande's ethnography, which shows that prospective Indian parents *do* want Brahman (high-caste) surrogates to gestate their gametes if possible—it's just that, in the words of the unstoppable Doctor, the market is harsh and "couples can't afford to be picky."

> Only one or two have said they are not happy with the surrogate we have given them—the way she looks, or her caste, or religion. Our philosophy is "take what you get" and if you don't like what you are getting, too bad for you.[9]

Whether they are familiar—let alone concerned—with caste politics or not, infertile people worldwide have grappled in very pro-Patel ways with the ethics of becoming consumers of the uterine productivities on offer in her country. A 2017 study of marketing techniques used by transnational surrogacy vendors in their attempt to hook intended parents—"We Want To Offer You Peace of Mind"— found that

> websites depicted surrogacy as a solution to a problem, privileged genetic parenthood, ignored the potential for exploitation, dismissed surrogates' capacity to bond with the fetuses they carry, emphasized that surrogacy arrangements are mutually beneficial, ignored structural inequalities, and depicted surrogates as conforming to strict gender roles.[10]

Patel, for her part, adds the extra embellishment of a bromide or two about Nature: "there are two basic drives in life: to survive and to have a child."[11] It seems to be working: forums for parents indicate that clients of Dr. Patel's hospital are those who insist the most vociferously that they are at peace.

"For the Surrogates, Run by the Surrogates"

The Akanksha is not a charity. In addition to the surrogates, the payroll of Sat Kaival Pvt Ltd includes chauffeurs, stem-cell researchers, clinical housekeepers, nurses, obstetric specialists, cleaners, drivers, lab analysts, administrators, neonatal intensive care unit (NICU) staff, managers, cooks for the surrogate hostels, and many other staff. Until late 2015, the clinic spanned several small buildings. The institution was then upgraded to a gigantic multiplex at a new site on the outskirts of the small town. The cost of construction was cited at the time by Dr. Patel's husband, Hitesh Patel, as approximately $6 million. A visitor touring the site in 2015 was given double this figure: "$12 million, with a separate branch for stem cell research."[12] Patel has said that she intends on staffing the new multifunctional maternity hospital mostly with former surrogacy alumni: people who, by gestating the gametes of hundreds of clients between 2004 and 2015, generated profits sufficient to undertake this ambitious upgrade of the facilities. (Patel's honoring of this commitment is a matter that deserves future research scrutiny.) The idea, as repeatedly clarified for the benefit of various media sources, was to bring together offices, outpatient clinical facilities, delivery rooms, a NICU, gift shop, apartments for the infertility tourists, and dormitories for their gestational carriers all under one roof—a "one stop shop." In *House of Surrogates*, the bare skeleton of the dreamt-of super-hospital could be seen, springing up amid the slow bustle of construction laborers wearing hard-hats and saris. As Patel declares in that documentary, the "first-of-its-kind Institute for Surrogacy" is meant to realize her vision of "total care."

The Patels' underquoting of construction costs suggests, if nothing else, that the lack of social legitimacy currently attached to profiting monetarily from human gestation generates a certain sensitivity in Patel around the question of profits. In an outburst captured in *House of Surrogates*, Patel protested: "Whatever *I* am earning in the small clinic will be [the same] in the big clinic. Maybe it will increase marginally, 5 percent. Whatever I get, I will be *distributing*." I am interested in how this distributing is going. Those who, like me, have tracked the progress of the Akanksha corporation since 2012 might, at this juncture, remember the moment when Patel said: "I am already visualizing one step further ... one day, I am thinking of *a hospital for the surrogates, run by the surrogates.*"[13] It is not an unrealistic idea, even if it is not Patel's to voice. Sex workers in Calcutta and Mumbai, for example, have set up successful cooperative banks in which community members can safely deposit their earnings. Sharmila Rudrappa treats this as a viable surrogate-worker strategy, attesting to the victory for sex workers' struggle now secured in policy: "The state-owned Life Insurance Corporation of India provides life insurance for sex workers in Calcutta through a policy specially designed for sex workers."[14]

Is this what Patel really wants—especially if she is planning to concentrate her profit-making activities on her research and development laboratory? Of course it isn't. As the wealthy philanthropist and "feminist" eugenicist Katherine McCormick confessed in 1956—in the context of her involvement in coerced contraceptive experiments in Puerto Rico—containing a "cage of ovulating females" is already a headache.[15] Rabbits, McCormick complained,

> can be intensively controlled all the time, whereas the human females leave town at unexpected times so cannot be examined at a certain period; and they also forget to take the medicine sometimes—in which case the whole experiment has to begin over again—for scientific accuracy must be maintained or the resulting data are worthless.[16]

These are precisely the inconveniences Patel faces as a bioclinical innovator; her wording in candid, harried moments is often quite similar. Enrolling surrogacy alumna as housekeepers and administrative aides is one thing—but Patel is far more likely to "create employment" around the handling, storing, and routine testing of relatively inert matter like cord blood, stem cells, and placentas than she is ever to relinquish control over the ownership and direction of Akanksha's capital.

The level of "feminism," measured by a western standard, that is to be desired in the disposition of an Akanksha surrogate ultimately extends no further than her boss's comfort-zone; no further than the interests of her superior within what Silvia Federici terms the new international division of labor.[17] Recruitment criteria for a Good Surrogate, as Laura Briggs notices, closely resemble those for undocumented nannies; what clients seek is "loyalty,"[18] which is to say, exploitability and vulnerability to becoming trapped indefinitely in well-to-do metropolitan households (or, alternatively, *outside* of that home, on the wrong side of an immigration system far, far away). In the candid terms of a would-be employer writing in a 1993 *New York Times* article: "I want someone who cannot leave the country, who doesn't know anyone in [my city], who basically does not have a life ... I want someone who is completely dependent on me and loyal to my family."[19] Twenty-five years later, the trappings around this desire for total control over the surrogate may have changed, but its substance has not. First World Intended Parents' "posting of online 3-D and 4-D ultrasound images of 'their' fetuses gestating in the wombs of Indian surrogates"[20] functions as a form of cybernetic surveillance of the gestator. One surrogacy doctor was recently quoted as saying "these women are not sad, they are submissive."[21] Clients who think of themselves as feminists may struggle with their desire to hear that word, even if they are demonstrably reassured by it. They desire a supplementary guarantee that their chosen broker is somehow "different." With the help of additional phrases like "for the surrogates run by the surrogates" mitigating the "submissive" message, Patel has had considerable success in positioning herself as this guarantee.

The Sacred Thread, a book chronicling one customer's experience, pinpoints the central question for the "ethical" North American commissioning parent: "Is Dr. Patel's clinic a reputable institution?"[22] The rest of the book is an exercise in clearing its author's conscience—the answer is "yes." The *San Francisco Chronicle* similarly concludes a full-length feature with the words: "Jennifer's only real regret about the experience was that they hadn't turned to the clinic sooner."[23] In an article titled "An Appointment with Dr. Patel," *The Sunday Times* describes the doctor's sari, long hair, jewellery, and all-round aristocratic demeanor effusively.[24] Time and time again we find, in guilt-ridden ruminations about transnational surrogacy, a turn to Dr. Patel performing a salutary function, offering relief: a compromise between boycotting surrogacy on ethical grounds and not getting what you want. *This* clinic, clients have soothed themselves, represents an exception: Patel isn't in it for the money so much as for the joy of helping people: most of all "the women." This has by and large been the logic Patel sets up for the ritualistic unburdening of her customers' doubt. It allows for a repudiation of all other surrogacy clinics if necessary. Elsewhere there might be "womb-farms," but here, everyone has "that positive attitude."

However, Patel's rhetoric shifted in October 2015, when it was first reported that India's government would be withdrawing its special surrogacy visa for foreigners, making surrogacy available "only for Indian couples."[25] At that juncture, as one *Guardian* article conveys, Patel launched seamlessly from defending her clinic as different from all the rest into defending the industry as a whole. "There is no exploitation" *anywhere* in Indian surrogacy, she is quoted as saying; "it's a voluntary contract between human beings involving an exchange of money. What's wrong with that? It's a dignified earning. Instead of women working as maids, they can be surrogates."[26] Revealing the same low regard for the viewpoint of the human beings in question as the politicians in government, this moment signalled the strategic abandonment of Patel's narrative of her "surrogate-centered" clinic's exceptionality. Her interviews at this time charged that the announced legislation—including the later legislation ruling *all* commercial surrogacy illegal in India—would deal an unfair blow to humanity, to her newly expanded business, and to Indian national pride itself. Throughout her proactive personal media countercampaign of late 2015 through 2018, the doyenne of surrogacy continued to argue that the alternative in India is "women working as maids": an argument it is somewhat shameless for *her* to use if one recalls the footage showing that Patel employs maids in her own home.

If the Indian government's ruling that surrogacy must be "altruistic" sticks, we could reasonably expect it to embattle the surrogacy business of the Akanksha. However, it might become the case that surrogates get paid nothing while clinics keep receiving all the fees for IVF-EF, laparoscopies, and obstetric check-ups they were receiving all along. Besides, all signs point to a shift in Patel's business model. The Akanksha could readily stay afloat regardless of the legislative battle's outcome by pivoting onto the terrain of stem-cell research and (umbilical) cord-blood banking, an invidious new domain of privatization based on the idea that the stem cells in one's own umbilical cord contain invaluable properties for one's putative future health care needs. With over a thousand pregnancies having already provided the by-products—the pluripotent cells—for such research, it is hard to foresee Patel's multiplex not remaining in place to become a pioneer of the (further) desocialization of medicine. What is perhaps harder to imagine is how such laboratory work could still be incorporated rhetorically into a mission of feminist philanthropy.

"Doctor Is (Not) God"

What kind of person is this novice cord-blood banker? One Gujarat newspaper's encomium to Dr. Patel describes her history of "serving the poor" while still in secondary school at the Catholic Nirmala Convent in Rajkot. The Gujarat *Weekend Leader* featured Patel in its "Amazing Entrepreneurs" series as a "humanitarian ... hailing from a respectable family," the daughter of a "brave" Gandhian barrister and a mother with a "zeal for social work."[27] As readers were somewhat breathlessly informed, Patel "remembers visiting tribal habitations as a small girl and cutting the nails, cleaning the teeth, and washing the hair of the tribal people."[28] The *Leader*'s piece, in fact, reads as though Patel herself edited it: its title, "Giving a New

Life to Many a Childless Couple and a Livelihood for Women" is precisely her message. The journalist admiringly notes the Kaival Corporation's Rs. 29.40 crore ($4.4 million) yearly turnover but hastens to add: "Dr Nayana has refused to look at surrogacy as a money-spinner." What follows is a potted hagiography of Patel's trajectory in corporate management. From 1993, the reader learns, she courageously borrowed and invested in good-quality sonographic and embryoscopic equipment. This clearly helps illustrate Patel's desire for a "lifelong bond" with "her surrogates." And virtue such as this (the article clearly implies) is its own reward: now she maintains a charitable trust that "offers medical assistance ... to surrogates who might have medical problems ... provid[ing] school bags and books to their children."[29] Despite enormous acclaim, Patel "refuses" all opportunities that would expand her business "too fast"; she rejects franchise requests "even if it mean[s] losing revenue."

Historically, there have been some different "requests" that Patel turned down—precisely because they threatened her revenue. In 2013 the *Indian Express* quoted Patel as "planning to launch a new brand"—the Anand Surrogate Trust—to be run by former surrogates on an artisanal trademark, SurroMAA. "Around 20 women," she is quoted as saying, "will get trained in chocolate-making initially. We plan to produce nutritive ingredient-based snacks that can be consumed by mothers-to-be and infants."[30] There is no evidence that any SurroMAA chocolate-making happened. Regardless, in the corpus of television materials generated about her that year, Patel made use of the idea in order to couch surrogacy in the language of gender-mainstreaming and "empowerment" policy. Here viewers were presented with surrogacy as a way of investing in women: a "win-win" opportunity for girls to become entrepreneurs. The terms "gender-smart," "smart giving," and "smart technology" would not have been out of place alongside Patel's phrase "total care."

But only one year prior, the *Express* had described a more radical intention: "Patel had announced the formation of a *cooperative* with 100 surrogates."[31] The original plan here—unlike the putative co-op in Bangalore I mentioned—was for the micro-business to cooperativize confectionery manufacturing labor, not gestational labor. Even so: as one reporter notes, the surrogates "had to shelve the plans, owing to an inspection by the Indian Council of Medical Research (ICMR) ... when the clinic was guided against such a move."[32] Patel manifestly did not tell the *Express* who it was who "guided" her against allowing the surrogates' co-op to be established, nor what negotiations were involved in it being "shelved." What is clear is that, in formulating a substitute plan, Patel fell back on the rigid hierarchies of the charitable traditions she knew in childhood:

> My dream ... which I will start in June [2016], is educating the school drop-outs, the chai-wallahs, the slum children: bringing them, tempting them, giving them a different sort of audio-visual training and education, computers, banking and so on.[33]

This, needless to say, is standard philanthropic window-dressing. Mentioning the possibility of worker ownership seems to have been little more than a public relations exercise, since in practice the co-op idea was immediately replaced by the standard top-down charity, Anand Surrogate Trust. Even as murmurs about empowerment and democracy were blithely replaced with a "benevolent" hierarchy, the vague pronoun deployed by Patel in speaking for it became—increasingly—"we":

> We collect donations, we help the children of the surrogates get their education. We help the surrogates with any medical help, even a few years down the line, even if it is not gynaecological. We help them—with medical treatment, or cover up certain loans. Even their family member is sick, we help them—everything.[34]

Given the air of global self-importance Patel likes to cultivate, it should come as no surprise that she has sought to give a TED Talk. Patel's April 2016 appearance at the TEDx event at KIIT University in Odisha fell flat in many respects, but its "striving" rhetoric was successfully true to the medium. The TED Talks media platform exemplifies, as one scholar puts it, the rise of neoliberal citizenship and "celebrity humanitarianism."[35] The doctor told her audience:

Dream! ... Use your knowledge and skills for betterment of society. Don't wait, saying "this is my time to earn; when I'm retired, I'll start helping people." Helping the people starts when you are earning! ... And at the end of the day, you know, the more you give, the more you get back ... More returns will come to you ... Be a philanthropist right from day one. I don't say "go bankrupt" or "don't help your family." Family comes first! But simultaneously, start your social service, don't wait for retirement ... And bless the critics ... Change is always not accepted at first ... Go ahead ... Never give up, because life is all about struggles ... Stop not, until the goal is reached![36]

Listeners are promised the satisfaction of having fat personal dividends "at the end of the day" while simultaneously submitting to the moral admonishment to give this wealth away—keep it circulating!—almost *in advance*. As with her remarks in the slum, Patel's speech confronts us with a vision of cyclical endlessness that naturalizes capitalism by means of spiritual, almost ecological imagery. Indeed, the final words in this speech quote a popular sloka of Swami Vivekananda: "Arise, awake, and stop not until the goal is reached." Vivekananda was a key figure in the middle-class nationalist movement within Hinduism that has been described as "bourgeois Vedānta" with "colonial roots."[37] This interpretation of Vedic philosophy, which deems "life [to be] all about struggles," has proven easy for Indian philanthrocapitalists to pair with the class-erasive message that we are "all in it together" (facing two basic drives). Meanwhile, capitalism's structural insatiability dictates that most "goals" never stay still (and as such can *never* "be reached").

Appreciating surrogates' own sense of the central participation of "god's labor" in their job (especially the "everyday divine") is not at all incompatible with skewering the class-blind framing of surrogacy as "gifts for global sisters."[38] It is patently obvious that Patel's employees are, in fact, routinely invited to deify *her* a little bit. Patel occasionally betrays monomaniacal lapses, even on camera, in which she likens *herself* to god. In her pronouncements on the "two basic drives," after all, we are ultimately hearing statements on the dizzying, quasi-messianic importance of her vocation. According to her own understanding, Patel deals in two things: on the one hand, the desire for *life* (the economic means to reproduce a life worth living for one's existing children) and, on the other, the desire for a specific new life or lives (not just any progeny but progeny of certain genetic parentage). Ministering to these "incontestable motivations," to borrow Heléna Ragoné's phrase, is essentially doing god's work under the embryoscope.[39] Godlike, Patel facilitates the fulfilment of both "primal" drives—bringing disparate questing hearts together in symbiotic unity.

As a public relations gambit, it is magisterial: the sheer neatness of this universalist "two basic drives" formula (1. for a better life, 2. for renewing "life itself") obscures the fact that Patel is actually splitting them. She is rendering "a new life" and "the ability to live" oppositional to one another. Their separateness and commensurability is accomplished through a discursive act of "sectioning" that mimics not only the cut of the scalpel (quick and timely for the "parents," long and painful to heal for the worker) but the distribution of liability that has become standard in nonphilanthropic neoliberal business. Risk is shouldered squarely by the laborer-cum-entrepreneur; not least, the risk carried by a C-section. Russia Today filmed instances of the liability release statement Patel makes to surrogate-recruits while signing them up in her office. The surrogate is told firmly: "*You* are responsible. If something happens, the clinic is not responsible. I am not responsible. The parents are not responsible."[40] So it is here, backstage, that the secret is revealed: Patel does not satisfy both parties' (or classes') libidinal imperatives. It is here, in the hidden abode of production, that workers are told: "Doctor is *not* God."[41]

That this egalitarian "win-win" framing has made headway on a global stage in legitimating commercial surrogacy is a testament to the diabolical canniness of Nayna Patel. Perhaps more than anything else, her mastery lies in having brought this trade—a living for a life—out of the purview of the biopolitical state and under the aegis of the firm. It would be foolish to doubt the force of feeling Patel inspires. She has an international coterie of often fanatically devoted former clients online. Grateful parents write dedicated blogs about their journey to Anand, promote her speaking tours to the United Kingdom and United States, and comment proactively in her defense on forums at Dr-Patel-Surrogacy.com—"Dr. Patel's Global Support Group"—or on the Akanksha Facebook page.[42] (One January 2016 comment reads "you are the one healing all the pain.") Speaking of pain, as we've seen, there is a large unspoken quantum of it that Patel contractually externalizes. Perversely, however, even some surrogates say things like "you are the one healing all the pain" to Doctor-Madam. "Nisha" in *Ma Na Sapna* says "she is more import-ant to me than my mother or my god"; while "Aasima" declares: "All of us here support Dr. Patel."[43] Most accounts depict a close-knit, happy (albeit reverently hierarchical) sorority in which even a regular assembly might end with the spontaneous cry: "everybody, touch her feet! She is our mother goddess."[44]

The anti-surrogacy activists visited in Chapter 2—like their Indian counterparts—view her as more of a demon; a baby-seller, an exper-imental creator many times worse than Dr. Frankenstein. And Patel's business does involve alchemizing new realities (though that is not the reason it—or any capitalist firm—is diabolical). Actually, from the anti-surrogacy point of view, we have still not glimpsed the central, and the most breathtakingly profane, moment in Nayna Patel's "ontological choreography."[45]

In the *Google Baby* scene with which we began, Nayna and the pediatrician are busy with their task when the mobile phone rings again. This time, the first man answers—"Hallo? Please hold"; then turns, in order to press the phone to Nayna's masked face. She traps the phone under her chin while continuing work with the suturing needle. Her blood-covered hands seem more than able to deal automatically with the unconscious body of her surrogate employee, while, separately, her voice deals with the person who has rented a similar body's capacities. The substance of what we hear her say in the very act of stitching up an abdomen creates a certain obvious but unconscious irony. She uses business English: "Yes, I'm so sorry, doctor, but, you know, it's *not an easy procedure.* It's a very *complicated* procedure, is surrogacy, and they should understand all the implications. Yes. Bye-bye, no, most welcome, bye-bye. Bye."[46]

What irony! Briskly sealing deals while physically sealing up a womb, the faintly bored-sounding Dr. Patel paradoxically asserts the high level of skill involved in the latter. She asserts, above all, that it is *her* highly skilled labor that defines the "surrogacy" process—not the surrogate's gestational creativity.

Here comes the clincher. Having just taken a baby out of a person's body, Patel nonchalantly issues the instruction: "Now take the baby *out to the mother*." This arresting illocution is the uncanny apogee of a performance, captured in *Google Baby* and already repeated innumerable times in real life. The author of this "repro-tech" operation flags exactly what she is doing: making parents. Dr. Nayna doesn't just produce babies. She cuts and draws, makes and breaks relationships of parentage; creates claims and nips others in the bud. Nonchalance is part and parcel of the communicative strategy. By enacting, for her implied and explicit audiences, a form of everyday surgical midwifery that is fused with a banal boss-employee relationship, Patel familiarizes us with the practice of clinical labor—on her own terms. This performance essentially consists of clinical labor's *manager* telling us, on the workers' behalf, that all of this is already real (so get used to it!). What we saw was not a mother; it was surrogacy. Motherhood was born, but the new mother was not the woman on her back. Nor was she the one talking on her mobile phone—the omni-mother—wearing surgical scrubs, standing upright. The real new mother, in fact, was not even in the room. She—if indeed it is a she—is waiting in the lounge at reception.

Leave Your Husband, Love Your Boss

Picture the scene: seated in the back of a car, wearing sunglasses, Patel is delivering a thundering segment for Russia Television. She does not pause to hear criticism—she knows already what's on your mind. "To my critics I say: *Can YOU give this poor couple a child? Can YOU give this poor woman's family a better life?* When you do, I will STOP doing SURROGACY!"[47] Or take this barrage to the BBC in 2008: "Are they [the surrogates] murdering someone? No. Are they doing a robbery? No. Are they doing some immoral act? No. Then what are they doing? They are doing a GOOD ACT by giving a baby to someone!!"[48]

These rants misunderstand the object of a putative anti-capitalist critique and unintentionally reveal the sheer poverty of a moral code that subordinates means entirely to ends, judging right and wrong on the sole basis of individual aspiration, the sanctity of individual property. Nevertheless, as early as 2007, such was the determination of the Akanksha-as-social-business to express its altruistic mission on its website that it was outright claimed: "The surrogates receive the full amount for their surrogacy, the clinic taking nothing at all."[49] (This text is now only accessible via the website's cached history.) Gosh, the full amount? If this were the case, one might well ask, how do the Patels themselves subsist, and how do they pay for their air conditioning? Why shouldn't the lucky surrogates *pay* for the privilege of their literacy and money-management training at the Akanksha? Believe it or not, the latter has certainly occurred to Dr. Patel: "… while Akanksha Infertility Clinic helps counsel the surrogates on money matters, we neither expect a single rupee of it nor would we take any. This service is for their benefit." Remember: the new Akanksha boasts a multi-million-dollar research facility on its top floor. For a clinic in the habit of "taking nothing at all" while remaining dedicated to not "expanding too fast," it cuts an astonishingly vast, white, futuristic figure on the ex-urban landscape. What is going on here?

What we're looking at is an attempt by Lady Bountiful (CEO) to legitimize her tranche of India's surrogacy market within the developmentalist discourse of "philanthrocapitalism." The latter term refers to the logic by which individual entrepreneur's progressive causes, such as women's empowerment, are celebrated more or less openly as strategies for capital accumulation (and vice versa). With her TED Talks and her Vivekananda quotes, the strategy that Nayna Patel is experimentally embodying qua industry figurehead is undoubtedly a philanthrocapitalist one. And while surrogacy-as-philanthropy remains a contested framing, it is already one that has smoothed the path for many a "compassionate consumer."[50]

The portmanteau *philanthrocapitalism* could in many ways describe most image-conscious members of the upper classes throughout colonial and modern history. However, it tends to be used to refer to more recent, "neoliberal" fusions of charity with business—where the promotion of entrepreneurship *is* the anti-poverty strategy and is often mediated by billionaire celebrity personalities. According to the 2008 handbook *Philanthrocapitalism: How the Rich Can Save the World*, for example, nonprofit and political activities are ultimately to be rejected in favor of (as *The Economist* has it) "doing well by doing good"—"win-wins" initiated through rich people investing in ("smart giving") something intangible never named as labor.[51]

The archetypal "social entrepreneur" is perhaps Muhammad Yunus, founder of the Grameen Bank. Self-designated "Banker to the Poor," Yunus repackaged capitalism entrepreneurship at the turn of the millennium as an "anti-poverty" approach, soon to become development orthodoxy. In lieu of boosting welfare spending or macro-infrastructural investment, Grameen-style "giving" involves offering tiny high-interest loans to individual women. (Poor brown women are constructed as more "fiscally responsible" than poor brown men.) A powerful oratorical free-market rhetorician, Yunus received a Nobel Prize despite ample evidence of debt's ill effects on women's lives and microcredit's inability to transform structural poverty.[52]

Dr. Patel can claim to be a banker to the poor like Yunus, not so much because she literally opens bank accounts for her employees (although she does), but because she brokers a form of biocapital—embryos—linked to an opportunity to take a risk, enabling proletarians to capitalize on their biological assets. I'm not the only one to have spotted the similarity: Nadkarni muses that "Dr. Patel's view of surrogacy as a form of empowerment resembles much-vaunted microcredit programs, which solve the problem of women's poverty by enabling women's entrance into largely unregulated and exploitative informal sector work."[53] With "doing well by doing good," or "doing good by doing well" as the dominant underlying motivation for the Akanksha's expansion, Patel's mission as a self-styled altruistic employer has already charted a high-growth trajectory. Surrogacy work is now routinely presented to the Indian recruit as a form of adventurous risk management—the risk in question being poverty, caste, and class disadvantage—where the risk-taker's strategy is dependent in turn on her ability to effect successful waste management—the "waste" being her "fallow" womb.[54] To paraphrase the words of another surrogacy clinician, Patel "only needs a uterus" to help everyone realize their potential.[55]

There aren't many public players visibly interested in cutting through the numerical vagueness surrounding projected increases in Patel's direct income. Private attorney Harjit Sarang enthusiastically interviewed Patel in the immediate aftermath of the BBC Four broadcast. In that saccharine exchange, Patel performed her signature tactic: ventriloquizing critics the better to (sensationally) refute them. "People think that I am making this grand new project to get more money!" she expostulated to Sarang, "NOTHING LIKE THAT!! It is not going to increase [here, she abruptly tails off] ... to the extent that they think. It is to give more employment."[56] Perhaps sensing opportunities for "more employment" herself, Sarang—a surrogacy lawyer—sympathized and heartily assented to this framing. It is hard to imagine a more vivid artifact of the cultural taboo against bourgeois femininity expressing mercenary motivations or openly engaging in the pursuit of profit.

Does the proletarian femininity that Patel "uplifts" have any more room to breathe, or is it rammed into the bourgeois mold? One of the glibbest, most insidious foreign ideas about the "house of surrogates" is that it is a kind of women's commune. Granted, surrogates spend six or seven months gestating and living together, resting, socializing, and earning money while their husbands take over all their daily tasks back home. So it is tempting to imagine a kind of an "anti-family" in which women are finding refuge in each other away from their usual unpaid reproductive duties, excusing themselves from their respective households and capitalizing on something that "good" women are not supposed to capitalize upon: wombs. The temptation to romanticize this grows especially strong in light of the cheerful misandry that can frequently be glimpsed in much of the footage. Surrogates' husbands are the butt of frequent jokes, be they living or deceased. (Remember, *all* the surrogates are either married mothers or widows.) If alive, these husbands often suffer terrible dressings-down at Patel's hands in her office. A certain glee around this is evident in all western documentary films about Patel's establishment, for instance, in the moment in *Wombs for Rent in India* in which Patel extracted nervous laughter from a gathering of sixty or so surrogates with the line: "Ah! A HUSBAND is ALWAYS a PROBLEM!"[57] In *House of Surrogates*, Patel is visiting newly enrolled surrogates in their separate dormitory when, in response to an account of one husband's drunken brutality and mendacity, she tells the woman: "Just *leave* him!"[58]

Admittedly, it is difficult not to enjoy all this. A delighted American and British media tends to strike a seductively celebratory tone about it that is easily swallowed (not unlike the message of *Lean In*) if one fails to notice that it is only *working-class* heterosexualities that are being mocked and undermined, only *working-class* relationships with children that are being strained and separated. Predictably, smaller-scale and more locally rooted media efforts have on the whole managed to be more thoughtful and respectful than have western ones when addressing this area. For example, in one scene, an Indian interviewer with the collective VPRO Metropolis cautiously approaches a woman preparing chilies on the floor of the Akanksha dormitory and addresses her in her own language. It is not at all implied that there is anything to laugh about in her response to his questions: "If you had my drunk and abusive husband, you would also enlist as a surrogate."[59]

In 2009, Patel invited a Delhi theater company to Anand to give a special performance of a play about "Fool Gulabi," a headstrong surrogate who defies her husband. *Fool Gulabi* was attended by 100 of her employees, and such was the comically misandrist and poignant splendor of the depiction that, as Patel reportedly enthused afterwards, "I could hear all my surrogates clapping."[60] Whereas fee-skimming agents or bosses aren't mentioned in her account of what so moved them to mirth, Patel's anecdote reinforces the line that intrafamilial male encroachment over women's money presents the biggest problem in surrogacy. (It is a pattern alleged to be rife in microfinance—enabling advocates to pin blame for its failures solely on brown men.) In contrast with both her obfuscatory stance on brokers and her respectful attitude to her own husband, Dr. Patel proactively targets the endemic phenomenon "no-good husbands." There is a name for this leadership strategy: triangulation.

Certainly, life inside the Surrogate House enables a temporary form of defiance toward a husband.[61] It provides temporary escape from motherhood in the act of generating motherhood for someone else. But there are trade-offs involved. The heterotopia over which Patel presides is defined by its moderately defiant stance toward heterosexual proletarian marriages, not patriarchy as a whole. And what husband bashing accomplishes, in context, is not particularly liberatory anyway. It primarily obfuscates other relevant dynamics—notably, the intrawomen class relations between Patel and the surrogate workers. The sisterly call at the Akanksha may be to "leave your husband," but it comes at the cost of loving your boss.

Doing It for the Children

In championing the procreative rights of relatively affluent infertile heterosexual couples, Patel appeals variously to a humanist register—in which the barren body receives the intrinsic "right" of reproductive "care"—a determinist register—positing two basic "drives"—and a socio-spiritual one—in which people's purpose on earth is proliferation. All these various forms of legitimation, as far as she is concerned, sanction commercial surrogacy as a means of "acquiring one of the most intimate aspects of human life—the parent-child relationship"[62]—for those that can afford it. Be it at cord-banking conferences or TEDx symposia, her universalist biomedical framing of her arguments conceals the reality of whose childlessness counts. Patel might cry (or so she alleges) over the gametes she ushers from petri dish to fallopian tube, but she seems unmoved by how, in the absence of world revolution, some gametes are simply never going to make the trip. Put differently: some infertilities are not even *visible*, let alone in a position to elicit tears. To say that Patel is merely silent with regard to reproductive justice is therefore a grotesque understatement. As far as Patel is concerned, she washes her hands of responsibility for structural relations because she deals in *families* (and inside a family, so the ideology goes, there can be no stratification). But it is precisely the family, this bourgeois norm that capitalist society naturalizes and imposes on everybody, that privatizes and stratifies social misery, structurally obstructing the flourishing of "collectivized means of material survival that bring us into relation with each other in bonds of solidarity and care."[63]

But in some cases, surrogacy's entire economy actually does take place inside a single family. When this occurs, surrogacy is partially segregated from capitalism and confined within a single legal, affective, and usually also genetic, unit: a sister gestating for a sister (or sister-in-law), an aunt for a niece, and so on. Despite the paucity of data on surrogacy markets, it is safe to say these cases are still in the minority worldwide, even though some governments (notably the United Kingdom's and India's) would currently like to confine the whole industry within the bounds of "altruism." Given Patel's fierce opposition to the Indian iteration of that anti-commercial legislation, it is instructive to notice that it is nevertheless precisely such a case that she has chosen to center narratively in her "story of the Akanksha clinic." Make no mistake: the vast majority of the arrangements she has brokered in her career involved strangers entering into a commercial contract for payment across significant difference or distance. In contrast, the famous and often-repeated origin-story of Patel's sphere of specialization is a tale with *intra*familial rather than interfamilial and altruistic rather than commercial characteristics.

In Patel's own words, this formative case is a British-Indian one involving Non-Resident Indians from the suburban town of Ilford in Essex, England. Most strikingly, the surrogate was Radha Patel, no relation of Nayna Patel but not unlike her in some ways. Accounts in British newspapers varied in placing Radha Patel between 43 and 47 years of age. Says the doctor of her double, the company's "maiden" grandma:

I always thought that it [surrogacy] is a headache. But then I had this first couple from UK, where the girl was Indian, and they could not find [or] afford a surrogate in UK. For three months they searched for a surrogate in Anand, and Delhi, and could not find one. And therefore the girl's *mother*, that is, the *grandmother*, delivered the twins for the daughter. And when I saw the end-result, I was *really happy*! Because the husband was ready to divorce that girl …[64]

As an instance of a grandmother surrogacy, the 2004 case was only the fifth in global history, a fact proudly emblazoned on the Akanksha's original website. The above is transcribed from a February 2016 Russia Today segment, but similar renditions appear elsewhere in which Patel clarifies that the girl was "beautiful" and that the husband "wanted his wife's genes or was ready to throw her out."[65] Patel's account varies, and at least one element suggests factual slippage: there is the claim, for instance, that the clinic was named "Akanksha" after this auspicious first baby, when in reality they were twins, and their names were Neal and Nandine.[66] Regardless, these narrations betray considerable identification with the grandmother-surrogate, whom she outright eulogizes: "What will a mother not do for her children? … She did it, and then she came out in the open and she said … 'There's nothing wrong about it.'" The *positive attitude* of the morally irreproachable grandmother-surrogate remembered and honored in Patel's autobiographical speech clearly provides a deep well of inspiration for Dr. Patel when she boasts (in her TEDx Talk) of the shame-free "community" in Anand "out in the open." But this narrative of destigmatization sits uneasily with the *other* Mrs. Patel's widespread insistence on anonymity at the time, for fear of stigma.[67]

What happened after the illusory "Baby Akanksha" surrogacy? Patel talks us through the thought process that made her realize that surrogacy could in fact be scaled up, while preventing it from being a "headache":

Not all females are that lucky, that they can have family or a friend who can do it. So then I thought: that this is not a bad option, this is a good option! The birth certificate will have the name of the genetic parents, not the surrogate. The surrogate has no *right* over the baby and no *duty* towards the baby, so the legal problem post-surrogacy is not there, adoption is not required, and neither can the surrogate *keep* the baby—that is very important. And finally, the cost. It is definitely one-third of the cost of surrogacy in the western world: the doctors, the clinics, the surrogates, everyone charges that much.

Here, extrapolation from the immaculate "grandmother" case—itself already bowdlerized—extends so far as to lose sight of it completely. In every case going forward, that is, in every case *except* this originary one, the surrogate will have barely any further contact with the family afterward, and she will be *paid*. When it comes to any other surrogate's daughter's infertility, for instance, the clinic will not arrange for it to be serviced (by her or anyone) for free. Needless to say, a price that is one-third of that in the western world is still a barrier to most people ever accessing commercial surrogacy. If Patel is not going to provide surrogacy for free or on a sliding scale, then she is merely paying lip-service to everyone's right to be helped while necessarily only elevating a limited, affluent constituency's appetite for babies to the status of a health care entitlement. Lastly, that Patel feels able to say that her surrogates "charge" one-third of what western surrogates do, as though they set the price themselves, is somewhat damning.

One woman is flimsy grounds for Patel's claims that she supports stakeholder control over her surrogacy business. Nevertheless, it is the affluent, dignified, and immaculate figure of Radha Patel who seems to be animating Dr. Patel's statement that she would— "in a heartbeat"—serve as a surrogate herself, "even without the desperation"[68] ... *on her children's behalf.* Unencumbered by too much historic specificity, the tale of the British-Indian lady and her daughter from 2004 was evidently chosen to be the metonym for all surrogacy because it accomplishes an astonishing representational elision of the internal gulfs between commercial and altruistic surrogates. The unpaid altruistic surrogate who is *doing it literally for her child* stands in inconspicuously for all surrogates, who are doing it *economically* for their children.

There is a striking contrast between the fervor the clinician deployed to save this middle-class couple from divorce and the pseudofeminist dismissiveness she deploys toward working-class marriages. Patel typically recounts—whether or not this is true—that Radha proudly gestated her son-in-law's genes *in order to save her daughter's marriage*. Was this definitely such a worthy cause? Patel seems to have assumed so, with gusto. Yet, rather than fighting equally hard for conjugal harmony between the illiterate villagers in her area, whom she uses economically, she actively encourages their divorces, as we've seen. And it's not as though there aren't couples of that class who inspire affection. One useful counterpoint to Patel's anti-working-class-husband shtick appears in *Ma Na Sapna*. One surrogate's husband, Pinto, is shown caring for his wife (and for their child) in all kinds of ways. Pinto helps Papiha in her postpartum recovery by carrying her pumped breast-milk from floor to floor, feeding and massaging her, and earnestly asking the clinic to be allowed to do more. Ideally, he says, he would feel that he is actually *participating* in the job of surrogacy. "Is there nothing for us gents?" appeals Pinto to Dr. Patel via the interviewer, "Pay us less [than the gestators]! but hire us for something." Here is Pinto, struggling for admittance to a workplace in which surrogates are invited to leave their "bad" husbands (temporarily or permanently), only to sign themselves over to the megalomaniacal matron of a permanent all-girls' sleep-over club that demands submissive participation in the hypervalorization of bourgeois marriages and their "universal" procreative ideal. Papiha and Pinto's partnership, in my view, enacts a touching resistance to this faux-feminism.

Director Valerie Gudenus seems to agree, persistently shining a querying, probing light on the presented image of a happy sorority united in piss-takes about lazy men. Although removed in 2016, the Akanksha website carried text for several years describing the "nurturing environments" and "camaraderie" of the spaces surrogates inhabit, stating that they are "run by a former surrogate who had a vision to care for her 'sisters.'"[69] But one scene in *Ma Na Sapna* shows a surrogate ("Champa") describing her utter hatred for the place. There is even an outright brawl captured, in which surrogates beat and hurl abuse at one another. Gudenus seems to be giving us the option, then, of understanding Surrogate House not so much as an anti-family then, but rather as—precisely—a *family*, with all its attendant psychological violence, structural conservatism, and normative efficacy. More so even than "what kind of family?" the most pertinent question for the doctor is perhaps: what does it *mean* to call something a family? When Patel claims "I keep them [the surrogates] like my daughters"[70]—what does that mean? If the people Patel calls "my surrogates" are to play the part of children, then what kind of parent is she? A disciplinarian one, it would seem. This is a typical utterance: "Before you leave this house each of you must learn to write your signature. Otherwise you won't get your money. Got it?"[71]

The parental rationale is almost explicit; the broker "Divya" in *Wombs in Labor* quotes Patel as saying, "how you train them, that is what makes surrogacy work."[72] She is not referring to handicrafts per se, but to the molding of subjectivity. In addition to promoting literacy, Patel trains surrogates to espouse the right neoliberal ideology and to harbor the correct desires, first among which is the aspiration to private property. For, indeed, besides the priceless gift of helping others, the rightful allure of the surrogacy opportunity, for surrogates, is deemed to be a house of one's own. The myth exists, seemingly generated by Patel, that a single go at surrogacy will generate a down-payment sufficient for a plot of land and a deed. As a symbol of a new life, this fictive *house* sticks in the mind as surrogacy's just reward. Interviewed about their motivations, surrogates' almost always respond: "I came here because we need to build our house."[73] In *Ma Na Sapna*, seconds after Papiha has undergone a caesarean section, Patel briskly asks her: "Happy? What will you do with the money?" A semi-conscious Papiha answers from where she is lying, simply: "I will buy a house." Patel nods in approval. "Where will you buy it? In Nadiad?" "Yes." "Hmm," Patel counters, sceptically: "Your husband seems ... OK. Some husbands spend it all." "No, no, I will buy it for sure," promises Papiha. It falls to Madhu, the agent, to speak the truth behind Patel's back: "Who can speak up to her [Dr. Patel]? I've told her four or five times: *No houses are available for that money, Madam.*"

What, besides personal enrichment, *drives* Patel? The answer would seem obvious: in Patel's office, photos of babies hang as calendars. A blond baby forms the back of a clock. A mural artwork depicts a figurative white feminine form enveloping, in its arms, a large number of multicolored smaller forms with swollen bellies. Patel (the white figure in this montage, presumably) does not brook arguments that call into question baby-making's inherent virtue. Of prospective customers who cannot conceive she has said: "they suffer so much, they are just like vegetables."[74] So it would seem definitive that this idea—that infertility is death—is what provides the overarching, legitimating rationale for Patel's industry. I do not wish to imply that the babymania isn't real, and yet, having seen how Patel reacts to *propertylessness*, I have my suspicions that something a little different is afoot. Of all the pluripotent germs that stand to be ushered toward growth under her high-powered lens, is the one that Patel is perhaps most devoted to the germ of home-ownership? Is it perhaps for the sake of swelling the ranks of the home-owning middle-class that she invests herself so obsessively in the successful development of the cells she manipulates under the lens? Is it because there is a phantasmatic *house* attached to every blastocyst that she sheds tears whenever embryo transfers fail?

5

"She Did It for the Money"

That we are so prone to getting exercised about the putative unhappiness of paid surrogates might reflect our unwillingness to confront the unhappiness in our own untenable and unjust (unpaid) gestational relations. It's an open secret that the impossible generosity demanded of gestators and mothers under capitalism is always collapsing into toxicity and blackmail because it is a trap. At least, as Roxane Dunbar-Ortiz averred in 1970, if "motherliness" is desirable at all, it is surely "desirable for everyone, not just women."[1] But then, in a sense, wouldn't it cease to exist? The precarization of labor under contemporary capitalism is clearly succeeding at making larger and larger swathes of the workforce work emotionally, unremittingly, and sometimes even part-unconsciously, in a gruesome caricature of generosity. But even as more and more people join the ranks of multiplatform "whores" in the new economy, the violent moral animus against doing certain things for money shows absolutely no signs of abating.

The principle subjects of Deepa Dhanraj's coruscating film *Something Like a War*[2] are participants in a Bangalore-based feminist consciousness-raising group. We encounter them drawing pictures of their bodies and "dream households" on a giant piece of paper spread on the ground, in colored pencil. Subtitled for an anglophone audience, their dialogue develops a vision of emancipated feminine sexuality, of communities in which daughters "hold the reins to the house" and of social norms revolutionized by principles easily recognizable to the western viewer as those of contemporary Reproductive Justice. The group is particularly disgusted with the imperative for women in India to be generous and accommodating both when it comes to making babies *and* when submitting to procedures aimed at preventing them from making babies. Caught between the natalist pressure coming from her in-laws on the one hand, and the anti-natalist pressure coming from the state on the other, all the while terrorized by a value system that deems women without sons (specifically) to be disposable, "what is a woman to do?" the collective angrily demands. And "what about women who can't have children? Where is their place?" Above all, the "yearning for motherhood" that women experience appears (by their own account) to be far less metaphysical than legend would have it. Under present conditions, says one woman, Gyarsi Bai, "We need children because we have no other resources. We have no wealth, no assets. So children are our wealth, our land, our only source of income. That is why the poor need children. Why else?" Says another: "If you want to, you can be a mother, [but] motherhood cannot be imposed on anyone ... [Personally,] it stuck in my throat like a bitter fruit." Sharing the care of children with one another, redistributing their respective joys and burdens, is the broad strategy the Bangalore collective defines toward overcoming the structural abuses of "generosity."

It is has hitherto been common for some Reproductive Justice activists to argue that "having babies for profit is a lie"[3]—as, famously, did Johnnie Tillmon of the National Welfare Rights Organization in the early 1960s. The idea here is obviously to flatly contradict eugenicist class hatred by claiming that poor people (unlike rich ones) have nothing but selfless and idealistic motivations when they have kids. But this is just as obviously a lie, too. It's always been a bad strategy for that reason—even before the rise of commercial gestational surrogacy—and especially given the validity and defensibility of accounts like Gyarsi Bai's of why "the poor need children." In the Indian context, the fact that there is no welfare system in place by which families can receive an immediate "profit" per baby, only a hoped-for future dividend in income, doesn't change the fact that arguments like Tillmon's are wrong. Rather, it proves that they are wrong not just morally but factually, since they deny the existence of motivations like Gyarsi's.

It seems relevant to the politics of "stealing from the government," too, that the women in *Something Like a War* are responding—as survivors—to the Indian government's coercive roll-out of Norplant (a disastrous experimental contraceptive) in the 1970s. In many parts of India, as Sharmila Rudrappa has researched, cash-for-sterilization drives were followed up a couple of decades later with cash-for-babymaking. The same populations whose reproduction was "desisted" are now being enlisted in the bodily "assistance" of wealthy people's reproduction, and in both scenarios, already-existing offspring are supposed to benefit. An Indian mother cannot be accused, as US mothers can, of seeking money through the very act of having kids (being a "welfare queen"). Yet her soul may still be weighed and found wanting if her reproductive organs pass under the clinician's hands: "she did it for the money" must still be sanitized by virtue of "she did it for her children."

The belief that kids must be ends in themselves and never means to an end is one that places impossible constraints on reproducers and inevitably leads (to return to the US context once more) to progressives throwing people like Nadya Suleman, a.k.a. "Octomom," under the bus. Who was Octomom? "To summarize in the language we were all then coming to learn," writes Mark Greif:

> Nadya had leveraged her disability payments into six babies, collateralized them (as a state liability likely to pay revenues for years to come), and then quite brilliantly leveraged those six babies into eight more.[4]

It wasn't that Greif himself would usually think this way, or that he hated Suleman, just that, "doughy as she was still from pregnancy, soft-spoken, rabbit-eyed, naively mendacious," she was (apparently) "so easy to hate." Altogether, it's hard to tell whether this is the toxic "language we were all coming to learn" during the 2008 financial crash, or simply phobic language the writer has no interest in unlearning. Would single business tycoon Mitsutoki Shigeta also be said to be "pullulating" with the sixteen babies he commissioned from Thai surrogates to be his genetic heirs?[5] No; he wasn't parlaying the intimate labors of his body into what can still be demeaningly referred to as "handouts."

Greif adds that "many thought [Octomom] had done it for the

money," signalling that he himself would never think that. But *why not* think that? Obviously, she did it for the money. And so what? If solidarity with a Nadya Suleman who "did it for the money" is impossible—because she fleeced the taxpayer by taking family values too far with her corporeal generosity turned monstrous—then solidarity will surely be unthinkable when it comes to commercial surrogates, gestators who not only are in it for the cash but aren't even signing up to mother the upper-middle-class babies they've made. And if Reproductive Justice is going to exclude "irresponsible decision-makers" from its constituency, then those of us who would communize reproduction will have to march under another, wilder banner. "Suleman's violation," Natalie Fixmer-Oraiz explains, consisted in this: "not only did she gain access to the infertility clinic, a space of reproductive choice never intended for her, but once there, she proceeded to make all of the 'wrong' (unruly and undisciplined) choices."[6] She implanted all the embryos, and their implantation was unexpectedly successful. Finally—this being her failure of "generosity" toward the state—she demanded all the pay. By putting herself in the role of a consumer of infertility medicine *and* full-time "mom," she encroached on upper-middle-class women's territory and departed from the script (hardworking, under-provisioned) that forms the condition of most anti-racist feminists' support for mothers of color. Under reproductive stratification, many a woman of color is forced to be the "worst" of mothers and the "best" of nannies. Suleman, a kind of antihero, successfully gamed the system and was neither.

The disciplinary notion of the "bad mom" is obviously a problematic one; however, the theft of proletarian time *is* deleterious to the social reproduction of marginalized groups. Queer radicals like Laura Briggs or Alexis Pauline Gumbs—who ultimately vindicate and celebrate queer proletarian social reproduction—extensively document how the oppressions and constraints faced by immiserated parents can damage caring relationships and squash the joy out of life. Even so, they insist, it is crucial for the Reproductive Justice movement to forcefully articulate the idea that "good" parenting is not synonymous with unlimited-availability parenting on the bourgeois model. Maternal love is irreducible to the (nonblack) image of the eternally present, cis-heterosexual, solicitous housewife. To pretend otherwise, as they show, is to entertain fundamentally normative if not eugenicist ideas that can only ever be used to legitimate the removal of kids from poor families and associated punishments.

An example from popular culture springs to mind: despite her intensely loving, principled, and comradely relationship with her daughter, the depiction of a sex-working, shoplifting, semi-homeless single mother in Sean Baker's *The Florida Project* (2017) prompted all too many voices to approve the expropriation of the movie's six-year-old protagonist by social services in the final scene.[7] Or, to give another example, Assata Shakur in her autobiography describes the surprisingly widespread view that incarcerated black radicals in the 1970s should, morally speaking, abort their pregnancies rather than birth babies destined to be so proximate to "crime."[8] Lest we forget: babies can and are beautifully mothered (thanks in part to community solidarity-surrogacy) in the absence of "stable homes," both through and around prison bars. Besides, stable homes are very often far from the utopias they are supposed to be.

To this day, the idea that inestimable ravages are wrought by maternal "absence" or "selfishness" is perhaps the most conspicuously class- and race-contingent piece of modern dogma in existence. Perceived neglect or deviance by white mothers is punished severely at the symbolic level since the stakes of its failure—white children—carry the most valuable freight; but nonwhite mothers, for their part, can practically do no right and carry the blame for every social problem even as they receive no economic incentive whatsoever to perform motherhood "better." Our collective lack of sympathy for even fleetingly "ungenerous," finite mothers—let alone those who abandon their babies in toilets—is also intriguingly species-exceptionalist: we have no problem cackling along and celebrating monumentally ungracious treatment of newborns among nonhuman species featured on *Planet Earth*. It's as though tales of the mad moms of the deep sea serve as a safety valve for human rage. Case in point: the multigendered, cunning, cannibalistic, perverse, and opportunistic diversity of "mothering" among other animals is entertainingly portrayed by Isabella Rossellini in her *Mammas* television series. "If I were a hamster," declares Rossellini in one skit, having munched up two of the smaller babies in the litter she's just expelled from her womb, "I would not have been considered a monster but a good administrator of strengths and resources."[9]

On a related note, Maggie Nelson confides: "Harry and I sometimes joke that women should get way beyond twenty weeks—maybe even up to two days after birth—to decide if they want to keep the baby. (Joke, OK?)."[10] Such proposals can seemingly only ever be a joke, even though, as Sarah Hrdy and Alison Jolly detail in their myth-busting sociobiological writing on "alloparenting," cooperation, and adaptive "disinvestment" (infanticide) in reproduction among humans, there is no such thing as a "maternal instinct." In the nonhuman realm, as Elizabeth Grosz contends, "The family has no preferred form."[11] We are too quick to forget how mutable our own preferences have been, historically speaking. The very name of our class of animals—Mammalia—originates, Jolly vouchsafes, "in Linnaeus's campaign for women to nurse their children at their own breasts, at a time when most of his own circle did not do so."[12]

Abolish the Family

Nowadays, the bourgeoisie tends to do its "own" breast-feeding—but what does it even mean, that word "own"? We saw earlier how the world's star surrogacy clinician's inaugural transaction constituted a mission to save a traditional marriage by founding a proper family through an incestuous arrangement in which the surrogate gave birth to her own grandchildren. It follows that, in order to implement a revolutionary critique of surrogacy, we have to interrogate its relationship with the notion of natural kinship (while criticizing that, too). Though the objects in question consist of moving parts that can't really be considered distinct, assisted reproduction's track record in human rights violations is dwarfed—by any measure—by the track record of the "natural family."

It's certainly not tenable to say that commodification of babies is the province of the "technological": in her study on pregnant straight women, Janelle Taylor found that the fetus becomes a commodity in people's minds regardless of whether the pregnancy is commercial. Certainly under capitalism, Taylor notes, "commodification is inextricably bound up with personification."[13] The promissory reward of capitalist pregnancy is that its upshot, in Firestone's terms, is a "baby all your own to fuck up as you please."[14] Formerly a collection of children, slaves, and docents, now a microfactory of debtors, the "family," frankly, already sucks—which is not to say that the mere absence of it in people's lives wouldn't in many ways be worse in the short term. ("A purely negative effort to destroy the family would simply result in starving infants."[15])

For many decades, scholars of feminist history have had ample access to archives, in both art and bureaucracy, recording the kind of experiences the custom of living in private households together with naturalized relatives has generated for humanity overall. The yawning history of so-called "unassisted" bio-kin provides the statistics, poems, songs, pamphlets, and novels detailing the discomfort, coercion, molestation, abuse, humiliation, depression, battery, murder, mutilation, loneliness, blackmail, exhaustion, psychosis, gender-straitjacketing, racial programming, and embourgeoisement. The private family is the headquarters of all of these. As far as the mountain of available evidence goes, the *natural* way clearly privileges making babies in the shape of personal mascots, psychic crutches, heirs, scapegoats, and fetishes, not forgetting avatars of binary sex. The findings are pretty clear, and the basis for our widespread "irrational exuberance about babies"[16] is difficult to fathom. The philosopher Nietzsche put the following explanation for it in the mouth of Zarathustra, expounding Woe: "'*I want heirs,*' sayeth everything that suffereth. '*I want children, I do not want myself.*'"[17] Increasingly, with Friedrich Nietszche and with Rebekah Sheldon, we have no choice but to understand this compulsion toward reproductive self-deferral as the deep, sublimated depression of a world in eco-catastrophe. As Elizabeth Freeman suggests, "kinship diagrams have no codes for wet-nursing, or visiting the sick, or tending to the aged"[18] (or, for that matter, queer people). Nevertheless, with Sheldon, we must push through to the realization that "it is not sufficient to renounce or to denounce the child."[19] Following José Esteban Muñoz, we must say: "as strongly as I reject reproductive futurity, I nonetheless refuse to give up on concepts such as politics, hope, and a future that is not kid stuff."[20]

Is a queer way of parenting possible, asks Shelley Park?[21] Which is to say, can we parent politically, hopefully, nonreproductively—in a comradely way? Can humans collectively enact this kind of "counter-social reproduction," a mode of "social reproduction against the reproduction of the social"?[22] Perhaps we have to assume that the answer is yes in order to find out. Certainly, the "techniques of dependency and renewal"[23] with which we replace kinship are going to have to be radically, relentlessly anti-natural. Care will have to come to the fore, ceasing to be the background of social life. In Helen Hester's formulation,

> xenofam ≥ biofam—the idea that families hospitable to otherness and synthesized across differences match or exceed those built on genetic coincidence alone—heads in the right direction, so long as we add the explicit caveat that so-called "blood relations" can *themselves* be xenofamilial through an ongoing orientation towards practical solidarity.[24]

After all, even bio-kin—who Donna Haraway calls "precious"[25] in an important qualification to her appeal to humanity to stop making them—sometimes turn out to be comrades, if we're lucky.

Bio-kin produced through surrogacy at least have the odds on their side in terms of being intensively wanted, planned, and financially pre-invested in. By the way: "It's not just the rich who use [assisted reproductive technologies]—not by any stretch."[26] Briggs finds that they are popular "among Turks in Germany, the middle classes of Egypt and Iran, indigenous people in the Andes, and people from all over Africa and Asia who can make it to the United Arab Emirates."[27] Natural kinship is itself already assisted, already a body modification technology, one that happens to militate at a structural level against queerness. In other words, as Janet

Carsten says in *After Kinship*, kinship steps in to help biology out: "Nature requires technological assistance."[28] A "surro-baby" is no more or less natural(ized) than any other. All babies are the effects of a "politically assisted procreation technology."[29] This is because normative parenting, or normative kinship, according to a foundational intervention by Gayle Rubin, makes bodies not only (or not even primarily) through procreation, but also through the process of gendering them male or female. This last is one of, if not perhaps *the,* most challenging aspect(s) of the horizon of queer parenting: the defeat of kinship as "a regulated system for making people look like they were born into an anatomical sex."[30] The magic of naturalization is robust.

In 2015, Madeline Lane-McKinley and Marija Cetinic articulated a movement toward a world in which "the distinction between mothers and non-mothers is radically challenged," appealing powerfully to an erotics of "radical kinship."[31] They are far from alone among twenty-first-century communist feminists to have called for resurrection of the goal of family abolition. There have lately been powerful calls for counter-familial institutions and communist centers of social reproduction such as an "anti-dyadic crèche" that would, by virtue of its integration with socialized health and reproductive-care providers as well as universities, meet all humans' basic needs for the first two decades of their lives.[32] Stressing the coercive function of the family in linking the working class to the state and in preparing its members for "the division and abuses of the workplace, or exclusion from it," Jules Joanne Gleeson and Kate Doyle-Griffiths observe that "even in the 'best' families, free of abuse" the family is the institution tasked with producing "racially/ethnically marked identities" and expressing the organized regulatory violence known as gender.[33]

Michelle O'Brien, for her part, emphasizes the significance of the fact that "queer life has flourished when people are able to find alternatives to their families for their survival" despite such survival being "sharply constrained by the gender-normative expectations built into social welfare programs and wage employment."[34] Unavoidably, as she elucidates, the form is a robust one and even cherished: "It is through the family that generations are reproduced ... and survive fluctuations in access to wage employment." But this is, O'Brien suggests, the nettle we have to grasp in "the fight for full gender liberation through the abolition and transcendence of capitalist society and the heteronormative family."

If it is easier to imagine the end of the world than the end of capitalism, it is still perhaps easier to imagine the end of capitalism than the end of the family. In the common rhetoric of anticapitalists, that second part of O'Brien's formulation ("and the heteronormative family") tends to be selectively forgotten. It just seems too challenging. Bioconservative thinkers, who thrive even in "revolutionary" institutions and networks, still far outnumber liberationist feminists. In a talk at a 2014 Marxist conference in London, one speaker made her disapproval of the return to family-abolitionist thought on the radical left intensely clear: "We are not," she said, "about to march around with placards saying 'Abolish the Family,' *which would be crazy.*"[35] But even if one doesn't think the slogan is crazy, one might still reasonably think—especially given the omnipresent hand-wringing nostalgia for it—hasn't the family kind of already abolished itself?[36] In fact, it hasn't: despite widespread reports of its epochal decline, as Sarah Brouillette pithily remarks, "this traditional family ... is not broken enough."[37]

In her history *Family Values*, Melinda Cooper thoroughly details her thesis that the key governmental unit of capitalism really does remain the family: it's just that the key characteristic of this gestation-organizing unit is its own perpetual crisis.[38] Like capitalism, as social reproduction theory aims to understand, private household-based reproduction is premised on fundamental contradictions that are constantly threatening to erupt. Much remains yet to be elucidated about how and why exactly "capitalism cannot survive without the family."[39] The revolutionary strategy we require in answering the question of how gestational and social reproduction will be untethered from one another remains almost entirely unwritten. For the purposes of this book, "family abolition" refers to the (necessarily postcapitalist) end of the double-edged coercion whereby the babies we gestate are ours and ours alone, to guard, invest in, and prioritize.

With that in mind, I want to revisit 1970s feminist science fiction on the basis that the many aspects of their repro-utopian visions that *aren't* directly dependent on automation are invaluable suggestions of the future, too often overlooked.

In Mattapoisett, the aforementioned society from Marge Piercy's 1976 novel *Woman on the Edge of Time*, care socialization doesn't preclude specialization. People of all genders are responsible for all children, but there is also Luciente, a dedicated "kid binder, meaning I mother everybody's kids."[40] As Luciente explains in their capacity as Connie's personal guide, it is not just that biological and social reproduction are now separate from one another thanks to the brooder; the point is that, thanks to that intervention, mothering has been communized. The assumption Piercy makes is that a further disaggregation of traditionally combined elements is desirable: sexual and parental aspects of social reproduction are kept at a remove from one another: "Comothers [coms] are rarely sweet friends [lovers] if we can manage. So the child will not get caught in love misunderstandings."[41] Ursula Le Guin's *The Left Hand of Darkness* assumes the same thing, limiting sexuality's sphere of influence—this time temporally rather than spatially—on the planet of Gethen, where the labor of child-rearing is shared equally between all adults. Gethenians are androgynous for twenty-six days out of every twenty-eight, and manifest either one of the two available sexes just once a month, for two days at a time, in order to experience pleasure and engage in planned procreation.[42]

Piercy and Le Guin's recipes for polymaternal radical kinship (respectively genderfluid and part-time agender) share characteristics with Firestone's nonfiction. Frustratingly, the only thing that tends to be remembered about the twenty-five-year-old "shooting star"[43] of New York Radical Women and Redstockings is her proposal that "childbearing … be taken over by technology." In reality, Firestone's flawed masterpiece also imagines a host of governing principles for living spaces based on the "diffusion of the responsibility for physical welfare"—not just responsibility for the physical production of babies—"over a large number of people."[44] Having a home somewhere must automatically entail, she said, an immediate right for every child and adult to "transfer out," the aim being to promote freedom and a generalized "weakening and severance of blood ties."[45] She conceded that someone "who undergoes a nine-month pregnancy is likely to feel that the product of all that pain and discomfort 'belongs' to her .... But we want to destroy this possessiveness along with its cultural reinforcements so that no one child will be a priori favored over another."[46]

Firestone's utopia represents what "adoption rights advocates" abhor the most. It is what they see when they look at surrogacy, because they sympathetically inhabit (in their minds) the position of the surrogacy-worker's poor child, who witnesses his mother's pregnancy and "sale" of the resultant baby and thereby infers—horror of horrors—that he himself (for some reason it always seems to be a "he" in this rhetoric) might be put up for sale. Children undoubtedly need stable commitments. But the worst thing in the anti-surrogacy activist's world, it seems, would be for children to realize that they are *contingently* rather than *automatically* their parents' children; the products of an active choice to care, rather than a necessity borne of Nature. How might we develop, together with children, an understanding that it is not nature but love, in all its contingency, that is the real source of the stability to which all children have a right? How could we collaborate with children in the abolition of adulthood? Lane-McKinley demands that we ask this question: "How would you talk to a child about family abolition?"[47]

A child, in turn, might want to talk to a gestational surrogate about the "destruction of this possessiveness." After all, we have at our disposal the cumulative testimonies of workers *straddling* the two spheres of baby-making: surro/non-surro, paid/unpaid, unitary/fragmented, maternal/nonmaternal. Those with experience of the latter category almost invariably possess experience of the former, because of industry guidelines stipulating that surrogates in most legislatures must be married and already mothers. It seems from their accounts that the prolonged separation from one's children during surrogacy work contracts is occasionally challenging and unpleasant. But ethnographers also report that some workers "find the mandatory dormitory stays quite liberating" rather than lonely and guilt-ridden.[48] Others (including husbands) are filling in, doing childcare, gaining fresh respect for the mother's everyday toil, and building bonds with her children that could well lighten her load far into the future. The children, meanwhile, have the opportunity to observe for themselves that they were labored over, wanted, and—on top of all that—adopted. Thus the sentiment Firestone paraphrases exclusively in terms of its use as blackmail—"To think of what I went through to have you!"[49]—might conceivably also be the source of a more comradely and emancipated relation between "mother" and child.

What do surrogacy veterans have to say about the two kinds of pregnancy they've known? If we scrutinize the discourses documented in the course of clinic workplace ethnographies, to see if analogizing the paid and unpaid spheres is common, we can see right away that gestational workers are in fact *highly* prone to asking, of surrogacy, "compared to what." Their reflections take the shape of (for example) pointed remarks directed at their in-laws, remembering what it was like to do what they are doing for no pay at home. Documentaries quite frequently depict surrogates who, in this way, retroactively reimagine their prior pregnancies as undervalued services. In Mumbai, Anindita Majumdar transcribes and translates "one of the surrogate mothers in my sample notes" saying that pregnant people in general deserve normal workers' privileges since, "after all, we are also doing work that involves the body."[50] Surrogates routinely make elaborate cases to their bosses for why their labors deserve better pay; sometimes taking the line that "pregnancy is different with medicine" because they have to be "more careful."[51] Alternatively, the difference is altogether erased: a surrogate might tell a support group online: "I made three babies for my husband and one for the couple from China—I celebrate all four birthdays."[52]

On occasion, a surrogate will converse with the fetus inside her body in an expressly simplified version of her native language—as a courtesy to it, because it is foreign. She might theorize surrogacy-labor as biologically more arduous than her ("own") prior pregnancies because of the IVF fetus's larger size—whether real or imagined—which, as Daisy Deomampo explains, is a racial coding associated with whiteness which clinicians use to justify performing caesarean sections in surrogacy.[53] Some surrogates develop strong opinions about styles of cooking that help with surrogacy pregnancy as compared to nonsurrogacy pregnancy. These skills become a kind of craft expertise, riffing off knowledge of pregnancy itself. In sum, for many, it is a completely casual matter to draw parallels between clinical pregnancies—pregnancies they have seen generating surplus-value directly for biomedical entrepreneurs—and unpaid pregnancies that swelled the ranks of their own families (only indirectly benefiting the capitalist class). Said one interviewee: "Any fool can have a baby [*sic*]—it takes a smart woman to get paid for it."[54]

A "smart" surrogate is likely to be at least somewhat prepared for the range of feelings (from indifference to grief) generated by her permanent separation from the baby in the clinical context. To someone like Orna Donath, author of *Regretting Motherhood*, this is a situation that should also prompt a broader question: When and how does gestation under capitalism generate—more generally—an *absence* of bonds between infants and adults; a genuine wish, going beyond "healthy ambivalence," not to mother the infant you've borne?[55] Because, manifestly, nonsynthetic outcomes of gestational labor are *not* confined to the context where nonrelatedness is the explicitly stated aim. A sense of alienation from the baby, and even dislike or disgust, is a massively common experience.

Maggie Nelson hypothesizes that, today, the violence of partum and the disappointment of postpartum constitute an untheorizable trauma. Essentially, romanticizing childbirth is a societywide psychic necessity, because, otherwise, we would not get over it. Because of the imperative to keep reproducing the species, there is a real structural need, she says, for humans to forget and simply move on with their lives, shackled irreversibly to the other members of the now slightly less minuscule population they call home.[56] As the wracked anonymity of a BBC news article of December 2016 collecting testimonies from "Parents who regret having children" confirms, the prescribed scripts for "successful" gestators are ones that censor regret and devastation, not only presuming but—*pace* Sara Ahmed—*demanding* happiness.[57]

Under the coercion of this oppressive happiness, Lane-McKinley and Cetinic advance the claim that it is actually "postpartum depression" that more accurately "describes the social conditions of mother-hood under late capitalism." Their utopian intervention, "Theses on Postpartum," is one that powerfully punctures the narrative—hegemonic even on the feminist left—that there could be such a thing as "worth it" or "not worth it" or "worth it in the end." If we are going to manufacture human beings, let us aspire to something more, something immeasurable, something beyond the idea of "worth it."

"Labor Does You"

At the Women's March on Washington, DC, in January 2017, Janelle Monáe warned that those who "have birthed this nation … can unbirth it if we choose." Sigrid Vertommen, theorist of "repro-sabotage," declared it a brilliant intervention, and it was.[58] In the name of reminding the 500,000-odd people in attendance of their power—both to deal death and to produce life—it makes sense to talk about choice. As a queer black artist, Monáe knows better than most that the conditions of possibility for this "choosing" are heavily circumscribed. Gestators' freedom is circumscribed not only by the policy horrors we're used to listing on our marches against Trump, but also—and more complicatedly—by the frankly less than perfect control we possess on an individual level over the work we do with our bodies. The statement "we can, if we choose," in short, strategi-cally exaggerates (un)birthers' agency. And this same tendency—to exaggerate the separation between humans and the things they are doing, as well as the degree of control—is true of lots of kinds of theory. As W. B. Yeats suggested, it is maddening not to be able to "know the dancer from the dance" (a reference, I always imagine, to the terrifying predicament of the girl who can't stop doing arabesques in the Hans Christian Andersen fairy-tale "The Red Shoes.")[59]

The flipside of this ontological anxiety, aroused by a dance and dancer being indistinguishable from one another, is the fantasy that surrendering entirely to one's work is a deeply beautiful thing. The reality for most of us is that there isn't much to love about the fact that the labors of creation and destruction move through their subjects more or less independently of their choice—like silk through a silkworm, as Marx famously said (without necessarily knowing much about the working conditions of silkworms) in praise of an "unproductive laborer" whose work was *Paradise Lost*.[60] Whom does it serve, in the present, to figure this dissolving of the self in labor as sublime and desirable? Unsurprisingly, women, queers, and people of color have often been the ones to correct these romantic prowork moments in Marx and in culture more generally.[61] They have pointed to the co-optation of this idea, notably in the neoliberal mantra that it is not only possible but morally imperative to "do what you love." In short, fighting for a world based on "fulfilment through work" is not a communist horizon, even if that goal remains beloved by some who share the commitment to abolishing capital. Laboring *shall* no doubt one day be more pleasurable than it currently is; humanity will be free. But the framing of struggle, in the meantime, remains a matter of finding ways to maximally eradicate work, not learn to enjoy it. And that, in turn, requires recognizing work for what it is—wherever it is—in the first place.[62]

In her memoir *The Argonauts*, Maggie Nelson visits the idea that "You don't do labor. Labor does you."[63] Or, to repurpose Yeats: *How can we know the mother from the fetus, the gestator from the gestation?* Bringing this tangledness of producer and product into dialogue with Monáe's call for an unbirthers' revolution is the difficult but necessary task, I think. How does one actually exert the political "choice" to refuse, in so circumscribed and nonsovereign a situation? How do we collectively develop the prostheses, techniques, and technologies that would *give* us more meaningful forms of agency around pregnancy? How do we do politics with the understanding that politics is also, simultaneously, doing us? And finally, how do we make it reliably okay for our comrades to enter into the many, many situations where they're being *done by labor*? Because, while the truth of Nelson's striking apothegm applies first and foremost to the labor of parturition, it also describes other work forms:

in *The Argonauts*, it includes her partner's labor of self-reinvention, the labor of writing and, in a complicated way, the process of dying.

Certainly the labor of "being in labor" "demands surrender"; it "runs you over like a truck," Nelson attests. "If all goes well, the baby will make it out alive, and so will you. Nonetheless, you will have touched death along the way. You will have realized that death will do you too, without fail and without mercy."[64] Which is why, when we take up the anti-reproductive struggle invoked by Janelle Monáe in America, we have to develop assistive apparatuses that can ease the process of dying. It is why we have to face up to the fact that, as Donna Haraway says, "sometimes it's important to kill ... it can be a good thing to do."[65] Birthing and unbirthing the world are overlapping projects. "We're not idiots," agrees a pregnant Maggie Nelson in annoyance at anti-abortionists' way of addressing those considering having an abortion: "we understand the stakes. Sometimes we choose death."[66]

The Argonauts describes Nelson performing pregnancy at the same time as her partner Harry remakes his sex. The title is the guiding metaphor for two parallel "gestational" processes, recalling the mythical ship the *Argo*, which remained *itself* even as, one by one, all of its parts were replaced while it sailed. In Nelson's autobiographical critical theory, birth, gestating, writing, parenting, and gender/sex transition are all asymmetrically mutual forms of holding and letting go. They are not meaningful or "worth it in the end" according to some sentimental calculus. They are labor-intensive and ambivalently gruelling, boring, and joyous. Maggie and Harry, gestator-gestatees, are simultaneously sailors and sailed vessels, fluid self-birthing and self-un-birthing subjects whose organs, muscles, and endocrinal systems move, shed, and morph.

Nelson's stress in both arenas is firmly on the collaborative character of production; the production, in this case, of selves. Gender transition is not an autonomous process one might achieve alone. The process of uterine becoming, likewise, involves a one-way partition (the placenta) yet isn't a one-way street. Thoughts to this effect are spelled out by another poet, Minnie Bruce Pratt, in the words she performatively addresses to the fetus hidden inside herself: "the sound of your blood crossed into mine."[67] Pratt's account is scientifically accurate. "Microchimerism" is the scientific term for the cross-colonization that takes place in pregnancy, whereupon the pieces of DNA left behind by the fetus float around the adult's body for the rest of their life. (I am also reminded of the description of a pregnancy in fiction writer Samantha Hunt's story, "A Love Story": "her blood and bones were sucked from her body."[68])

Pregnancy is about "intra-action, or the mutual emergence of entities in simultaneous practises of differentiation and connection."[69] Exactly this could also describe the diffuse productivities of the person in *The Argonauts* who self-administers testosterone, transforming his voice and his very bone mass while sweating skin-permeable testosterone onto (and into) his writerly, gestating lover. Simultaneously, the body of that gender-Argonaut's "same-sex" partner is being irreversibly colonized by strange DNA in the form of living fetal cells. As such, the famous lines—*They fuck you up, your mum and dad / They may not mean to, but they do*—require revision because, biologically speaking, they also apply in the opposite direction.[70] Gestation always implicates actants far more diverse, numerous, and queer than the figures implied by the words "mum and dad."

With her titular ship's repair-and-maintenance crew, it is as though Nelson is answering Christine Battersby's complaint that "we are lacking models that explain how identity might be retained whilst impregnated with otherness, and whilst other selves are generated from within the embodied self."[71] And while the metaphor of the metabolism of the mutant ship is genuinely fresh, it builds on previous descriptions of being pregnant, demonstrating immanently that authorship can only ever be coauthorship, and even including annotations or glosses on theory in the margin of the memoir. For Iris Marion Young, who, as it happens, does not appear explicitly in *The Argonauts*, pregnancy is one of the things that schools us (unpleasantly) in this communistic sensibility. "The integrity of my body is undermined ... I literally do not have a firm sense of where my body ends and the world begins."[72]

Pregnancy occasions, in Maggie Nelson's words, at once "a radical intimacy with—and radical alienation from—one's body."[73] Alienation per se is arguably not a problem—indeed, it has proven to be an appealing value to some feminists, notably the authors of a manifesto they even subtitled "A Politics for Alienation."[74] The point is: *Which* alienation? Controlled how? In anti-surrogacy feminism and ecofeminism, as Helen Hester notices, we are typically encouraged to give ourselves over to (alienate ourselves in) natural childbirth. In this view, "reproductive technology offers a disenchanted alienation, achieved via devolving epistemic authority to medical experts, whilst nature offers an (for some reason vastly preferable) enchanting alienation, achieved via the subjection of the impregnated body to forces beyond its control."[75] Like me, Nelson rejects this distinction between reproductive technology and "natural" pregnancy, and between the two alienations they represent. For Samantha Hunt, too, the point is that gestational biology is already a hostile takeover: "I'm ruled by elixirs and compounds I don't even know."[76]

But it's not just that the technophobic pronatural message is troubling, given the health risks associated with pregnancy and childbirth, and the risk of death, literally, that rises in proportion to one's loss of control over a pregnancy. The message fails to grasp the bothness, the cyborgicity, the queerness of the labor experience. The productivity made possible by nature and medicine's foreign rule is, in many ways, vindicating and miraculous: "My body made eyeballs and I have no idea how," speaks Samantha Hunt's narrator. "There's nothing simple about eyeballs ... 'Queer' once meant strange ... I am extremely not simple." Meanwhile, Nelson asks:

> How can an experience so profoundly strange and wild and transformative also symbolise or enact the ultimate conformity? Is this just another disqualification of anything tied too closely to the female animal from the privileged term (in this case, nonconformity, or radicality)?[77]

In a way, yes: but it seems to me that we might also want to regard the politics of gestationality more broadly, in terms of the erasure inflicted on the skillfulness of bottoms (in the sexual sense), the sub-jugation of that gender-distributed power we've called "circlusion."

The problem that "circlusion" corrects is essentially the over-valorization of agency in our imagining of labor-power, the excessive attachment we cultivate to our self-image as authors who exert control over their work. As we've seen, even Marxists who (in theory) know better would prefer to feel they have the upper hand over the labor process. Politically unsettling as it may be, however, it does appear that labor *does us*. Or so Nelson recalls being coun-selled several times during her pregnancy. This interpenetrative knot is an image of labor it would make sense to work from, as Marxists. It could serve as the model in relation to which other forms of earthly labor, when we investigate them, may or may not differ. In other words: rather than seek to shoehorn pregnancy into the falsely simple categories we have to delimit productive work, what if we faced up to the possibility that a far, far wider range of social labors than we might previously have thought is fundamentally akin to gestatedness, gestatingness, miscarriage, abortion? What if we really felt the politics of uterine work to be comparable to other labors? What strikes, riots, and occupations might we become capable of?

Notwithstanding the wildness of the labor that "does them," as things stand, waged gestators are not calling for rescue. This is remarkable, and while they don't have to command your reverence (as they do mine), it seems clear to me that they deserve the utmost respect. They are not calling for destruction of the industry that exploits their labor (at least, not in shorter order than any other industry). Ethnographies and workers' inquiries are quite unambig-uous on this point—and Chapter 2 detailed how frustrating it is that RadFem exponents of Stop Surrogacy Now policy appear unable or unwilling to read them.

The familial status quo is a far more deserving target for "our" opposition. (I say "our" here, optimistically, despite being uncon-vinced that collaboration between revolutionary and cultural feminisms is possible.) If revolutionaries want to transform that template, they must act to secure, not policy safeguards against

Surrogacy™, but rather, incentives to practice *real* surrogacy, *more* surrogacy: more mutual aid. We need ways of counteracting the exclusivity and supremacy of "biological" parents in children's lives; experiments in communizing family-support infrastructures; lifestyles that discourage competitiveness and multiply nongenetic investments in the well-being of generations.

Limits on Generosity

In a laudable challenge to (academic) neglect of (low-income non-white maternal) neglect, Rhacel Parreñas has documented a "care deficit" in the Philippines. This alleged crisis of care stems from the fact that so many Filipina mothers are located outside the country, far away, looking after other people's children in the Global North.[78] Asked whether they would ever leave their own future children with other family members in order to travel abroad, as their mothers had left them, Parreñas found that most daughters said they would not. Yet Briggs questions whether we can extrapolate a completely straightforward narrative of "tragedy" from this data, suggesting that more often than not, low-income transnationally dispersed families really are doing all right when they say there are doing all right (which they mostly do say, at least in Parreñas's study). Highlighted by Briggs, for instance, are the ways such families take for granted a wider range of "alternative" caring intimacies that are often based on a looser gender division of labor than that of the traditional bourgeois nucleus.[79] She proposes that we give credence to the children's professed appreciation of their mother's migration-based sacrifice, and their judgment, when proffered unprompted, that they are okay. To talk of a "care deficit" with "devastating ... life-long" impact on kids is to risk reiterating, Briggs thinks, a conservative ideology about where care—exclusively—comes from, underestimating the success and tenacity of proletarian forms of care-surrogacy. Mothers who work abroad do not in and of themselves a care catastrophe make.

Nor are mothers generally unbounded in their generosity, even if that seems to be the only social basis for praising them. Such praise is a form of policing. When the Thailand-Australia surrogacy scandal known as "Baby Gammy" broke in 2014, the person unwillingly cast as the "Mother Courage" in the story was the surrogate-turned-adoptive-parent, an employee of Thailand-Surrogacy Ltd, called Pattharamon Chanbua.[80] The multiple embryo transfer she had undergone had resulted (as is common) in the implantation of twins. Late in the contract pregnancy, the clinic apprised the Australian commissioning parents of the male fetus's trisomy 21, whereupon they sought a partial refund, requesting that it be aborted. However, the surrogate, Pattharamon, refused this option. After the birth, and a highly dramatic tussle, Pipah (the other twin) was brought to Australia, and Gammy stayed. He is now a kid with Down syndrome living—in contravention of the most fundamental rules of Surrogacy™—with Pattharamon's Thai extended family.

While the dominant narrative around all this involved Pattharamon "instinctively" coming to the rescue of an abandoned fair-skinned infant whom she'd borne in her womb, and featured a lot of horrified castigation of the heterosexual buyers for their behavior (especially, and rightly so, when it came out that one of them, Mr. Farnell, had a conviction for child abuse), in my opinion what Pattharamon actually said and did, while generous, was much more interesting than that. In adopting Gammy, Pattharamon acted on behalf of a collective and was very clear about placing limits on her generosity. She adopted Gammy, not automatically or out of "instinct," but on the seemingly pragmatic, self-respecting, and comradely basis that the household she belonged to outside Bangkok would be the better place for him, given the ableism and hostility of the baby's Australia-based genetic parents. When interviewed on TV, her main message was directed not at the gawking public but to other impoverished people in Thailand, especially feminized service- and sex-industry workers and potential surrogate recruits. Pattharamon articulated a warning about predatory, proprietary wannabe-parents and an appeal to the necessity for mutual aid: we have to help ourselves, she said; "no one will help us."

Pattharamon Chanbua is, as I have argued elsewhere,[81] an example of a structurally queer parent and recalcitrant surrogate who quietly transcended Surrogacy™, causing sufficient bioconservative alarm that surrogacy was banned in Thailand shortly thereafter. On the other hand, some of the most reactionary upholders of normative ideas about maternal sacrifice are to be found among the surrogacy industry's "labor aristocracy"—US-based gestational freelancers. I've already mentioned the existence of an extreme version of generosity even unto death—giving "the gift of life" as a calling in life—which goes all the way back to antiquity. Much ancient Greek thought imagined a primal sex-dyad, "man" and "woman," as being endowed with a special mission for each involving bloody valor: childbirth and war respectively. Risking death in birth-labor and risking death on the battlefield were the twinned fundamentals of civic virtue, each in its own way critical to building and defending the polis. Although it enjoys popularity among anti-black fascists and briefly structured 1970s and '80s Black Nationalist opposition to abortion, this image of the two duties of national honor being a conjugal labor dichotomy had largely disappeared as an overt referent in modern societies. The Reproductive Justice scholar Jennifer Nelson discards it actively when she states: "an act of valor for a woman need not take place inside of her."[82]

However, with the rise of commercial gestational surrogacy, it seems to be making an interesting comeback. In a context of twenty-first-century US wars of invasion and occupation, troop deployment "overseas" and attendant revivification of pronatalist, imperialist sentiment on the domestic front, something like this discourse accompanies the surge of commercial surrogacy work among communities of spouses of US Army personnel, commonly known as "military wives." As Elizabeth Ziff explains: "when [infertility] agencies first began targeting military spouses as surrogates, military healthcare (TriCare) covered surrogate pregnancies, which ultimately lowered the cost of surrogacy for the intended parents."[83] Being subject to intense demands around "morale" and participation on the part of the army, this population of voluntaristic recruits is one that defines itself by its culture of sacrifice, valor, emotional strength, discipline, accountability, and, above all, endless waiting. Having conducted over thirty interviews, Ziff reports: "for this group of surrogates, the common notion of 'military first' becomes 'surrogacy first' and the specific military experience of deployment is easily transposed onto the surrogate experience."

It gets worse. In a different, broader study of the predominantly North American forum SurroMoms Online, it was found that participants "uphold the nuclear family as the building block of society"[84] with a ferocity unequalled anywhere else. Predictably enough, discursive norms on SurroMoms Online are shaped significantly in reaction to hegemonic formations of whorephobia and moral reproach (as described in the context of anti-Octomom sentiment); yet this does not fully excuse the strategy of the response. Instead of defending themselves as workers with rights and power, upper-middle-class surrogates are doubling down on the ideology of maternal generosity and going the "respectability" route in deeply anti-communist fashion. Far from agreeing with Claudia Card that "we need to pluralize the term 'biological mother,'"[85] SurroMoms naturalize the cult of the one mother, the "real" mother, whose possession of her baby is total. If we take a step back, it should strike us as particularly strange that a surrogate-worker-support forum would collude in this anti-polymaternal ideology. As "full spectrum" doulas never tire of advocating, we produce lots of things through our wombs that aren't living babies, yet weave worlds. But such truths—the truths of collective parenting, collective mourning, and full-spectrum reproductive autonomy—are precisely the ones that one cannot make money off, perhaps inherently so, but certainly at present.

Clearly the SurroMoms' hireability as workers—"fetus sitters,"[86] they sometimes say—depends on their reliability as nurturing angels who would never harm or covet a fetus. It isn't exactly hard to understand why, if SurroMoms Online is head-hunted by clinicians and intended parents, that participants are elaborately constructing an image for themselves as accommodating helpmeets who *devoutly* respect the property rights of parents named in the contract and would never "steal." An online "surromom" in California will typically receive a lot of praise and agreement on the forum for posting a statement like "This baby is not mine." One SurroMoms Online-er who is bearing twins posts: "These are not my babies to give away!

They aren't mine!" Another writes: "I am offering the risk of my LIFE for people to have a child. That is the gift I offer."[87]

It's hard to know how representative of freelance surrogates these hundreds of thousands of competitive assertions of self-sacrifice on SurroMoms Online really are; how much of what is on display is a "front" belying something queerer. One can easily find examples of support among surromoms around conflictual negotiations with intended parents—so it's not exclusively a sea of disciplinary chiding. But willfully happy-striving and cultlike conformity does seem to be the name of the game on SurroMoms Online, as when for instance shame is poured on one "Surro" who shared with the forum her desire not to have her intended parents present at the birth itself (girl, "it's still their pregnancy").[88] Surromoms, it seems, *do* define what they do as work, but they do so precisely in order to perform surrender to it. Given the prevalence of Christian piety on the forum, it makes sense that the other major literature in which refusing abortion is theorized as a duty and a commitment for pregnant people, namely the field of "pro-life," also frequently speaks of the "work of pregnancy" in terms of embracing holiness as work, and work as holy: "creating with God."[89]

The heated response that is still elicited whenever a book on maternal regret, such as Donath's, comes out—or even one on mere maternal ambivalence such as Sarah LaChance Adams's—is proof enough of these scholars' central thesis: that testimonies of unrepentantly unwilling mothers retain a persistently sacrilegious character and that there is next to no tolerance in society for discourses that denaturalize the law of maternal generosity or seek ways to support mothers who want out. Even words like Mai'a Williams's from the introduction of the anthology *Revolutionary Mothering* are enough to offend some readers: "Birth is smelly bloody dirty messy bestial … It isn't sweet. It isn't romantic … life itself broke you apart, shattered you and made you the earth that made your kid possible … for better or for worse."[90] And very often it really is "for worse." Of the infamous deserters of white bourgeois mid-century motherhood, perhaps the least reproached are the suicides, like Sylvia Plath. Here is her account of parturition resulting in no redemption, no rush of euphoria, no consolation:

I felt this black force blotting out my brain and utterly possessing me. A horrible fear it would split me and burst through me, leaving me in bloody shreds, but I could not help myself, it was too big for me ... I had nothing to do with it. It controlled me ... A great wall of water seemed to come with it ... The afterbirth flew out into a Pyrex bowl, which crimsoned with blood ... We had a son. I felt no surge of love. I wasn't sure I liked him.[91]

Or think of the suicide-by-abortion captured in Richard Yates's novel *Revolutionary Road*.[92] Or the way Eva Khatchadourian experiences motherhood in *We Need to Talk About Kevin*. That narrative (a successful movie, originally a novel by Lionel Shriver) made waves by raising the important point that—regardless of your provision of "unconditional love" and tireless generosity—your kid might be sociopathic, reactionary, and cruel, just like anybody else.[93] If your horrible pregnancy doesn't abort itself, if your horrible kid doesn't kill himself (as is the case, traumatically, in *Kevin*), can it really be that, as a mother, you are expected to endure more than a decade of your life in a household with no "immediate right," recalling Firestone, to "transfer out"?

There's a reason, remarks Laura Briggs, why

Adrienne Rich opened her classic feminist text on mothering *Of Woman Born* with a story of a woman slitting the throats of her three children on her suburban front lawn and the terrified, whispered acknowledgment of the mothers Rich knew that they all had had days when they felt like doing something similar.[94]

Ann Lamott tells us twenty-five years later that "a friend" of hers "looks at her child and thinks: I gave you life. So if I kill you, it's a wash."[95] The life-giver's right to kill is a surprisingly common formula; for instance, it appears in the New Jersey surrogacy tele-drama *Baby M* when Mary Beth Whitehead is fleeing the police with the rich couple's baby: "I gave her life! I can take her life away!"[96] But this brings us to the standpoint-specificity of necropower's positive potential. When Mary Beth utters this formula, it is nothing more than a melodramatic propertarian threat. It is not motivated either by hatred, a need to be free of the baby, *or by comradeliness toward it*, as can also be the case—albeit in infinitely worse human predicaments, such as that famously explored by Octavia Butler in *Kindred*[97] or Toni Morrison in *Beloved*.[98]

The sense that "unbirthing the nation" and unmaking babies would overall constitute a good thing is a perspective that belongs— not exclusively but specifically—to the Movement Mothers marching in Washington, DC, because their children have been murdered by the police. Or, as Barbara Bush shows, while taking pains not to romanticize infanticide, it might be something slaves in the British Caribbean decided upon: to take life away again from those they had birthed under slavery because *that* was the generous thing to do.[99] While it is a perspective echoed elsewhere,[100] it is nevertheless deeply disappointing to me that Rich could write the following: "[gestation under capitalism] is exploited labor in a form even more devastating than that of the enslaved industrial worker who has, at least, no psychic or physical bond with the sweated product, or with the bosses who control her."[101] Rich here manages to unfavorably compare the lot of racially unmarked "mothers" such as herself to that of historic slaves (who may or may not be pregnant, though Rich does not seem to have considered this). She completely flattens the racially stratified context in which the "validity" of necropolitical actions (such as baby-killing) is necessarily determined.

Rich's theorizing, like that of Maria Mies and Ariel Salleh and countless others, runs on nostalgia for a putative *unalienated* child-birth of which women of all classes and races have been robbed. And while radical and ecofeminism often stands accused of "biologism," ironically, biologism—that is, better acquaintance with the bare biology of human gestation—is more than capable of putting an end to that fantasy.

Staying with the Violence

A Tamil-language newsclip aired in early 2014 by a small broad-caster, RedPix 24x7, reported on the urgent need for free legal aid for surrogacy workers in Tamil Nadu and the problem of predatory middlemen. In conclusion, it proclaimed: "Pregnancy is a dangerous business."[102] It is rare to find theoretical biologists who not only agree with this but possess good public-facing communication skills, but one such person—affiliated with Monash and Leuven universities— stands out. In literal contradiction of prevailing cultural idealizations of maternal generosity as boundless, Suzanne Sadedin explains in her interventions at *Aeon* and *Quora* that "the mother is a despot: she provides only what she chooses."[103] (I'm not at all sure, admittedly, that the one thing follows from the other.) Sadedin's point, put another way, is that our maternal anatomy is perpetually defending itself, *decreasing* sugar and blood pressure in response to the fetus signalling for more. Human gestators are technically "less generous" in this sense than are most nonhumans; they have to be, because human fetuses, "tunnelling towards the mother's bloodstream," fight and override every "no" they encounter. They disable our immune system with floods of cortisol and constrict our blood vessels (if necessary) with the help of toxins, causing kidney or liver damage and stroke. In short, the unborn routinely deploy all manner of "manipulation, blackmail and violence" in their contribution to being made.

Seen through the gynophobic eyes of certain authors of medical textbooks, Sadedin's language unfortunately does resonate with woman-punishing suspicions propagated by influential doctors in the 1950s and 1960s about the inconvenience for babies of having to exist inside the hostile environment of the womb, where they are "attacked." Fascinatingly, it also resonates with the most deeply conflicted, not to say schizoid, elements of self-styled "biological" feminism. It has been—at least in England—self-designating "Radical Feminists" vehemently opposed to transgender rights (such as Fair Play For Women) who have gleefully shared Sadedin's piece on social media in the context of news stories concerning uterus transplants for trans women.[104] The erroneous idea here—which completely misreads Sadedin—seems to be that those already equipped with uteruses (i.e., "real women," according to transphobes) are naturally able to cope with the "1,000 cancers" gestation unleashes on the human organism, whereas the recipient of a donor uterus, for some reason, is not.[105] By and large, this lobby-group's antipathy to all technological assistance in the obstetric domain makes it clear that the everlasting persistence of pregnancy's injury and mortality rate would be a price anti-trans feminists are willing to pay for the satisfaction of excluding trans women from the health care system and the legal sphere of womanhood. While patriarchal scientists have sought, and still seek, to extract pregnancy from the brutal terrain of the uterus, in short, it is for similarly misogynist reasons that certain feminists hug that violence tightly to themselves.

But even beyond these twinned poles, it is a problem that Sadedin relies upon some of the same metaphors of violent overwhelming, combat, competition, and male-female antagonism that were so popular in the mainstream stories about sexual reproduction famously analyzed by Emily Martin (inaugurating a whole field of study on the politics of fetal representation).[106] In the mid-twentieth-century scientific and medical canons parsed in *The Woman in the Body*, Martin found that the fetus appears as a jolly little soldier, a bumptious intruder, and a cute emissary of the binary "otherness" of the father's genetic difference, lost in the mean enemy territory of the mother's body. Fetal violence toward maternal anatomy was wholly naturalized in these casually sexist texts, and maternal-fetal antagonism was also never imagined as a relationship *internal* to the laboring maternal body (on the contrary, as so many scholars have shown: "the lady vanishes").

All these tropes have been instrumental in stabilizing the pernicious notions of fetus-as-subject so beloved of "pro-life" movements and weaponized in their attacks on reproductive rights. Worryingly, such notions also visibly live on in the minds of some brokers in Surrogacy™, with the twist that consumers of any gender can now be positioned where the malevolent male "father" used to be in the obstetric (not to mention RadFem) imaginary; while the laborer whose labor power is circulating becomes more and more like an invitingly empty space—"only a uterus," as one clinician put it.[107] So, despite other changes, the gestational body in representation stays more or less where she was, her "generosity" only growing more and more perfect as the various discourses around assisted reproduction are competitively refined. On the one hand, there is the disconcerting hypergenerosity of the "military wife" surrogate, shouting "surrogacy is worth sacrificing for."[108] On the other, as two exceedingly genteel commissioning parents from Oxfordshire suggested—referring to the Indian woman engaged in gestating their gametes 7,000 km away, whose name they didn't even know—there is the perspective that goes beyond sacrifice to pure object-instrumentality: "she is only the vessel."[109]

But it is to miss the point to infer from Sadedin's startling story that getting into gestating willingly is so irrational as to be "bad," or that fetuses are to be blamed, or that human gestators aren't *extraordinarily* "corporeally generous" despite (or perhaps because of) the limits they place on that generosity. This is not an undialectical "anti-pregnancy" intervention: it is an argument for amplifying, rather than simply staying with, the trouble. Staying with the violence of gestating, rather than excluding it from our affections, is necessary not because the violence is somehow natural but precisely because it need not be. It observes that when we have gestated, we have been at pains to place acceptable limits on our own colonization; forced to work absurdly hard to stop a beneficiary of our labor from taking more than we are willing to give, the argument suggests that that is both similar to labor relations everywhere, and less than okay.

The rise of surrogacy notwithstanding, even upper-class white females continue to do gestation and to experience it as depressing and perilous. "How did we humans get so unlucky?" might be the pivotal evolutionary question for Sadedin. But "what do we do about this violence, and how can we *help* one another?"—is the other question it yields for a (gender-, race-, and class-abolitionist) repro-utopian politics. The anti-romantic understanding of pregnancy need not erase what's "positive" about it. At the same time it has the potential to sharpen our understanding of the knottedness and contradictoriness of social reproduction and of the fact that we can't put off tackling this complexity until "after the revolution."

What is key for me is that Sadedin's insights can be framed as a demand for solidarity with gestators—a call for the very unalienated childbirth some feminists think we would already have if only technodocs got "off our backs." In refuting *them*, I don't just mean that the products of gestational labor are intimate aliens confronting their makers; I mean that the process itself is necessarily going to estrange the laboring body in every society except a society where that labor's independent existence is wrestled into *maximal* gestator control. There's no cause to be phobic or reactionary about the ways in which "labor does you," or to pursue the mirage of perfect control and autonomy. The debilitating invasion of the produced, during gestation, might after all have an ecstatic, masochistic rush to it. But while consent is always an ideal rather than a reality, in any intimate session based on domination and submission the set-up has to be carefully rigged for the purposes of striving toward that ideal. To achieve something like unalienated gestation, an environment that has secured "free abortion on demand without apology" would be a start, but isn't in itself good enough; the services of abortion and birth ("full spectrum") doulas, biohackers, and gynepunks should be a universal given, as should be research into ways to prevent things like *placenta accreta* (where the placenta grows attached to the body). While all hitherto existing societies have probably only known alienated gestating—even celebrating that disempowerment—biology is quite literally not destiny. As Vicki Kirby speculates, it was culture all along.[110]

How do we mold an *is* out of an *ought* we have largely yet to imagine with regard to gestational nature/culture? That is to say: How do we remake pregnancy according to principles that may themselves be as-yet-unthinkable? I've suggested in this chapter that we start by grasping how morbidity is part of the mutuality of life's work. I've explored the agonism of gestation as it plays out at the molecular level and is concretized, in turn, by social forms that could conceivably be transformed. What remains to be said is that, if insisting on gestator-fetus agonism leads to a certain degree of subjectification of the fetus (be it as a heroic or parasitic figure), then the challenge to which we must rise involves affirming a politics that has a place for the killing of subjects—a politics of abortion that resists "preemptive compromise"[111] on the question of what it is exactly gestators sometimes kill. In the absence of such a discursive step, there can be neither gestational strike nor gestational riot.

6

Another Surrogacy Is Possible

Among the disproportionately female populations that have been cast as surplus to capitalism's labor requirements, the fertile and the infertile alike suffer the consequences of abysmal maternal and reproductive health care provision. But in the liminal and transitional space of the Akanksha clinic, for the duration of their hired custodianship of valuable biocapital, Indian women are lavished with an intensity of high-quality medical care they never experienced for their unpaid pregnancies. In India, infertility is estimated (as elsewhere) at about 10 percent.[1] Hysterectomies, however, are more common there than anywhere else in the world. Indian women's reproductive health has been attacked through structural underprovisioning, which the anti-natalist measures I've repeatedly mentioned only compound. No country accounts for as many maternal deaths as India. Amit Sengupta finds that "women are truly invisible to the public health system—the latest available data indicate that just 17.3 percent of women have had any contact with a health worker."[2] And if Indian gestators are the most competitive service providers for outsourced prenatal maternity ("the world's back womb"), it is perversely because they continue to die in childbirth at record rates for lack of care. It is this prior lack of care in turn which—perversely—legitimizes the medical appropriation of their motherhood.

These are the presently developing patterns that are lubricated by discourses of universal humanism such as Patel's. While there is no reason to single out surrogacy work for anti-capitalist excoriation, we must take issue with any suggestion that her actions even come close to fulfilling her (or anybody's) obligations as a feminist. With garment factories as the prevalent alternative source of employment for the women she studied, Rudrappa found that "surrogacy was ...

more meaningful for the women than other forms of paid employment."[3] Needless to say, however, this finding does not so much vindicate Patel as point to the kind of nuanced sensibility required if we are to develop an antidote to Patel's and her Stop Surrogacy Now enemies' shared preference for moral blackmail.

The promise of a hospital "for surrogates run by surrogates" opens the question of who the "patient" in infertility care is taken to be. As Rudrappa notes: "The [Indian Assisted Reproductive Technology] Bill specifically defines a patient as "an individual/ couple who comes to an infertility clinic and is under treatment for infertility."[4] Surrogate mothers, who bear the brunt of reproductive interventions, including caesarean deliveries, are specifically not patients. By explicitly transferring the suffering in medical intervention from the mother to the commissioning individual(s), the Bill ignores that surrogate mothers are "the ones whose bodies are the most heavily manipulated by medical technologies." It ignores the fact that the women in question are among those worldwide most deprived of—most entitled to—medical care *in their own right.* The Human Rights Law Network raises this in its workers' inquiry against Dr. Patel, stressing the riskiness of both pregnancy generally and C-sections in particular. Demands levied at the Akanksha through the farm laborers' union, according to this report, include a demand for pay equivalent to that of American surrogates, to compensate for this elevated risk to human health. And why not? Women's wealth is supposedly a top priority for the UN, and babies, as we know, are "priceless."

In the iconoclastic view of Dr. Gunasheela, this would represent a start, but not enough. Dr. Sulochana Gunasheela was a medical pioneer in southern India notable for both for her reproductive justice advocacy and her support for decriminalizing and progressively regulating surrogacy in the domestic national frame. And in her opinion, the "problem" with "womb farms" hinges primarily on the question of who is doing the farming and running the farm. Sharmila Rudrappa's book *Discounted Life* rightly puts a spotlight on Gunasheela, laying out the reasons she advocated the formalization of Indian third-party reproduction. In Gunasheela's eyes enterprises like Patel's opportunistically exploited the context of the Indian state's anti-natalism and the colonizing imaginary that sees in India a "surplus" of reproductivity. Whereas Patel says her employees gestate "instead of working as maids," Gunasheela saw a situation in which surrogates need to struggle together *where they are* (including as maids) for better conditions. Gunasheela's arguments point toward worker autonomy, not training programs and literacy initiatives dreamed up by management. However well-intentioned, enlightened bosses like Patel can never effectively bargain on behalf of reproductive workers in their confrontation with patriarchy and capital. Recall the portrayal of Patel by the recruiter, Madhu, in *Ma Na Sapna*: "We tell Dr. Nayna to increase the payment, but she isn't doing it ... Who can stand up to her?"[5] A good question.

Surrogate recruits face serious obstacles to redressing their labor power's relative cheapness. But Oprah's blessing does not protect Patel from the presence of a living international legacy of more radical and class-conscious feminisms, which threatens to upend the illusion of orderly harmony at her clinic. As other Indian feminists have long explained, their reproduction has been systematically "desisted" by the state even as new actors have sought to enlist their bodies in various ways (now including surrogacy) to *assist* the reproduction of others.[6] Patel, we've seen, hails the desire for a baby as a "basic human right."[7] Proponents of reproductive justice such as Gunasheela and Sama in India, and Loretta Ross and Dorothy Roberts in the United States, have long strategically deployed this type of universalism against itself, drawing attention to the fact that poor people's procreative rights are undefended and, as such, nonexistent.[8] Contemplating lives like Gunasheela's helps us see that Patel's declaration of feminism was already (of course) locally contested. Controversially from the point of view of Euro-American and Australian feminists, Gunasheela preferred commercial to altruistic surrogacy. The fee, she thought, seizes at least some payment for a practice already socially entrenched in Indian society whereby impoverished women act as "traditional" surrogates in wealthy households—precisely the practice to which the Bharatiya Janata Party now wants to revert.[9]

The share of the undisclosed profits of the Akanksha taken home by surrogates must be extremely low. Foreign clients pay the clinic approximately $30,000 for their procreational package (Indian clients pay 20 percent less); surrogates contribute to their board and receive between $2,500 and $5,000, a wage for their gestational labor which works out as an hourly rate of approximately $0.5. Notwithstanding the operating costs of the clinic with its microscopes, freezers, incubators, ultrasounds, and monitors, its specialist staff and full-time surrogate house, one can guess that the Akanksha has hitherto been far from a workers' co-operative—a point bitterly underlined by the fact that Patel and her family live in a mansion, while surrogates can't buy a house with what they are paid. The utopian phrase *"for the surrogates, run by the surrogates"* may still, for all that, come back to haunt the person who spoke it. As her hollow promise unconsciously demonstrates, discursive space has opened up in which gestational contractors, aided by others, can assert their power. Substantial social stigma around womb rental remains to be overcome, but materially speaking the core obstacle facing Nayna Patel's employees is the patrician Patel herself.

If the Akanksha survives the ban on foreign surrogacy clients, and even the ban on commercial surrogacy *in toto*, it will supersede the illustrious milk-making co-operative Anand Milk Union Limited (AMUL) as Anand's signature industry. The famous worker-controlled dairy and its 1970s "White Revolution" are still synonymous in the local area with a host of emancipatory effects on gender relations, on account of AMUL's policy of buying exclusively from women's dairy collectives. Patel pays lip service to AMUL as a source of inspiration. But if elaborations on the plan for a "hospital for the surrogates, run by the surrogates" really exist, they cannot readily be located. The phrase, as we saw, appears to have been an apotropaic gesture toward an idea that was once briefly floated (a 100-strong co-op) before giving way to something more modest (a twenty-women private trademark) and finally becoming eclipsed by a plethora of charitable collections and banking tutorials. Far from turning the management of the hospital over to the gestators, the intention of today's Anand Surrogate Trust is clearly to diversify and increase the productivity of surrogates, creating self-responsible individuals who are in themselves a bulwark against their own dissent.

To dream of surrogates running surrogacy is to change forever the very meaning of the word "surrogate." Materially and semiotically, it poses the question: what (if anything) could surrogacy be under conditions of cooperation and horizontality? Followed to its conclusions, the motto "for the surrogates, run by the surrogates" undermines the necessary link between surrogation and subordination. Though the noun "surrogate" is synonymous with "substitute," a world in which deep, nonproprietary practices of mutual aid were generalized might be one in which *self-directed* surrogacy is not an oxymoron. Politically subjectivating surrogacy is one strategy for bolstering gestational theory and praxis that is predicated upon the collective, co-imbricative, transcorporeal creativity of social reproduction everywhere. The demand for a permanent auto-managerial role in reproductive medicine for its "clinical laborers"—whose acts of gestation have been the "cure" for global others—brings us nearer, I think, to apprehending the political challenge of collectively determining whose reproduction (in global terms) gets assistance, and how.

As Natalie Fixmer-Oraiz has pointed out, "the rhetorical dimensions of transnational gestational surrogacy have received less scholarly attention than its legal, ethical, structural, or ethnographic counterparts."[10] Disruptions of the communicative practices emanating from the sector are, she argues, necessary, because they consolidate worlds. This book has been one such attempt at rhetorical disruption. I believe capitalists' creative destruction of categories pertaining to life, rights, and labor can be matched and countered by those of us (including those of us in publishing and academia) committed to different ends. Deconstructing the internal logic of Nayna Patel's philanthrocapitalist speech has shed light not only on neoliberal feminism's schizoid maneuvering and the political economy of an important emerging industry, but even helps, in my view, to generate utopian alternatives. Excessive and unintended effects of her discourse (such as "it's a physical job") can help us see through the implied egregiousness—the "novelty"—of commercialized gestation and remind us to connect it to histories of materialist-feminist struggle around housework, care, and reproduction, notably Wages for Housework. I've argued that the name "Akanksha" encrypts a fable about an impossibly flexible woman (paid for yet volunteering for free; anonymous yet unashamed; traditional yet futuristic; a grandmother to her child, and so on) and that this fable functions to discipline actually existing gestational workers in the Surrogate House even though it doesn't remotely apply to their situation.

But it is not enough, in the end, to have enumerated ways in which capitalist reproduction is guaranteed, rather than challenged, by what Patel does. Naturally I hope that others will find useful my articulation of the web of ideas framing "surrogacy politics" in Patel's discourse, from philanthrocapitalism to (universalizing) feminism. From here, as I am all too painfully aware, the question must become: How can surrogacy be turned *against* reproductive stratification? Otherwise, just like the creative destruction of the surrogacy business itself, its critiques will turn out to be just one more case of *plus ça change, plus c'est la même chose*. Patel has earned the gratitude of thousands of people by systematically brokering the exchange of one family's circumnavigation of clinical infertility for a temporary amelioration in another's quality of life. And, as I have suggested, it is the prerogative of her workers—and of onlookers sympathetic to class-based feminist organizing in the Global South—to denaturalize the oppressive uneven geography upon which this brokering depends.

I hope this reading has posed a threat to Nayna Patel's philanthrocapitalism, recentering the liberatory desires for a just and liveable—classless—mode of social reproduction which her narratives seek to co-opt, distort, and obfuscate. If the Human Rights Law Project (HRLP) activists' report in Anand shows anything, it is that a laborers' perspective not only exists but is levelling demands. If successful in their struggle for life insurance and higher wages, surrogates will fix their sights on even broader horizons of reproductive justice for all. Reproductive expertise and assistance might be made locally available to those whose reproduction has historically been stamped out. Families who have helped other families might enact ongoing kinship through forms of solidarity more meaningful than payment.

"They Will Belong Only to Themselves"

Despite capitalism's worldwide hegemony, many people on earth are putting something like "full surrogacy" into practice every day, cultivating non-oedipal kinship and sharing reciprocal mothering labors between many individuals and generations. In particular, trans, black, sex-working, migrant, and queer communities have historically survived thanks to their skills in this sphere[11] (sometimes called "kinning"). Feminist kinning, or so Shulamith Firestone proposed in the context of the radical women's groups of the 1970s, selectively rehabilitates habits from the European Middle Ages where the "myth of childhood" didn't yet exist: "in every family the child was wet-nursed by a stranger ... parents reared *other people's* children for adult life."[12] Whether or not Firestone's genealogical theory checks out, open adoptions, radical crèches, "GynePunk" experiments, queer co-parenting households, and plain old neighbors have long been quietly at work building human subjectivities beyond the dyadic template ("oddkin," in Donna Haraway's phrase). The common idiom about raising a child, "it takes a village," is an everyday way of acknowledging that the template is and always was a fantasy; a person is not the result of a mother and a father simply adding together their unique identities of "flesh and blood" and genes.

In academia, the word "repro-normativity" has been belatedly formulated, largely off the back of black and lesbian feminism, as a way of articulating the cultural edifice that is palpably disrupted by practices such as open adoption or—to an extent that is yet to be determined—conceivably also by a surrogate-led surrogacy. Like all big concepts, repro-normativity is a blunt, geographically imprecise instrument: created in one specific (settler-colonial, postplantation) setting and, as a result, not always fully adapted or applicable to others (such as postcolonial ones). Having described particular nodes of its functioning throughout this book, my recourse to it now is minimal. In reaching for the shorthand, care needs to be taken to avoid insinuating that repro-normativity was always around. Many of the practices that sustain and refine alternative modes of kinship predate anti-capitalism and weren't originally projects to "abolish" or "queer" anything at all. Such non-normative rather than anti-normative traditions tend to be survivors of distinct histories of violent settlement, dispossession, forced adoption, anti-natalism, and enslavement.[13] They require salvaging or (as two indigenous American scholars put it) "reclaiming and recovery."[14] The point is that relationships with children built in the wake of forced estrangement from authorized ownership have, some indigenous and black feminists contend, more than just a special need for revolutionary mothering: they have, perhaps, proto-communist potential as well.

Inventive kinning has taken place in every corner of the planet ever since the institution of marriage started being forcibly imposed on poor, indigenous, and colonized people. Or, in the words of Elizabeth Freeman: "racial, ethnic, and working-class communities have maintained expansive notions of kinship that supersede the genealogical grid."[15] In the United States, Freeman notes, the main energies behind counter-kinning stem from resistance to the state "forcing African Americans to comply with the hetero-nuclear model of family in order to qualify for the entitlements of full citizenship."[16] Condensed in Saidiya Hartman's unforgettable phrase, this means that "Slavery is the ghost in the machine of kinship"[17]—and for Christina Sharpe, our capitulation to kinship relations in their current configurations "is the continued enfleshment of that ghost." Sharpe demands that we refuse to reconcile with kinship, "refuse to feast on the corpse of others" and, instead, remake the world. For, as Hortense Spillers has uncomfortably reminded thousands in "Mama's Baby, Papa's Maybe," captive persons of African descent were wrested from their kinship structures and therefore unintelligible as gendered (and thus human) beings.[18]

That unintelligibility, in its own way, has been reclaimed as precious, to the point where it has been defended against the predations of an Assisted Reproductive Technology sector that would seek to provide cut and dried, certified relationships to populations to whom these had not hitherto been granted. People know that "poor, uneducated and dark-skinned women ... [are] not normally ... valued in the reproductive market, except as gestational surrogates"[19]; they aren't stupid. In the 2017 report of "Generations Ahead"—a "national convening of women of colour and indigenous women" on reproductive assistance—it was concluded that "these technologies create an environment that equates parenthood with biology and challenges Black women's notions of family and community."[20] For decades, within the black American community known as the Flats famously studied by Carol Stack, it has been found that "family is as family does." Out from the rubble, out from the ghostly wound of unrecognized non-kinship and sub-gender, Mai'a Williams suggests, "Black midwives, granny midwives, unlicensed midwives saved us as a people and helped our communities give birth to revolutionaries, agitators, militants, freedom fighters."[21] In the more sober formulation of Laura Kessler, "Family caregiving can be a form of political resistance or expression, especially when done by people ordinarily denied the privilege of family privacy."[22] Once again, practices of what Kessler calls "transgressive care" are "quite prevalent," she writes, "in African-American communities."[23] For Alexis Pauline Gumbs, the central pillars of these transgressions are the "Mamas who unlearn domination by refusing to dominate their children."[24]

Anti-authoritarian oddkin everywhere, not only in black communities in the Global North, have been experimentally sketching and tentatively building reproductive communes on a micro scale. From northern India to Aotearoa, recalcitrant elements have routinely refused to make the bonds among them based on transgenerational "othermothering," nonbinary gender and polygamous marriage legible for the purposes of state categorization.[25] Most famously, "non-genealogical modes"[26] of relatedness remain a cultivated norm in specific pockets of the earth much-beloved of kinship anthropologists. In *The Gender of the Gift*, famously, Marilyn Strathern says of Mt. Hagen, Papua New Guinea, that "mothers do not make babies." Rather, in the absence of all "reproductive technologies," Mt. Hageners "share substance" with and collectively labor to bring forth a being who is already socially connected with lots of people and not at all "corporeally continuous" with its parents. "Melanesian women are not seen as the sole agents of childbirth," Strathern reports; "children are the outcome of the interactions of multiple others."[27]

Even in cities, substance sharing through neighborhood-based open foster-care and adoption networks is common. In Cameroon, someone recently explained to a visiting academic that "a child has many mothers"[28]; in Nigeria, the analogous phrase noted in the 1970s was "several mothers."[29] Admittedly, these appealing-sounding realities aren't always straightforwardly political. From the Caribbean to Palestine to the Philippines, people have stressed how their multiple-parent practices are not pure realizations of their intentional collective ideals but also simply pragmatic instances of making-do by way of adaptation to military and transnational capitalist predations.[30] Polyparental abundance can, alas, become stretched and distorted under market pressure until it resembles neoliberal resilience and work flexibilization. Across increasingly dramatic distances, working-class communities are emptied of mothers by the bourgeois demand for mothering-labor. In this way, equitable polymaternal practices operating at the grassroots level tend to collide in inexpressibly painful ways with the kind of dis-avowed perversion of polymaternalism that operates in sharply polarized class societies. This is the socialism or "full surrogacy" of the rich that sees wet nurses, nannies, ayahs, and mammies serving upper-class children as full-time "second mothers" while leaving their own children in the care of several already overburdened others.

The collective labor of reproduction and regeneration involves a quantity of killing: maybe always, but definitely under colonialism, capitalism, and patriarchy. For example, fourteen-year-old Bresha Meadows killed her father because she, her siblings, and her mother needed him dead in order to live.[31] The proactive morbidity of social reproduction does not just touch abusers, though, and some-times indeed mothers—in all thoughtfulness—do kill children. One infamous account of the organization of generational care in a shan-tytown in Brazil in the 1990s holds that fully half the babies born were turned into "little angels" by their mothers—deaths "without weeping"—because they were never going to make it in such a harsh environment.[32] Proletarian and peasant practices around death and birth typically rub shoulders—and no wonder, given how frequently the two coincide across the disease-, disaster-, and poverty-ravaged geographies of human life. When catastrophes roll in, reproductive shelters afford "survival pending revolution," and sometimes not much beyond. Often though, while situations necessitating "disaster communism" are not exactly enviable, it is obvious that what people are producing in them is joy, rest, conviviality, art, eros; a life worth living against all odds.

Like social centers and crèches, abortion clinics are a key ingredient of this: too few of us understand how critical "abortion doulas" are therapeutically speaking in underprovisioned communities or refugee camps. Society dismisses the abortion doula at its peril.[33] To gestate and birth someone, in Spanish, can be expressed in a phrase that evokes uncovering, relinquishment, and perhaps death: *dando a luz,* "give to the light." In Argentina, the many-gendered Mothers of the Plaza de Mayo have cultivated a politics of collective mothering whose militant demands for healing of the living is inseparable from their memory of and care for the dead. There is laughter to be found, too, in navigating the vicissitudes of co-mothering in a hostile world. In 1977, in the journal *Lesbian Tide,* the black lesbian feminist Diane Bogus, perhaps inspired by her own name with its evocation of nonauthenticity, coined the wonderful term "mom de plume" which further opens up the horizon of surrogacy's possible meaning. Bogus, in that movement newsletter, was giving a name to "the labor of mothering *without the name of mother* performed by many nonbiological mother figures"[34] in her milieu, despite the ongoing epidemic of white supremacist violence they faced.

Moms de plume, repairers of devastated communities and crafters of new ones, are—now as then—drawing on reservoirs of local, sometimes ancestral, kinning experience while simultaneously responding to deep trauma and confronting the need for ever deeper revolutionary transformations of the home. "We can learn to mother ourselves" was Audre Lorde's promise to those who "were not meant to survive."[35] To some of us this apparent appeal to "do-it-yourself" autonomy or perhaps individual self-help might not seem at first blush like a particularly radical statement. (I am a white European social reproduction feminist, and my first reaction to this was, I'm sorry to say, a concern that it sounded individualistic.) But, as I've learned, this is a grave misreading, shaped by an underlying preconception of mothering as structurally individual and conservative that comes primarily from a white culture that Lorde is not presumably first and foremost speaking to.

In the first instance, Lorde is not thinking individually—she does not say every*one* should mother her*self*—and, secondly, many of us should not be so sure we know what "mothering" is. Maternity has been theorized by the inheritors of Audre Lorde as nothing short of bomb-making. Christy NaMee Eriksen's 2010 poem about mothering-as-insurrection, "My Son Runs in Riots," imagines her infant's body as a petrol bomb: one she wishes she had had the historic option of assembling as something less destructive. Eriksen's poetry, in which gestating and breast-feeding is weapon-building, and black mothers are pétroleuses by default, also defines plural maternity in and against murderous attacks by the police: "when you watch the video / It's tough to tell whose son it is."[36] Reproduction itself in this context is an insurgency of the commons—personal yet plural, intimate yet inclusive. Over the past three decades, black feminist theorists of revolutionary mothering such as Gumbs have levelled a stinging reproach to the anti-maternal strands of family abolitionism within Marxist feminism and queer theory.[37] Distinguishing hegemonic motherhood from counterhegemonic practices of (for example) "mamahood" or "mamihood," Gumbs historicizes the figure of the impoverished deviant black single mother as already queer.

Such mothering in the United States is "a queer thing," says Gumbs, because "the practice of American slavery has fundamentally ripped the work of mothering from the bodies of Black mothers ... fully denying them any of the authority of motherhood."[38] She is echoing Angela Davis: "The reproductive role imposed upon African slave women bore no relationship to the subjective project of motherhood."[39] Thus, what Gumbs calls queerness is exactly what other communists have called "surrogacy." Davis and Anita Allen have both argued, for example, that black mothers post-Reconstruction were always already "surrogates."[40] Far from implying a quest to simply appropriate for black women the property rights white women enjoy in relation to *their* children as an end in itself, however, the terms of this social struggle and its goals have been powerfully described by the more radical fringes of the Reproductive Justice tradition as family-abolitionist and polymaternal. Fighting in the name of an unnatural, radical "mamahood" might well involve, on occasion, the strategic assertion of "property in the body." But its vision of property is at root a commoning one. (I submit one might conjure it, too, with the slogan *full surrogacy now.*)

A pamphlet by Jeffner Allen hints at what a practice of broader, multiracial, and many-gendered feminism, allying with queer black "mamahood" against motherhood, might entail: "In breaking free from motherhood ... I no longer give primacy to that which I have produced."[41] In discussions of assisted reproduction, academics of all persuasions have liked to pay a cautious, oblique kind of lip service to this idea, specifically, by quoting the deceptively radical-seeming opening line of Kahlil Gibran's verses from *The Prophet*, known as "On Children": "Your children are not your children."[42] Patricia Mahlstedt and Dorothy Greenfeld began this trend in 1989, in the journal *Fertility and Sterility*. Paula Gerber picks it up in a 2015 TED Talk in defense of legalizing and regulating surrogacy; Diane Ehrensaft does it in her book on "building strong families"[43]; and surrogacy abolitionists do it on the Australian website Online Opinion. In all these instances, it should be said, the radical purport of the thought is not followed through, but rather, is undercut with the help of a consolatory, quietist interpretation of the second line: "Your children are not your children / *They are the sons and daughters of Life's longing for itself.*" Since the message of line 1 is too uncomfortable, this addition, with its appearance of an appeal to "life itself," seems to serve those of us who want it to as a retraction; a contradiction, too, of the labor theory of gestation.

Refreshingly, however, Sweet Honey in the Rock, a black lesbian feminist a capella freedom band, set the whole poem to music in 2010 and gave the idea that "your children are not your children" renewed, subversive polymaternalist meaning.[44] In their song, the emphasis is less on the verses' repro-normative futurism ("You are the bows from which your children as living arrows are sent forth") than on the comradeliness and plurality of the endeavor ("they belong not to you"). But indeed, Sweet Honey in the Rock's own queer black tradition is the one from which academics commenting on surrogacy should be quoting. Black feminist polymaternalism's contention—a contention far more explosive than Kahlil Gibran's—is that an assault on the whole system of kinship-as-property might be waged with formidable clarity by the survivors of capital's concerted attempt to turn humans themselves into property while separating those bodies from the babies they bore. The power that can be salvaged from this wreckage was reflected in the oft-forgotten resolution of the Third World Lesbian and Gay Conference in 1979: "all children of lesbians are ours."[45] And it was the Sisterhood of Black Single Mothers that proclaimed, with regard to children: "They will not belong to the patriarchy. They will not belong to us either. They will belong only to themselves."

Coming Knocking

Despite her claims that she "wants them [the surrogates] to become self-sufficient," Dr. Patel markets "her surrogates" on the basis that social and geographic distance will make it near-impossible for them to later "come knocking" (her words) on the doors of families their laboring bodies have made possible. The question, then, is how to disrespect and denaturalize that distance, or perhaps, how to undermine its production in the first place. Through factory strikes and social movements—whose brand of feminism radically supersedes the "business feminism" of Dr. Patel—those who might have deemed themselves destined to remain at the butt-end of noncooperative value-chains are forcing the horizon open for a recasting of reproduction. Anti-rape campaigners, dispossessed women, industrial unionists, and farm laborers have lately begun to step up the intensity of their struggles throughout India. In this climate, "coming knocking" might be exactly what surrogates organize themselves to do. Leftists, meanwhile, can abet them by "coming knocking" on the closed doors of neoliberal feminist ontologies.

Siggie Vertommen illustrates in the most vivid possible way how the position one occupies in a localized geography of two-tier reproductive injustice determines what "sabotage" will entail. For an incarcerated Palestinian, for instance, "producing life through IVF can actually be an act of sabotage."[46] Although pronatal anti-colonialist discourses have been criticized by Palestinian feminists as patriarchal, the secretive pro-fertility practices in Gaza have themselves been feminist instances of resistance, Vertommen finds. Families and their allies have organized sperm-smuggling operations covertly in collaboration with sympathetic clinics who will carry out the in vitro for free. Meanwhile, on the other side of the security walls, the contrary yet directly continuous act of solidarity and sabotage has been understood to be the promotion of anti-natalism among Israelis in Tel Aviv. Such is the mission of Gays Against Surrogacy, a group in Tel Aviv whose members "refuse" to give birth to white settlers and soldiers. Wearing "No Kidding" buttons and carrying Gay Pride banners declaring a commitment to sodomy, the queer Israeli activists in question see themselves as the disgusted, anti-reproductive children of apartheid settler-colonialism itself; they represent the occupying power's recalcitrant chicks, come home to roost.

Deboleena Roy, too, is doing something experimental of this kind when she asks whether the gestational legacies of the 1984 Bhopal disaster might not be returning to political prominence more than thirty years later. Roy is inquiring into the poisonous creativities involved in surrogacy practices in Bhopal, where repro-tourism arrangements often implant embryos created through conjugated North American and European germ-cell materials into the wombs of Indian surrogate gestators whose placental biomes have been transformed as a result of their or their relatives' exposure to methyl isocyanate (MIC) at the time of the gas leak at the American gas plant. More precisely, Roy is tacitly probing the wickedly uncomfortable possibility that what goes around—flowing catastrophically from the US headquarters of Union Carbide into the bodies of people in Madhya Pradesh—ultimately comes around thirty years later, contaminating the surro-babies commissioned from wombs in Madhya Pradesh and sent back "home." What does the vertical transmission of genetic aberrations mean in the context of surrogate-fetus encounters, she asks. "Can it be imagined that a MIC-mediated chemical infrastructure of reproduction in Bhopal is rupturing our ideas of fixed racialized and gendered biologies?"[47]

This returns me to the question of postgenomic biologies' inherent (or non-inherent) utopian, or at least anti-anti-utopian, possibilities. Like Rebecca Yoshizawa, I see a political freight to the recognition—in microchimerism and related transcorporeal phenomena—of "diffuse responsibilities for fetal–maternal outcomes that extend beyond mothers to the biosocial milieus of pregnancy.[48] To me, the answer to Roy is yes, it is imaginable that toxic surrogacies are forcing a rupturing of ideas regarding what transpires in the transcorporeal genesis of race, gender, identity, and species. The next question we would have to pose, however, is if and how such a "rupture" could be captured by gender- and whiteness-abolitionist revolutionary ideas, instead of something worse than what we've currently got. As the reactionary anti-surrogacy argumentation of Kajsa Ekman seems to sense, there may be radical, chaotic consequences to exposing the falseness of the surrogacy industry's guarantee that a buyer's baby will not emerge to greet them full of somebody else's blood and guts. Ekman is perilously close to hitting on the nonpropertarian possibilities of the form when she writes, plaintively: "If *all* biological claims were rejected, it would be incredibly difficult to decide whose the child is."[49] Yes, exactly, yes!

There is a simple but infrequently noted kind of beauty to the fact that the gestating body does not necessarily distinguish between an embryo containing some of its own DNA and an embryo containing none. Previous chapters explored how what does distinguish the two scenarios, assuming the latter is commercial, is the intensity and degree of alienation of the work discipline, and argued that *that* was where the revolution had to occur. The implosion of the firm distinction clinical capitalists attempt to maintain—between "surrogacy" and "pregnancy"—itself generates the curiosities that may eventually lead to the distinction's revolutionary undoing. Hence the questions lit upon by Kathleen Biddick, simply by looking at surrogacy sideways: "Can distributed maternity appear only as the effect of oppressive institutions and technologies? Can we imagine distributed procreation as transformative and productive of differences?"[50] Or Gilbert Meilaender: "vicariousness ... is an essential part of creative human love ... Can we have a person [the fetus] who is not the bearer of (at least some) rights?"[51] Or Mitchell Cowen Verter: "Can we not embrace a non-patriarchal vision of the home as a site for the enactment of responsibility for the needs of ourselves and other people, a place for caring, refuge and hospitality; a model for empathetic sociality?"[52] After all, in Meilaender's formula, we inevitably "do live off others who never invited us to do so or granted us any rights thereto." Therefore *lose your kin*, urges Christina Sharpe; remother yourself, fashion yourself into an ancestor to strangers untold, and become new parents' offshoots.

We have need of fictions, artworks, and dreams to help us train our minds to the question of what those prospects look and feel like, lighting the way. Clearly, the "sodomitical maternity" of Maggie Nelson's *The Argonauts* holds pride of place in my personal carrier-bag as I walk this road. Another source of inspiration I'll now mention is a sculpture series by Patricia Piccinini made of silicone, polyurethane, leather, fiberglass, plywood, and human hair—"Big Mother," "Undivided," and "Surrogate."[53] These pink humanoid wombats with their gestational pouches, teats, and human neonates are the artwork that inspired Donna Haraway's essay "Speculative Fabulations for Technoculture's Generations." As Haraway perceived: these are "helpful aliens."[54] They are immoveable and undeniable, and we are compelled to acknowledge them quietly lying down beside "our" children at night. Do you have a problem with that? As the curators of the M/others and Future Humans exhibition in Melbourne propose—Piccinini among them—the work of "brooding, birthing, and rearing bodies" is not intrinsically gendered; rather, it is, in Haraway's words, "wet, emotional, messy, and demanding of the best thinking one has ever done."[55] Here is a more-than-human manifestation of the powerful, naked, hermaphroditic, corporeally generous labor of which we are all capable but which, in Kalindi Vora and Neda Atanasoski's theorization, is becoming more and more distorted, more and more concealed through automation, in the phase of capitalism we might come to know as "surrogate humanity."[56]

As Haraway memorably reflects, gazing at these comradely simians: "The point for me is parenting, not reproducing. Parenting is about caring for generations, one's own or not; reproducing is about making more of oneself to populate the future, quite a different matter."[57] The horizon Piccinini opens up is one of multi-species—cyborg—reproductive justice.[58] The surrogates require our care yet are co-parents with us, they are our carers and (at the same time) menacing aliens. Piccinini "fabulates" the impossibility of the human "individual" by evoking a kind of continuum of incestuous, bestial or chimeric, gestation. Her creatures beckon us toward the same buried "narcosexual" knowledge and pleasure of pregnancy hinted at by Preciado in his account of witchcraft, which seeks to revive dynamic communist ecologies of "techno-gestational" bio-hackers and "biocorsaires." These cyborgs, transsexuals, and other leaky creatures who are always already inside your home gestating your kids. Piccinini's installations distill an uncanny, vaguely dystopian vision of the future, but the question I glean from them is not *whether* surrogates will intimately produce us one day: it is, rather, *how* we should respond to them and hold them—since they're already here. They make a mockery of the idea that children "belong" exclusively to you—or indeed to anyone.[59]

Weighed down by the array of new challenges posed by Infertility Inc., world legislation around biological filiation, property and heredity has never looked closer to buckling. Not only was *mater semper certa est*, that legal principle by which maternal status is unambiguous, thrown into disarray by the first test-tube baby, it continues to be eroded every year, for example, by breakthroughs in somatic cell nuclear transfer that now enable multiple genetic "authorship" of a child. While there is nothing necessarily anti-propertarian about this *per se*—quite the reverse, in fact, if gene pools are to be divvied up in the sphere of child-futures like stock shares—it is amusing to note how news-items like somatic cell nuclear transfer elicit essentially the same fretful, monogamist arguments that one hears trotted out to discredit "polyamory," arguments whereby the multiplication of parties simply dooms the business of human relationships to bewildering complication. For Claire Horner, for instance: "the presence of multiple stakeholders in the reproductive arrangement and the separation of reproductive roles and rights between the intended parents and the surrogate create the potential for conflict that may not otherwise arise in traditional reproduction."[60] Good. Already, as Shelley Park somewhat gleefully puts it, the practice of surrogacy has often instantiates two (or more) "monstrous mothers."[61] Now, bioethicists are having to scramble to devise "ways to promote a blended system in which altruism and commercialism, science and sentiment, love and profit, gift and commodity can coexist."[62] Perhaps the experts may be overtaken from below.

I wish to confess that I am also coming knocking. The probable origin of my years-long pursuit of alternative—utopian—surrogacy is a memory from childhood I only lately realized I've been harboring. It is a memory that pertains to a traumatic conversation with my father. He was driving me, my mother, and my brother home from an amateur play that some friends had staged in their garden. Musing incredulously on its themes, I recall cheerfully asking from the back seat: "but, Dad, it's ridiculous. If you found out that we [my brother and I] were *actually* the biological children of the milkman, you wouldn't love us any less all of a sudden, would you?" I had meant it as a rhetorical question only. But there was a stony, awkward silence that made clear to me I was not going to get the answer I needed. I felt so devastated that, for the rest of the drive, I could not speak.

7

Amniotechnics

To my knowledge, all humans in history have been manufactured underwater, in amniotic fluid. Think about it: How do you bring a body to life? Filmmakers and fiction writers have always implied that you need to have a tank. Dr. Frankenstein's adult baby—and knock-off versions of him—is animated in a bath full of electric brine. The effort that goes into husbanding that body of water is self-evidently thought of as creative labor. Pregnancy, though, is much less commonly thought of as a magical Frankensteinian tank. Amniotic fluid (in Latin: *liquor amnii*) is initially a mix of water and electrolytes and later sugar, scraps of vagrant DNA, fats, proteins, piss, and shit. As pre-borns, our embryonic mouths, noses, and lungs are filled with this "liquor." We move our tiny diaphragms and intercostal muscles in a dedicated rehearsal of future breathing, but we do not breathe. Nor do we drown. It is said that some escapologists and deepwater divers will try to slow their heart rates by "remembering" this time before fear—this state of nonantagonism toward water—to calm themselves enough to perform their tasks.

A live birth took place at Standing Rock. It was, reportedly, an event in which dozens of midwives participated. "Our first home is water," said some of these midwives—Melissa Rose, Yuwita Win, Carolina Reyes—patiently repeating this message to reporters and broadcasters who crowded around; "water is our first medicine."[1] It is under the banner of "water protection" that 2016's epochal mobilization of Indigenous people in the United States and supporters has taken place: a blockade of the Dakota Access Pipeline. If there were just one slogan for the mass revolt, it would be the Lakota phrase "mni wiconi": water is life.[2] Less commonly known is the fact that Mni Wiconi is also the actual name for a potable water pipeline that risks contamination and corrosion, in three places, from the planned oil pipeline. As well as representing an ideology, Mni Wiconi is thus a literal preexisting infrastructure serving several parts of nearby indigenous reservations: ecology and technics. Water Protectors vindicate the need and desire for water-provisioning technology over the interests of swifter fossil fuel transport.[3]

Theirs is, I feel tempted to say, a cyborg concept of water—water as social and presocial, water as companion technology, water as both medium and message. The cyborg "hydrofeminist" Astrida Neimanis paraphrases it like this: "if we are all watery, then we all harbor the potential of watery gestationality," because "gestationality need not take the form of a human reprosexual womb: we may be gestational as lover, as neighbor, as accidental stranger."[4] In fact, it is the contention of Neimanis's book *Bodies of Water* that not only "may" we be gestational; we *must*. "We learn gestationality from water," writes Neimanis, but we urgently need to learn *better*: the question is, "How might we, in partial dissolution of our own sovereign subjectivity, also become gestational for this gestational milieu?"[5] One possible answer: by supporting Water Protectors. A spirit of ecorevolutionary hydrofeminism, or full surrogacy, animates the live rebellion against crude oil routes threatening the integrity of lakes like Lake Oahe and rivers like the Missouri.

Water typically abandons a pregnancy and drains away—heralding the beginning of pregnancy's end—because of a signal from fetal body chemistry, which at the same time forces the liquor out of the fetus's lungs in preparation for their meeting the unwet world. In a C-section, it is a scalpel that releases the water. In each scenario, exit from *liquor amnii* and the death (by stretching) of the oxygen-providing umbilical cord trigger an irreversible and rather bittersweet development: the replacement of water by air in certain core pipelines of our anatomies. Yet even as we become land-dwelling animals for whom drowning is an ever-present danger, humans remain overwhelmingly water. "Underwater" is the only word we have in English to refer to what is really a state of being "inwater," water-in-water. It frightens more than it attracts. After all, it might be fine for fetuses—as the *National Geographic* video (discussed earlier) or the countless water births captured on

YouTube attest—but it is extremely dangerous for people to be filled with baby-making water. And a person does not suddenly become an amphibian by virtue of becoming pregnant. Yet she (or they, or he) is flooded from the inside: control of the circulation overridden, arteries jammed wide open, blood pressure forced into overdrive. A plug forms, to seal as much as a liter inside the vessel that is the amnion, the placental tank.

Gestation, like all labor, is cyborg, because watery. Water, like surrogacy, "is facilitative and directed toward the becoming of other bodies ... [but] not necessarily tied to the female human."[6] It is an unbalanced techno-social co-production involving less than two but more than one. Lest that sound cozy, recall the molecular biologist's testimony, that the unborn *Homo sapiens* deploys all manner of "manipulation, blackmail and violence" as its contribution to being made. Deploys against whom? After all, as pre-persons, these tiny animals are part of the mother. Though the DNA might be utterly distinct, fetuses are—during pregnancy and for a while afterwards—concretely a part of their holder-nurturers, almost a kind of organ. The idea that two discrete selves exist in pregnancy seems linguistically necessary to describe what happens there, but it is factually dubious. Given advances in understandings of chimerism (cellular cross-colonization between organisms) and symbiogenesis (interspecies cooperation) in recent years, it almost seems eccentric to believe in individual autonomy nowadays, let alone in fetal autonomy. The word "individual" by definition never referred imaginatively to gestators anyhow.

Our wateriness is our surrogacy. It is the bed of our bodies' overlap and it is, not necessarily—but possibly—a source of radical kinship. To an extent, bodies are always leaky, parasited, and non-unitary, as the vital and varied flora of bacteria in every body, not just gestating ones, demonstrates. In the accounts of earthly life given by biologists such as Lynn Margulis, we are all revealed to be disconcertingly pregnant, multiply-pregnant with myriad entities, bacteria, viruses, and more, some of whom are even simultaneously gestating *us* (or rather, providing some crucial developmental functions on our behalf).[7]

It is impossible to deny, however, that fetuses (themselves full of parasites and symbionts) distinguish themselves from other animals. They do so brutally. According to some etymologists, the word "amnion"—which refers to the inner membrane of the placenta, a sac of water analogous to the Promethean tank in the sci-fi fantasy—is a diminutive of the word for lamb (amnos) ... as in little lambs to the slaughter.[8] According to others, "amnion" derives from ἀμνίον, the Greek for a bowl or bucket in which the blood of sacrificed animals (or human offerings) was collected.[9] Clearly, the Greeks were confused about who the lamb is in the situation, since the last thing the contents of the amnion resembles behaviorally is a little lamb, meek and mild. Furthermore, there are many interlocking bowls and membranes "down there." The amnion doesn't fill with blood, ever, except in some types of abortion; menstruation is a feature of the endometrium; and it is between the placenta's outer membrane, the chorion, and the endometrium, that the sacrificial blood is typically "caught" during hemorrhage. Who holds and catches whose blood? Who rips into whom? Doctor or monster? Gestator or gestatee? What's certain is that monsters rampage, as Mary Shelley wrote, because of a lack of care. It was probably ultimately the man of science, denied the chance to be a mother, who was the more destructive monster on the rampage.

I call "amniotechnics" the art of holding and caring even while being ripped into, at the same time as being held. Amniotechnics is protecting water and protecting people from water in the spirit of full surrogacy. I want a generalized praxis of this, which doesn't forget the importance of holding mothers and thwarted mothers and, yes, even wannabe "single fathers" afloat in the juice; breathing but hydrated; well-watered but dry. I hope it is possible even for fantasists of ectogenetic progeny, like Frankenstein, who have dreamed of a birth unsullied by a womb, to become capable amniotechnicians in time. Their worldviews may not hold water, but I think they too have to be held. Let them too experience, in Sylvia Plath's words, "9 months of becoming something other than [them]self, of separating from this otherness, of feeding it and being a source of milk and honey to it."[10]

Let us assume that it is possible for any of us to learn that it is the holders—not the delusional "authors," self-replicators, and "patenters" —who truly people the world. "Water management" may sound unexciting, but I suspect it contains key secrets to the kinmaking practices of the future. Just as with water, we've consented too much to the privatization of procreativity. Surrogates to the front! By surrogates I mean all those comradely gestators, midwives, and other sundry interveners in the more slippery moments of social reproduction: repairing boats; swimming across borders; blockading lake-threatening pipelines; carrying; miscarrying. Let's all learn right now how comradely beings can help plan, mitigate, interrupt, suffer, and reorganize this amniotic violence. Let's think how we can assist in this regenerative wet-wrestling, sharing out its burden.

Reproductive justice and water justice are inseparable. The substance of this connection, however, is often wrongly ascribed to the type of primitivism-tinged "goddess" ecofeminism that too often roots its claims in tacitly colonial and sex-essentialist imaginaries of nature so as to be non-challenging to white environmentalists.[11] By way of antidote, The radical midwife Wicanhpi Iyotan Win Autumn Lavender-Wilson (henceforth Wicanhpi) theorizes this relationship with the help of a long line of decolonial science and materialism:

> It was through the work of Fanon and Memmi, LaDuke and Deloria, that I came to midwifery. As Dakota people, we understand that "mni wiconi" is not some fluffy abstract concept designed to fuel some hokey pseudo-spiritual practice. [C]lean water has the power to heal, contaminated water has the power to kill.[12]

For me, these words illuminate amniotic water as something that "complexity" theorist John Urry might call a "global fluid."[13] Rather than equate water with a universal concept of "life," Wicanhpi approaches liquid as the historic ground of life in particular. Techniques for curating amniotic water, as she suggests, must integrate the dual meaning of "care" (pain and relief) and the double power of medicine (poison and cure).

We have to make sure there isn't too much, or too little [amniotic water]. From the lead-contaminated water poisoning the children of Flint, Michigan, to cancer caused by [perfluorooctanoic acid] contamination in the water of Hoosick Falls, New York, to Newark public schools giving lead-contaminated water to their entire student and staff population ... to the consequences of uranium mining, nuclear waste facilities, fracking, oil spills and outdated public works systems ... [water politics] is and has been a lived reality for many Indigenous nations for the past several decades.[14]

Crucial to the practical awareness of pregnancy's liquid molecular joy and violence is, as Dakota midwives like Wicanhpi suggest, consciousness of its embeddedness in global structures of social reproduction. Pregnancy is bound up with colonialism, white supremacy, capital, and gender—but also resistance.

The work of social reproduction brings forth new hope for revolutionary struggle, but also produces new lives for oppressors to suck and crush. A birth under unlivable conditions can be a kind of obstinacy—a rebellion—but it would be wrong to assume it is always so. Take the concrete lack of freedom not to gestate faced by thousands of people migrating into Europe from Syria and sub-Saharan Africa currently. Following the "democratic" decision to stop the Mare Nostrum policy of saving people, the Mediterranean has become an open grave. A bad amnion, an utterly unviable one that catches the blood of migrant mothers and babies indiscriminately:

An Eritrean woman, thought to be about twenty years old, had given birth as she drowned. Her waters had broken in the water. Rescue divers found the dead infant, still attached by the umbilical cord, in her leggings. The longest journey is also the shortest journey.[15]

The woman's name, according to this article, was Yohanna. She and 367 other dead people were found on this particular day in 2013 off the coast of Lampedusa. Had Yohanna made it ashore to give birth, I hope that she would have been okay. Much-needed organizations like Care for Refugee Interim Baby Shelters (CRIBS) are helping get people out of the sea, and the fetuses inside them out, while also helping secure the free, safe contraception people are obviously entitled to.[16]

CRIBS reported in 2016 that, in some refugee camps in Greece, the rate of caesarean section was up to 90 percent. Even as they performed these dangerous surgeries, which take months to recover from, CRIBS lamented that organizations like the Red Cross were doing nothing to help refugees not to get pregnant again (and again, and again). For this and other reasons—including charges of doctors manually raping the people in their care—CRIBS was unambiguously critical of the Red Cross doctors on the ground with their fast scalpels. There's nothing wrong with a timely C-section, of course, but mud and rain and sweat and tears and garbage and permanently elevated adrenaline and cortisol levels are not the kinds of healing flows that a comradely amniotechnician would want to get in the vicinity of a leaky uterus on the run that has been sliced open seven layers deep. Reproductive justice seeks an end to criminally thoughtless cuts, both fiscal and obstetric.

Blood and amniotic liquor, baby-food and baby-drink and soil and brains and plants and river and sea are largely water as are people (60 percent of them). It's impossible to keep such damp beings cleanly apart. Yet Yohanna was murdered by a lack of borders as much as she was murdered by borders. Others are dying because of much smaller and more localized cuts. This call for amniotechnics is an insufficient response to this violence, but I still argue that we should cultivate thoughtfulness as to the technologies we use— borders, laws, doors, pipes, bowls, boats, baths, flood-barriers, and scalpels—in order to hold, release, and manage water. When is it time to release a boundary? When is it time to keep a space (cervixlike) firmly sealed? At what point (cervixlike) must the wall come down? When is a bandage ready to come off? How can a city be open to strangers and closed to tsunamis?

Research on michrochimerism "has the potential to destabilise the division between the gestational body and the surrogate," as Kalindi Vora suggests, and therefore, it "threatens the segregated authorship of the commissioning parents."[17] Authorship is always co-authorship; and we are all awash in a matrix of our collective labor. Well, but a note of caution is in order: affirming the "postgenomic" or so-called "new biologies" of mother-fetus relations does not necessarily pack an amniotechnical punch in and of itself. Sonja Von Wichelen warns that it is "premature" to suggest that new awareness of the ways the "surrogate body is biologically entangled with the fetus" will "bring non-reductive and non-deterministic understandings" of anthrogenesis and racecraft "and therefore revalue the surrogate." Rather, she speculates, it is more likely that the leaky subversions of postgenomic gestation will simply coalesce into "new biolegitimacies," co-opted by capitalism for the purposes of market "regulation."[18] While I am less pessimistic than von Wichelen about the uses of postgenomic consciousness (in part because, I take it, *revaluation* of the surrogate is not the endpoint of political struggle), I agree that there is no excuse for anything that could be mistaken as glib celebration of reprotech's leakiness as "queering race."

A communist amniotechnics would unbuild the fantasy of an aseptic separation between all these spaces and entities. It would be the art of timing desired or needful openings between them that are savvy, safer, and conducive to flourishing. Two decades on from the time—the first of many, as it would turn out—when my father asserted to my brother and me that he would not love us if we were revealed to not be, genetically speaking, "him," I can still feel the abyssal alienation of that moment. Yet, equally, in the aspirationally universal queer love of my friendship networks, in my queerly held and polymaternally tended flesh, I can sense the mutations of an incipient communization. Everywhere about me, I can see beautiful militants hell-bent on regeneration, not self-replication. Recognizing our inextricably surrogated contamination with and by everybody else (and everybody else's babies) will not so much "smash" the nuclear family as make it unthinkable. And that's what needs to happen if we are serious about reproductive justice, which is to say, serious about revolution.

There's a world worth living in, unfurling liquidly through the love and rage of—among other things—contract gestators' refusal to be temporary. Surrogates' struggle is a challenge to the logic of hierarchical "assistance" and a premonition of genuine mutuality;

it is an invading mode of life based on mutual aid. For if babies were universally thought of as anybody and everybody's responsibility, "belonging" to nobody, surrogacy would generate no profits. Would it even be "surrogacy" at this point? Wouldn't the question then simply be: how can babymaking best be distributed and made to realize collective needs and desires? Formal gestational workers' self-interest, like that of their unpaid counterparts, is an anti-work matter, and anti-work in the domain of care production is admittedly sometimes bloody. Their tacit threat to reproductive capitalism, whose knowledges and machinery they embody, takes the world a few steps toward queer polymaternalism. Terrifyingly and thrillingly it whispers the promise of the reproductive commune.

Note on Reproduction of Material

Some strands of this book have appeared (or are scheduled to appear) in other forms. Ideas have crossed over from essays written for other publications (for example, *Boston Review* (*Once and Future Feminist*, 33–37) and the Verso blog (see "Gestators of All Genders, Unite!" and "'Not a Workplace': Julie Bindel and the School of Wrong Abolitionism"). About half of the total research was originally directed toward *Cyborg Labour: Exploring Surrogacy as Gestational Work*, my PhD thesis in geography submitted to the School of Environment, Education and Development on November 4, 2016, defended on March 10, 2017, and archived at The University of Manchester. The analysis of *The Handmaid's Tale* in Chapter 1 develops the ideas in "Dreams of Gilead," a short polemic I posted at *Blind Field: A Journal of Cultural Inquiry*. The findings in Chapter 2 also undergird my article "Defending Intimacy Against What?: Limits of Antisurrogacy Feminisms," published in *Signs* 43: 1, 2017, 97–125. Elements of Chapters 1 and 4 expand on my article "Gestational Labors: Care Politics and Surrogates' Struggle," in S. Hoffmann and A. Moreno, eds., *Intimate Economies*, London, UK: Palgrave, 2016, 187–212. Parts of Chapter 3 are adapted from my article "Cyborg Uterine Geography: Complicating Care and Social Reproduction," published in *Dialogues in Human Geography*, 2018. Parts of Chapters 2 and 6 overlap with my article "International Solidarity in Reproductive Justice: Surrogacy and Gender-Inclusive Polymaternalism," published in *Gender Place & Culture* 25: 2, 2018, 207–27. The "fact and fiction" passage of Chapter 4 is a revised version of my article "How Will Surrogates Struggle?" *The Occupied Times*, no. 27 (occupiedtimes.org). The material on Dr. Nayna Patel was drawn from my article "Surrogacy as Feminism: The Philanthrocapitalist Framing of Contract Pregnancy," to be published by *Frontiers: A Journal of Women's Studies*. Chapter 7 ("Amniotechnics") was drawn from my article by that title, published in *The New Inquiry* (January 25, 2017), thenewinquiry.com/amniotechnics.

Notes

Introduction

1 Elena Ferrante, *The Days of Abandonment*, London, UK: Penguin Press, 2005, 91.

2 Chikako Takeshita, "From Mother/Fetus to Holobiont(s): A Material Feminist Ontology of the Pregnant Body," *Catalyst: Feminism, Theory*, Technoscience 3: 1, 2017.

3 Suzanne Sadedin, "Why Pregnancy is a Biological War Between Mother and Baby," *Aeon*, 4 August 2014, aeon.co.

4 BBC News, "Post-Natal PTSD: 'I relived childbirth over and over again'," November 28, 2018. On birth trauma in the US: Linda Villorosa, "Why America's Black Mothers and Babies are in a Life or Death Crisis," *New York Times*, April 11, 2018.

5 Susan Bordo, *Unbearable Weight: Feminism, Western Culture, and the Body*, Berkeley: University of California Press, 1993.

6 Ana Grahovac, "Aliza Shvarts's Art of Aborting: Queer Conceptions and Resistance to Reproductive Futurism," *MAMSIE* 5: 2, 1–19.

7 Erica Millar, *Happy Abortions: Our Bodies in the Era of Choice*, London, UK: Zed Books, 2017, 4.

8 Schurr, Carolin, "'Trafficked' into a better future? Mexico two years after the surrogacy ban," *HSG Focus* magazine, Universität St. Gallen, January 2018.

9 Associated Press, "Pregnant Cambodian Women Charged with Surrogacy and Human Trafficking," July 6, 2018.

10 Sharmila Rudrappa, "How India's Surrogacy Ban Is Fuelling the Baby Trade in Other Countries," *Quartz*, October 24, 2017.

11 See for instance Michelle Murphy's succinct overview of Margaret Sanger's trajectory in Michelle Murphy, "Liberation through Control in the Body Politics of U.S. Radical Feminism," in Lorraine Daston and Fernando Vidal, eds., *The Moral Authority of Nature*, Chicago, IL: University of Chicago Press, 2004.

12 Lee Edelman, *No Future: Queer Theory and the Death Drive*, Durham, NC: Duke University Press, 2004.

13 Laura Briggs, *How All Politics Became Reproductive Politics*, Berkeley: University of California Press, 2017, 127.

14 W. E. B. Du Bois, *Black Reconstruction in America, 1860–1880*, New York, NY: Free Press, 1992; Dorothy Roberts, *Killing the Black Body: Race, Reproduction, and the Meaning of Liberty*, New York, NY: Vintage, 1999.

15 Irene Lusztig, *The Motherhood Archives*, Komsomol films, 2013, 91 minutes.

16 Michelle Stanworth writes: "the term 'natural' can hardly be applied to high rates of infertility exacerbated by potentially controllable infections, by occupational hazards and environmental pollutants, by medical and contraceptive mismanagement ... [and thus,] the thrust of feminist analysis has been to rescue pregnancy from the status of the natural." Michelle Stanworth, "The Deconstruction of Motherhood," in Michelle Stanworth, ed., *Reproductive Technologies: Gender, Motherhood and Medicine*, Minneapolis: University of Minnesota Press, 1987, 10–35, 34.

17 The view that reproductive autonomy denatures Nature—be that a good or bad thing—is alive and well. On May 25, 2018, in the wake of the Republic of Ireland's referendum repealing the ban on abortion in that country, the prominent British philosopher John Milbank (@johnmilbank3) tweeted: "The terrifying number of women in favour of 'the right to choose' is evidence of the drastic denaturing of women that lies perhaps at the very heart of the capitalist and bureaucratic drive to depersonalise." Meanwhile, xenofeminist theorist Helen Hester has aptly criticized the various other bodies of "naturalist" thought—including ecofeminism—that have also relegated gestators to a romanticized state of disempowerment. Writes Hester: "The apparent suggestion that gestation and labour should be beyond one's control is particularly troubling." Helen Hester, *Xenofeminism*, Cambridge: Polity Press, 2018, 17.

18 Firestone's take on the wave of enthusiasm for Grantly Dick-Read, Lamaze, and related "returns to nature" is worth reproducing, despite the force of its contempt leading her prose into sloppiness: "The cult of natural childbirth itself tells us how far we've come from true oneness with nature. Natural childbirth is only one more part of the reactionary hippie-Rousseauean Return-to-Nature, and just as self-conscious. Perhaps a mystification of childbirth, true faith, makes it easier for the woman involved. Pseudo-yoga exercises, twenty pregnant women breathing deeply on the floor to the conductor's baton, may even help some women develop 'proper' attitudes (as in 'I didn't scream once')." Shulamith Firestone, *The Dialectic of Sex*, London, UK: Verso, 2015 [1970], 199.

19 Silvia Federici, *Caliban and the Witch*, New York, NY: Autonomedia,

2004; Barbara Ehrenreich and Deirdre English, *Witches, Midwives and Healers* (2nd ed.), New York, NY: Feminist Press, 2010. -

20   Mary Mahoney and Lauren Mitchell, eds., *The Doulas: Radical Care for Pregnant People*, New York, NY: Feminist Press, 2016.

21   Alana Apfel, *Birth Work as Care Work: Stories from Activist Birth Communities*, Oakland, CA: PM Press, 2016.

22   In a study of seventeen "natural birth" manuals, geographer Becky Mansfield found that "natural childbirth requires hard and very conscious work." Becky Mansfield, "The Social Nature of Natural Childbirth," *Social Science & Medicine* 66: 5, 2008, 1093.

23   Radical doulas have ideological enemies: so-called ProDoulas. Katie Baker has dug up the dirt on the new clique of cut-throat capitalists in the doula industry. Katie J. M. Baker, "This Controversial Company Wants to Disrupt the Birth World," *BuzzFeed*, January 4, 2017.

24   Mary O'Brien, *The Politics of Reproduction*, London, UK: Unwin Hyman, 1981.

25   Katharine Dow, "'A Nine-Month Head-Start': The Maternal Bond and Surrogacy," *Ethnos* 82: 1, 2017, 86–104.

26   Margaret Atwood, *The Handmaid's Tale*, New York, NY: First Anchor Books, 1998.

27   Asha Nadkarni, *Eugenic Feminism: Reproductive Nationalism in the United States and India*, Minneapolis: University of Minnesota Press, 2014.

28   Rebekah Sheldon, *The Child to Come: Life After the Human Catastrophe*, Minneapolis: University of Minnesota Press, 2016, 121. In her sections on Atwood, Sheldon spells out something that no one had quite spelled out before: "The Handmaid's Tale is a novel about reproductive technologies" (123). On this, see Sophie Lewis, "Enjoy It while It Lasts: From Sterility Apocalypses to Non-Nihilistic Non-Reproduction," *Science as Culture* 27: 3, 2018, 408–412.

29   For two examples, see Angelica Jade Bastien, "The Handmaid's Tale's Greatest Failing Is How It Handles Race," *Vulture*, June 14, 2017, and Evan Narcisse, "The Biggest Problem with The Handmaid's Tale Is How It Ignores Race," *io9*, June 20, 2017.

30   Bruce Miller, Remarks at Tribeca Film Festival (YouTube), 2017, available at novel2screen.net/2017/06/12/the-handmaids-tale-novel2 screens-sneak-peak.

31   Katie Rogers, "Trent Franks, Accused of Offering $5 Million to Aide for Surrogacy, Resigns," *The New York Times*, December 8, 2017.

32   Ellen Trachman, "The $5 Million Surrogacy Offer and Disgraced Politician Trent Franks," *Above the Law*, December 13, 2017.

33   This only became more ironic in light of Margaret Atwood's prolonged

and contrarian involvement in the defence of Steven Galloway, a professor of literature accused of rape at the University of British Columbia, over the course of which she routinely conflated left-wing and right-wing politics as equally distasteful. See Margaret Atwood, "Am I a Bad Feminist?" *The Globe and Mail*, January 13, 2018.

34 It should be said that this criticism is much less true of the Irish feminists who donned Handmaid attire in 2018 in the run-up to the referendum that repealed the (drastically anti-abortion) 8th Amendment. See Kelli Korducki, "'It Was "Handmaid's Tale" Type Stuff': An Exclusive Conversation With Irish Abortion Rights Activist Stephanie Lord," *Brit+Co*, May 29, 2018.

35 Some scholars of Octavia Butler, not unlike some fans of *The Handmaid's Tale*, draw from the histories of actually existing reproductive slavery in the United States—which directly inform such novels as *Kindred* and the short story "Bloodchild"—a kind of ahistorical overextrapolation and nihilistic certainty that "it was ever thus." To complicate matters, Butler has denied that "Bloodchild" is about either surrogacy or slavery, saying that she was only seeking to write a "love story between two very different beings" to treat the topic of male pregnancy. Her protagonist is a human man, Gan, who is the slave of a "dignitary who raised him from infancy to be her sexual partner and surrogate 'mother' to her young." Octavia Butler, "Bloodchild" in *Bloodchild and Other Stories*, New York, NY: Four Walls Eight Windows, 1995, 3–32.

36 In linking Octavia Butler's fictional surrogacy with surrogacy in the real world, the Du Boisian–Marxist scholar Alys Weinbaum has suggested that, with its dilution of class antagonism and emphasis on perverse consensuality in Tlic surrogacy, "Bloodchild" speaks directly to the "neoliberal reproductive dystopia" (Dorothy Roberts's phrase) she sees as currently becoming reality in the twenty-first century. For Weinbaum, controversially, it is also the masochism we see in play in "Bloodchild" that evokes the unethical situation of contemporary waged commercial surrogacy. Today's commercial babymakers, she says, "appear to 'freely' choose their subjection," just as Gan "freely" chooses to be the one ripped apart by his parent and lover (in other words, their choice is no choice at all). See Alys Weinbaum, "The Afterlife of Slavery and the Problem of Reproductive Freedom," *Social Text* 31: 2, 2013, 49–68; and Dorothy Roberts, "Race, Gender, and Genetic Technologies: A New Reproductive Dystopia?" *Signs* 34: 4, 2009, 783–804.

37 Peter Linebaugh uses this as a paraphrase for the work movement in his blurb for the re-issue of the Committee's texts, *Wages for*

Housework, The New York Committee 1972–1977: History, Theory, Documents, Silvia Federici and Arlen Austin, eds., Chico, CA: AK Press, 2018.

38 In *Discounted Life*, Sharmila Rudrappa recounts her dealings with the group of women whose plan was to pay themselves "fair wages" and "share the profits among all co-op members, all of whom would be surrogate mothers." Sharmila Rudrappa, *Discounted Life: The Price of Global Surrogacy in India*, New York, NY: New York University Press, 2015.

39 Angela Davis, "Surrogates and Outcast Mothers: Racism and Reproductive Politics in the Nineties," in Joy James, ed., *The Angela Y. Davis Reader*, Malden, MA: Blackwell, 1998, 210–21. Paul B. Preciado makes an analogous claim in *Testo Junkie*: "the institutions of heterosexual breeding (the heterosexual couple, marriage, social recognition of "natural" kinship), as well as their practices (coitus as biopenis/ biovagina penetration, followed by ejaculation), are techniques of culturally assisted reproduction that have been sociopolitically sanctioned and naturalized by tradition and law." Paul B. Preciado, *Testo Junkie: Sex, Drugs and Biopolitics in the Pharmacopornographic Era*, New York, NY: The Feminist Press, 2013, 300.

40 "Commercial Surrogacy Has Become a $2bn Industry," *The New Indian Express*, September 1, 2016.

41 Paula Gerber, "Arrests and Uncertainty Overseas Show Why Australia Must Legalise Compensated Surrogacy," *The Conversation*, November 23, 2016.

42 Daniel Politi, "Tens of Thousands Protest in Israel Over Denial of Surrogacy Rights for Gay Men," *Slate*, July 22, 2018.

43 Olivia Rudgard, "Surrogacy Reform Could Remove Automatic Rights from Birth Parents," *The Telegraph*, May 4, 2018.

44 Richard Lewontin and Richard Levins, *Biology Under the Influence: Dialectical Essays on Ecology, Agriculture, Health*, New York, NY: New York University Press, 2007, 239.

45 Donna Haraway, *Primate Visions: Gender, Race and Nature in the World of Modern Science*, New York, NY: Routledge, 1989, 352.

46 Marcia Inhorn and Soraya Tremayne, *Islam and Assisted Reproductive Technologies: Sunni and Shia Perspectives*, New York, NY: Berghahn, 2012.

47 Laura Harrison, *Brown Bodies, White Babies: The Politics of Cross-Racial Surrogacy*, New York: New York University Press, 2016.

48 Elly Teman, *Birthing a Mother: The Surrogate Body and the Pregnant Self*, Berkeley: University of California Press, 2010.

49 Laura Mamo, *Queering Reproduction: Achieving Pregnancy in the*

Age of Technoscience, Durham, NC: Duke University Press, 2007.

50 Amrita Banerjee, "Race and a Transnational Reproductive Caste System," *Hypatia* 29: 1, 2013, 113–28.

51 Zsusza Berend, *The Online World of Surrogacy*, New York, NY: Berghahn, 2018.

52 Pande, Amrita, *Wombs in Labor: Transnational Commercial Surrogacy in India*, New York, NY: Columbia University Press, 2014, 21.

53 Elizabeth Ziff, "'The Mommy Deployment': Military Spouses and Surrogacy in the United States," *Sociological Forum* 32: 2, 2017.

54 My engagement with "make kin, not babies" can be found in the article "Cthulhu Plays No Role For Me," *Viewpoint* magazine, 2017, viewpointmag.com. See Donna Haraway, *Staying with the Trouble: Making Kin in the Chthulucene*, Durham, NC: Duke University Press, 2016; and the subsequent revision of Haraway's argument, which continues our ongoing conversation, in Donna Haraway and Adele Clark, eds., *Making Kin, Not Population: Reconceiving Generations*, Chicago, IL: Prickly Paradigm Press, 2018.

55 Barbara Katz Rothman, *Recreating Motherhood*, New Brunswick, NJ: Rutgers University Press, 2000, 39.

56 Mamo, *Queering Reproduction*, 228.

57 Melinda Cooper, *Family Values: Between Neoliberalism and the New Social Conservatism*, Cambridge, MA: Zone Books, 2017; Laura Briggs, *Somebody's Children: The Politics of Transracial and Transnational Adoption*, Durham, NC: Duke University Press, 2012; Anglea Mitropoulos, *Contract and Contagion: From Biopolitics to Oikonomia*, New York, NY: Minor Compositions, 2012; Shelley Park, "Adoptive Maternal Bodies: A Queer Paradigm For Rethinking Mothering?" *Hypatia* 21: 1, 2006, 201–26.

58 Ryan Conrad, ed. *Against Equality: Queer Revolution, not Mere Inclusion*, Oakland, CA: AK Press, 2014.

59 Katherine Franke, "Theorizing Yes: An Essay on Feminism, Law, and Desire," *Columbia Law Review* 101: 1, 2001, 181–208.

60 The hostile intervention of trans-exclusionary (or trans-exterminationist) feminists associated with the groups Mayday for Women and Object! took place at the London event on October 28, 2017, closely resembled dozens of prior clashes at similar forums, and was amply documented on the LibCom website and on Twitter. A similar cast of anti-trans characters pushed to the front of the London Pride march in July 2018, brandishing the message "Get the L out" (that is, create distance between cisgender lesbianism and the transgender-infected umbrella group LGBTQ).

61 Gayle Rubin, "The Traffic in Women: Notes on the 'Political Economy'

of Sex," in Rayna R. Reiter, ed., *Toward an Anthropology of Women*, New York, NY: Monthly Review Press, 1975, 157–210.

62 On the nondyadic character of human sexuation, see for instance, Claire Ainsworth, "Sex Redefined," *Nature*, nature.com; or Amanda Montañez, "Visualizing Sex as a Spectrum," The Scientific American blog, August 29, 2017

63 Loretta Ross and Rickie Solinger, *Reproductive Justice: An Introduction*, Berkeley: University of California Press, 2017, 7.

64 Federici, *Caliban and the Witch*.

65 See Merve Emre, ed., *Once and Future Feminist, Boston Review Forum*, Boston, MA: Boston Review, 2018, including Emre's piece "All Reproduction Is Assisted" (7–32) and my response, "Mothering" (33–37).

66 Cheryl Chastine, "Cisgender Women Aren't the Only People Who Seek Abortions, and Activists' Language Should Reflect That," *Rewire*, March 18, 2015.

67 Ross and Solinger, *Reproductive Justice*, 7.

68 Takeshita, "From Mother/Fetus to Holobiont(s)."

69 Millar, *Happy Abortions*, 27.

70 Chastine, "Cisgender Women Aren't the Only People Who Seek Abortions, and Activists' Language Should Reflect That."

71 Millar, *Happy Abortions*, 279.

72 Silvia Federici, *Revolution at Point Zero: Housework, Reproduction, and Feminist Struggle*, Oakland: PM Press, 2012, 3.

73 It is to Michelle O'Brien that everyone should turn for a history of the positive and negative movements of "family abolition" throughout capitalist history: Michelle Esther O'Brien, "To Abolish the Family: Periodizing Gender Liberation in Capitalist Development," Endnotes 5, forthcoming. Writes O'Brien in her draft manuscript: "Abolishing the family [only] finds coherence today when joined with the movement against the other dominant means of working-class reproduction: the struggles to abolish the capitalist wage and the racial state ... Abolishing the family is the mass decommodification, collectivization and universal access to the material necessities of generational and daily reproduction."

74 Mario Biagioli, "Plagiarism, Kinship and Slavery," *Theory Culture & Society*, 31: 2/3, 2014, 84.

75 The Cyborg Manifesto was first published in 1985 in issue 80 of *Socialist Review* and then reprinted in Donna Haraway, *Simians, Cyborgs and Women: The Reinvention of Nature*, London, UK: Routledge, 1991.

76 Firestone, *The Dialectic of Sex; Marge Piercy, Woman on the Edge of Time*, New York, NY: Fawcett Crest, 1983 [1976].

77 Ibid., 233.
78 Ibid., 199.
79 Piercy, *Woman on the Edge of Time*, 106.
80 This token question about justice in the supply-chain provisioning fully automated luxury repro-utopia was inspired by Laura Mamo and Eli Alston-Stepnitz's discussion of the project of queering reproductive justice. "From what towns, communities, and countries will the biomaterials be drawn? ... How can we be accountable to the collaborative reproducers who provide biomaterials necessary [for procreation]?" Laura Mamo and Eli Alston-Stepnitz, "Queer Intimacies and Structural Inequalities: New Directions in Stratified Reproduction," *Journal of Family Issues* 36: 4, 2014, 10.

2. But Aren't You Against It?

1 Deborah Grayson, "Mediating Intimacy: Black Surrogate Mothers and the Law," *Critical Inquiry* 24: 2, 1998, 525–46, 539.
2 Anita Allen, "The Black Surrogate Mother," *Harvard Blackletter*, no. 8, Spring 1991, 17–31, 22.
3 Ibid.
4 Ibid., 23.
5 Ibid.
6 Valerie Hartouni, *Cultural Conceptions: On Reproductive Technologies and the Remaking of Life*, Minneapolis: University of Minnesota Press, 1997, 132.
7 One other TV accolade Patel commonly mentions by name is National Geographic's 2012 *Womb of the World*, whose focus, similarly to Oprah's, wasn't so much the titular "womb" as the faces of the Canadian, Spanish, and Australian childless clients (tagline: "How far would you go to have a baby?").
8 A six-minute video clip (YouTube), produced by RedPix 24x7, interviewing the director of the small charity G-SMART, V. K. Karthirvan, and unnamed surrogacy workers. Translated for the author by Dr. Velaitham Umachandran.
9 Michal Nahman, *Extractions: An Ethnography of Reproductive Tourism*, Basingstoke, Hampshire, UK: Palgrave Macmillan, 2013; Amrita Pande, *Wombs in Labor: Transnational Commercial Surrogacy in India*, New York, NY: Columbia University Press, 2014, 22.
10 Julie Bindel, the prominent campaigner against trans and sex worker rights, gave a speech in February 2016 (transcribed at the Byline website) in which she said: "One of the most disturbing things I've

heard from commissioning parents was from this man who insisted upon a caesarean birth with all of his children's births ... they [it is not clear who "they" is] told me it was because they didn't want any of their children coming in contact with a woman's vagina because they found that so disgusting." Bindel does not state whether the disgust was voiced by "this man" or simply imputed to him by somebody else.

11 Amulya Malladi, *A House for Happy Mothers*, Seattle, WA: Lake Union Publishing, 2016.

12 On May 24, 2018, the day I published my blog outlining my opposition to RadFem anti-prostitution and anti-surrogacy ideology, Julie Bindel (@bindelj) sent several tweets implying that I believe baby markets to be wonderful and abortions to be, economically speaking, a "waste." "If we follow her [Sophie Lewis's] logic, she would be arguing that women with unwanted pregnancies should hold onto them and give birth and sell the baby at the end. She loves surrogacy. That's her logic about women's bodies and the marketplace."

13 Sharmila Rudrappa, "India Outlawed Commercial Surrogacy: Clinics Are Finding Loopholes," *The Conversation*, October 23, 2017.

14 Madeline Lane-McKinley, "The Idea of Children," *Blind Field: A Journal of Cultural Inquiry*, August 2, 2018, blindfieldjournal.com.

15 Geeta Pandey, "India Surrogate Mothers Talk of Pain of Giving Up Baby," bbcnews.com, August 15, 2015.

16 Kathi Weeks, "The Vanishing Dialectic: Shulamith Firestone and the Future of the Feminist 1970s," *The South Atlantic Quarterly* 114: 4, 2015, 740.

17 Priya Ramani quotes Dr. Gautam Allahbadia, director of the Rotunda surrogacy clinic, as saying "This is not a litigious society" in order to reassure commissioning parents that there is little risk of the surrogate going to court in the "unlikely event" of a misunderstanding or mishap. Priya Ramani, "The Art of Making Babies," *Live Mint*, April 1, 2011.

18 Sharmila Rudrappa, *Discounted Life: The Price of Global Surrogacy in India*, New York, NY: New York University Press, 2015.

19 Melissa Gira Grant, *Playing the Whore: The Work of Sex Work*, London, UK: Verso, 2014.

20 Daniela Danna, *Contract Children: Questioning Surrogacy*, Stuttgart: Ibidem Press, 2015, 9.

21 Renate Klein, *Surrogacy: A Human Rights Violation*, Victoria, Australia: Spinifex Press, 2017.

22 Libby Brooks, "Scottish Plan for Every Child to Have 'Named Person' Breaches Rights," *The Guardian*, July 28, 2016.

23 Charlotte Krølokke and Michael Petersen, "Keeping It in the Family:

Debating the Bio-intimacy of Uterine Transplants and Commercial Surrogacy," in Rhonda Shaw, ed., *Bioethics Beyond Altruism Donating and Transforming Human Biological Materials*, London, UK: Palgrave, 2017, 189–214, 198.

24 Rudrappa, *Discounted Life*, 169.

25 Feminist International Network of Resistance to Reproductive and Genetic Engineering, "WOMEN'S EMERGENCY CONFERENCE ON THE NEW REPRODUCTIVE TECHNOLOGIES: Resolution," Report entitled "International Conference Lund-Sweden, July 1985," 233. PDF archived at Finrrage.org (accessed October 11, 2018).

26 Gena Corea, "Junk Liberty," in Patricia Hynes, ed., *Reconstructing Babylon: Essays on Women and Technology*, Bloomington: Indiana University Press, 1991, 182.

27 Elizabeth Kane, *Birth Mother*, San Diego, CA: Harcourt, 1988.

28 Corea, "Junk Liberty," 178.

39 Ibid.,181.

30 Ibid., 179.

31 Ibid., 180.

32 Renate Klein, "What's New about the 'New' Reproductive Technologies?" in Gena Corea et al., eds., *Man-Made Women: How New Reproductive Technologies Affect Women*, Bloomington: Indiana University Press, 1987, 64–73, 71.

33 Brooke Beloso, "Sex, Work, and the Feminist Erasure of Class," *Signs* 38: 1, 2012, 47–70. See also Sophie Lewis, "SERF 'n' TERF: Notes on Some Bad Materialisms," *Salvage Quarterly* no. 4, 2017, salvage.zone.

34 Alice Echols, *Daring to Be Bad: Radical Feminism in America 1967–1975*, Minneapolis: University of Minnesota Press, 1989.

35 Sarah Franklin, "A Feminist Transatlantic Education" in Kathy Davis and Mary Evans, eds., *Transatlantic Conversations: Feminism as Travelling Theory*, Farnham: Ashgate, 2011, 15–21 17.

36 Michelle Stanworth, ed., *Reproductive Technologies: Gender, Motherhood and Medicine*, Minneapolis: University of Minnesota Press, 1987, 16.

37 Juliette Zipper and Selma Sevenhuijsen, "Surrogacy: Feminist Notions of Motherhood Reconsidered" in Michelle Stanworth, ed., *Reproductive Technologies: Gender, Motherhood and Medicine*, Minneapolis: University of Minnesota Press, 1987, 118–138, 136.

38 On Dworkin and Mackinnon's trans-inclusivity (notwithstanding their whorephobia), see Alexis Shotwell, "Misogynist Trans-hating: Neither Radical nor Feminist," 2018, alexisshotwell.com.

39 Zipper and Sevenhuijsen, "Surrogacy," 125.

40 Ibid.

41 2015/2016 European Parliament Resolution on Human Rights, item 114, posted November 30, 2015; see also the "Parentage/Surrogacy Project" at The Hague Conference on Private International Law, 2015.

42 Cited in Sharmila Rudrappa, "Reproducing Dystopia: The Politics of Transnational Surrogacy in India, 2002–2015," *Critical Sociology*, 2017.

43 Sara Farris, *In the Name of Women's Rights: The Rise of Femonationalism*, Durham, NC: Duke University Press, 2017.

44 Laura Agustín, *Sex at the Margins: Migration, Labour Markets, and the Rescue Industry*, London, UK: Zed, 2007.

45 Lisa Woll, "The Effect of Feminist Opposition to Reproductive Technology: A Case Study in Victoria, Australia," *Reproductive and Genetic Engineering* 5: 1, 1992.

46 Laura Briggs, "Reproductive Technology: Of Labor and Markets," *Signs* 36: 2, 2010, 361.

47 See for instance the July 27, 2018, Reuters story, "Italy's Families Minister Targets Same-Sex Surrogacy."

48 Kalindi Vora, *Life Support: Biocapital and the New History of Outsourced Labor*, Minneapolis: University of Minnesota Press, 2015. See also Sophie Lewis, "Review: Life Support by Kalindi Vora," The Antipode Foundation, 2015, radicalantipode.files.wordpress.com

49 Rudrappa, *Discounted Life*, 174.

50 O. A. Makinde, O. Olaleye, O. O. Makinde, S. S. Huntley, and B. Brown, "Baby Factories in Nigeria: Starting the Discussion Towards a National Prevention Policy," *Trauma, Violence and Abuse* 18: 1, 2015, 98–105.

51 Amrita Pande, "Gestational Surrogacy in India: New Dynamics of Reproductive Labour," in Ernesto Noronha and Premilla D'Cruz, eds., *Critical Perspectives on Work and Employment in Globalizing India*, Singapore: Springer, 2017, 267–82.

52 Vora, *Life Support*, 169.

53 Ruth Walker and Liezl van Zyl, *Towards a Professional Model of Surrogate Motherhood*, London, UK: Palgrave, 2017.

54 Laura Kipnis, *Against Love: A Polemic*, New York, NY: Vintage Press, 2003, 141.

55 Briggs, "Reproductive Technology," 370.

56 Dion Farquhar, "Feminist Politics or Hagiography/Demonology? Reproductive Technologies as Pornography/Sexworks," in Bat-Ami Bar-On and Ann Ferguson, eds., *Daring to Be Good: Essays in Feminist Ethico-Politics*, London, UK: Routledge, 1998, 185–98, 192.

57 Nancy Lublin, *Pandora's Box: Feminism Confronts Reproductive Technology*, Lanham, MD: Rowman & Littlefield, 1998, 73.

58 Marilyn Strathern, "Introduction: A Question of Context," in Jeanette Edwards, Sarah Franklin, Frances Price and Marilyn Strathern, eds., *Technologies of Procreation: Kinship in the Age of Assisted Conception*, Oxford, UK: Manchester University Press, 1993, 10.

59 Kajsa Ekman, "Being and Being Bought: An Interview with Kajsa Ekis Ekman," interview by Meghan Murphy, *Feminist Current*, January 20, 2014, 162.

60 Ibid., 152.

61 Zipper and Sevenhuijsen, "Surrogacy," 119.

62 Ibid., 137.

63 Paul B. Preciado, *Testo Junkie: Sex, Drugs, and Biopolitics in the Pharmacopornographic Era*, trans., Bruce Benderson, New York: Feminist Press, 2013, 120. Preciado lists this "certainty that maternity is a natural bond" amid dozens of other items (including Valium, Cinderella, and breast cancer) under the typically dizzying heading "some semiotechnical codes of white heterosexual femininity belonging to the postwar pharmacopornographic political ecology."

64 Sarah Hrdy, *Mother Nature: Maternal Instincts and How They Shape the Human Species*, New York, NY: Ballantine Books, 1999, xviii.

65 *Eggsploitation*, dir. Jennifer Lahl, Center for Bioethics and Culture, 2010.

66 The official trailer for *Breeders* can be viewed at youtube.com/watch?v_5GNNCqs52jFU.

67 *Breeders*, dir. and prod. Jennifer Lahl and Matthew Eppinette, Center for Bioethics and Culture, 2015, 52 minutes.

68 "Surrogacy Is Child Trafficking," Festival of Dangerous Ideas (YouTube).

69 Ekman, Klein, Tankard-Reist, eds., *Broken Bonds: Surrogate Mothers Speak Out*, Melbourne: Spinifex.

70 In her 2014 address, Ekman gave a gloss on what she said was a "Marxist" concept: "Reification. What is that? It was used by the Hungarian Marxist Lukács. And what he means by reification is when you commodify part of human life itself, as one is in work. I think this concept most applies to surrogacy. Because you're reifying something that used to be just part of life."

71 Ekman, "Being and Being Bought."

72 Ann Stoler, *Carnal Knowledge and Imperial Power: Race and the Intimate in Colonial Rule*, Berkeley: University of California Press, 2002; Margaret Jolly and Kalpana Ram, eds., *Maternities and Modernities*, Cambridge: Cambridge University Press, 1998.

73 In the vocabulary of Preciado, in *Testo Junkie*: The "techno-reproductive and techno-gestational division of labor" accompanies

and defines "all processes of filiation"; it's simply "more obvious when it comes to current practices of medically assisted reproduction" (298–300).

74　Rudrappa, "Reproducing Dystopia," 2017.

75　Alys Weinbaum, "The Afterlife of Slavery and the Problem of Reproductive Freedom," *Social Text* 31:2 (115), 2013, 49–68.

76　Angela Davis, "Surrogates and Outcast Mothers: Racism and Reproductive Politics in the Nineties," in Joy James, ed., *The Angela Y. Davis Reader*, Malden, MA: Blackwell, 1998, 210–21.

77　Preciado, *Testo Junkie*, 287.

78　Ibid., 288.

79　"Female Erasure," femaleerasure.com.

80　Susan Stryker and Stephen Whittle, eds., *The Transgender Studies Reader*, New York: Routledge, 2006, 131. It is deeply regrettable—not to mention, in light of what Maria Lugones calls the coloniality of gender, theoretically incoherent—that some of the trailblazing texts of black feminism, such as Dorothy Roberts's *Killing the Black Body* (New York, NY: Vintage, 1997), cite Raymond and her deeply binarizing sex-essentialism complimentarily.

81　Isadore Schmukler and Betsy Aigen, "The Terror of Surrogate Motherhood: Fantasies, Realities, and Viable Legislation," in Joan Offerman Zuckerberg, ed., *Gender in Transition: A New Frontier*, New York, NY: Plenum, 1989, 235–48, 240.

82　Debra Satz, *Why Some Things Should Not Be for Sale: The Moral Limits of Markets*, Oxford, UK: Oxford University Press, 2012.

83　For an in-depth discussion of FINRRAGE's strengths and (mainly, unfortunately) weaknesses, addressing peer criticisms of their actions as well as theoretical retrospectives from erstwhile participants, see Sophie Lewis, "Defending Intimacy Against What?: Limits of Antisurrogacy Feminisms," *Signs* 43: 1, 2017, 97–125.

84　Patricia Spallone and Deborah Steinberg were two FINRRAGE activists who spoke out against the class- and race-blind tenor of the leadership's favoured formulations. See Patricia Spallone and Deborah Steinberg, *Made to Order: The Myth of Reproductive and Genetic Progress*, Oxford: Pergamon, 1987. The differences internal to FINRRAGE, as well as their relation to external forms of technophobia and techophilia in feminism, are analyzed in Lublin, *Pandora's Box*.

85　Farris, *In the Name of Women's Rights*; Kamala Kempadoo, "The Modern-Day White (Wo)Man's Burden: Trends in Anti-trafficking and Anti-surrogacy Campaigns," *Journal of Human Trafficking* 1: 1, 2015, 8–20; and Elizabeth Bernstein, "Militarized Humanitarianism

Meets Carceral Feminism: The Politics of Sex, Rights, and Freedom in Contemporary Antitrafficking Campaigns," *Signs* 36: 1, 2010, 45–71.

86   Neda Atanasoski and Kalindi Vora, "Surrogate Humanity: Posthuman Networks and the (Racialized) Obsolescence of Labor," *Catalyst* 1: 1, 2015.

3. The World's (Other) Oldest Profession

1   Silvia Federici and Nicole Cox, *Counter-Planning from the Kitchen*, New York, NY: Falling Wall Press, 1975, 9.

2   Alyssa Battistoni, "Free Gifts: A Political Theory of Social and Ecological Reproduction," PhD thesis Yale, 2019.

3   Charlotte Shane, "Men Consume, Women Are Consumed: 15 Thoughts on the Stigma of Sex-Work," *Jezebel*, January 9, 2015.

4   Because of the absence of political economy in these accounts, the reader tends to be confronted suddenly with a fleeting admission that it isn't (unfortunately) up to us as embodied individuals endowed with labor power to be caught up in the maelstrom of capitalist accumulation. Instead, we get the meager wish that humans—or rather, the bodies of cis women—"shouldn't" be "viewed" as workers (or "workplaces"). Viewed? By whom? By what? By capitalists? No, by other feminists. For more on the slippage between "is not" and "should not be viewed as," specifically in the SWERF and TERF (and SERF—surrogate-exclusionary radical-feminist) oeuvre of Julie Bindel, see my essay "'Not a Workplace': Julie Bindel and the School of Wrong Abolitionism," versobooks.com/blogs.

5   Sharmila Rudrappa, *Discounted Life: The Price of Global Surrogacy in India*, New York: New York University Press, 2015, 168–69.

6   Kathryn Russell, "A Value-Theoretic Approach to Childbirth and Reproductive Engineering," *Science & Society* 58: 3, 1994, 304.

7   Amrita Banerjee echoes this account in relation to a clinic in Mumbai: "surrogates must learn to "de-structure" the normal clocks of their lives, and "re-structure" their lives around the standardized "maternal clock" of the industry." Amrita Banerjee, "Race and a Transnational Reproductive Caste System," *Hypatia* 29: 1, 2013, 124.

8   Kelly Oliver, "Marxism and Surrogacy," *Hypatia* 4: 3, 1989, 112.

9   Ibid., 113.

10   Marvin Glass, "Reproduction for Money: Marxist Feminism and Surrogate Motherhood," *Nature, Society, and Thought* 7: 3, 1994, 286.

11 Ibid., 288.

12 Mary O'Brien, *The Politics of Reproduction*, New York, NY: Routledge & Kegan Paul, 1981, 175.

13 Ibid.

14 Bronwyn Parry, "Narratives of Neoliberalism: 'Clinical Labor' in Context," *Medical Humanities* 41, 2015, 36.

15 Ibid., 34.

16 Ibid., 35.

17 Amrita Pande, *Wombs in Labor: Transnational Commercial Surrogacy in India*, New York, NY: Columbia University Press, 2014, 11.

18 Malcolm Harris, *Kids These Days: Human Capital and the Making of Millenials*, New York, NY: Little, Brown, 2017.

19 O'Brien, *The Politics of Reproduction*, 208.

20 Harris, *Kids These Days*, 34.

21 "Dr Nayna Patel," HARDtalk with Stephen Sackur, BBC World News, first broadcast November 17, 2013, 30 minutes.

22 "The Israeli Mom Behind Google Baby," *Israel 21c*, October 27, 2011.

23 "Dr Nayna Patel," HARDtalk.

24 Ibid.

25 *Outsourcing Embryos*, executive producers Bradley Levin, Bill Maher, Eddy Moretti, and Shane Smith, Vice Series, HBO, 2015.

26 Laura Harrison, "'I Am the Baby's Real Mother': Reproductive Tourism, Race, and the Transnational Construction of Kinship," *Women's Studies International Forum* 47, 2014, 145–56.

27 Note the striking paradox of the Akanksha Hospital's particular discourse of racial integrity: in declaring that "you can always tell" a baby is "pure white," one could say that it is negating the very corporeal labor surrogates do—the very labor the charismatic boss is selling to her clients.

28 *Outsourcing Embryos*.

29 Sarah Huber, Sharvari Karandikar, and Lindsay Gezinski, "Exploring Indian Surrogates' Perceptions of the Ban on International Surrogacy," *Affilia* 33:1, 2017, 69–84.

30 Sharmila Rudrappa, "Reproducing Dystopia: The Politics of Transnational Surrogacy in India, 2002–2015," *Critical Sociology*, online first, 2017.

31 Ibid.

32 Michael Petersen, Charlotte Krøløkke, and Lene Myong, "Dad and Daddy Assemblage: Resuturing the Nation through Transnational Surrogacy, Homosexuality, and Norwegian Exceptionalism," *GLQ* 23: 1, 2017, 83–112, 94.

33 Ibid.

34 Associated Press, "Norway's Crown Princess Minds Gay Friend's Surrogate Twins," *thejournal.ie*, December 4, 2012.

35 Radha Sharma, "IVF Bundle of 'Anand' for US Lesbian Couple," *Times of India*, November 9, 2014.

36 Petersen, Krøløkke, and Myong, "Dad and Daddy Assemblage," 96.

37 TIME Red Border Films, *Outsourcing Surrogacy*, youtube.com, uploaded September 26, 2015.

38 Pande, *Wombs in Labor*, 72.

39 Ibid., 66. The claim also appears in *House of Surrogates*, dir. Matt Rudge, BBC Four, 2013. 90 minutes.

40 "Dr Nayna Patel," HARDtalk.

41 *Outsourcing Embryos.*

42 *Ma Na Sapna*, dir. Valerie Gudenus, ZhDK, 2013.

43 Sama, "Comments on the Proposed ART Bill," 2008, samawomens health.in; Human Rights Law Network, "Surrogacy in Anand: A Fact-Finding Report," April 27, 2012.

44 Pande, *Wombs in Labor*, 95.

45 Ibid.

46 *Outsourcing Embryos.*

47 *Womb for Rent*, BBC World Service, 2011.

48 Ibid.

49 *Made In India* fieldnotes: madeinindiamovie.com.

50 Amrita Pande, "Commercial Surrogacy in India: Manufacturing a Perfect Mother-Worker," *Signs* 35, 2010, 969–92.

51 PC Vinoj Kumar, "Giving a New Life to Many a Childless Couple and a Livelihood for Women Renting Their Womb," *The Weekend Leader*, October 19, 2015.

52 *Wombs for Rent in India*, Russia Today, 2015, available at youtube .com/watch?v=PSXZSdMmRdg.

53 *Ma Na Sapna.*

54 Abby Rabinowitz, "The Trouble with Renting a Womb," *The Guardian*, April 28, 2016 (quoting surrogacy clinician Sukhpreet Patel).

55 It is Kalindi Vora who noticed first the peculiar framing of Indian women's wombs as "empty" and "wasted" if "unused": see Kalindi Vora, "Re-imagining Reproduction: Unsettling Metaphors in the History of Imperial Science and Commercial Surrogacy in India," *Somatechnics* 5: 1, 2015, 88–103; and Kalindi Vora, "Surplus Wombs and Biocapital: Indian Surrogacy and the Transnational Distribution of Mothering," Paper presented at the annual meeting of the 4S, Crystal City, VA, November 28, 2014. Asha Nadkarni's study, too, notes that surrogacy commerce in clinics like Patel's is framed as freeing the labor

potential of otherwise unused wombs: see Asha Nadkarni, *Eugenic Feminism: Reproductive Nationalism in the United States and India*, Minneapolis: University of Minnesota Press, 2014.

56 Cyra Choudhury, "The Political Economy and Legal Regulation of Transnational Commercial Surrogate Labor," *Vanderbilt Journal of Transnational Law* 46: 1, 2015, 2.

57 Pande, *Wombs in Labor*, 7.

58 Nick Dyer-Witheford, *Cyber-Marx: Cycles and Circuits of Struggle in High Technology Capitalism*, Chicago: University of Illinois Press, 1999, 105.

59 Myra Hird, "The Corporeal Generosity of Maternity," *Body & Society* 13: 1, 2007, 3.

60 Michelle Murphy, "Reproduction" in Shahrzad Mojab, ed., *Marxism and Feminism*, London, UK: Zed Books, 2015, 287–304, 289.

61 Nathan Stormer, "Looking in Wonder: Prenatal Sublimity and the Commonplace 'Life'," *Signs* 33: 3, 2008, 667.

62 Nancy Scheper-Hughes, "The Ends of the Body: Commodity Fetishism and the Global Traffic in Organs," *SAIS Review* 22, Winter–Spring 2002, 61–80, 62.

63 Rebekah Sheldon, *The Child to Come: Life After the Human Catastrophe*, Minneapolis: University of Minnesota Press, 2016, 3.

64 Mary O'Brien, *The Politics of Reproduction*, London, UK: Unwin Hyman, 1981, 177.

65 Tsipy Ivry, "The Pregnancy Manifesto: Notes on How to Extract Reproduction from the Petri Dish," *Medical Anthropology*, 34: 3, 2015, 286.

66 Margrit Shildrick and Deborah Steinberg, "Estranged Bodies: Shifting Paradigms and the Biomedical Imaginary," *Body & Society* 21: 3, 2015, 14.

67 Melissa Wright, *Disposable Women and Other Myths of Global Capitalism*, London, UK: Routledge, 2006, 2.

68 Heather Jacobson, *Labor of Love: Gestational Surrogacy and the Work of Making Babies*, New Brunswick, NJ: Rutgers University Press, 2016, 45.

69 Laura Briggs, *How All Politics Became Reproductive Politics: From Welfare Reform to Foreclosure to Trump*, Berkeley: University of California Press, 2017, p.103 (referring to Alex Kuczynski's controversial article "Her Body, My Baby," *The New York Times*, November 30, 2008).

70 Kathi Weeks, *The Problem with Work: Marxism, Antiwork Politics, and Postwork Imaginaries*, Durham, NC: Duke University Press, 2011.

71 Pande, *Wombs in Labor*, 212.

72 This piece of advice to "expectant mothers" in the context of 1950s US natalism was featured in Irene Lusztig's film *The Motherhood Archives*, Komsomol films, 2013, 91 minutes.

73 Russell, "A Value-Theoretic Approach to Childbirth and Reproductive Engineering," 296.

74 Ibid.

75 The abundance of books and articles published over the past three decades under the title "Labor of Love"—each referring to a different market, ranging from dating to catering—reflects the "feminization of labor" under late capitalism. Many of these works unfortunately do little more than demonstrate the insufficiency of "visibilizing labor" without integrating that visibility into a strategy for revolt. When it comes to pregnancy qua labor-of-love, it is entirely possibly to chart a persuasive course showing that it is work, without then expounding any political consequences of that claim. Ultimately, for such writers, the reign of work doesn't demand rectification.

76 Silvia Federici, "Wages Against Housework," Bristol: Falling Wall Press and Power of Women Collective, 1975.

77 *Mother!*, dir. Darren Aronofsky, Protozoa Pictures, 2017, 121 minutes.

78 Rosalind Petchesky writes: "Much controversy surrounds the question of whether and where slave women engaged in abortion, birth control, or infanticide as ways of reappropriating their bodies and resisting the master's domination. It is difficult to know when we are justified in reading into such actions a conscious expression of the idea that 'my body is my own,' especially when dealing with oral cultures that did not record their reasons or defend then- actions in philosophical terms. Yet convincing accounts show slave women in the British Caribbean deliberately rejecting the role of mother and slave breeder. The persistence of low fertility rates among Caribbean slaves, despite pronatalist incentives, may well have been the result of herbal methods of birth control and abortion brought from Africa." Rosalind Petchesky, "The Body as Property" in Rapp, Rayna, and Faye Ginsburg, eds. *Conceiving the New World Order: The Global Politics of Reproduction*, Berkeley: University of California Press, 1995, 398.

79 *Made in India*, dir. Vaishali Sinha and Rebecca Haimowitz, PBS, 2014, 93 minutes. Quotations are taken from madeinindiamovie.com.

80 Satinder Chohan's play is also (what lack of imagination!) entitled *Made in India*.

81 Melinda Cooper and Catherine Waldby, *Clinical Labor*, Durham, NC: Duke University Press, 2014.

82 Elizabeth Anderson, "Is Women's Labor a Commodity?" *Philosophy & Public Affairs* 17: 1, 1990, 71–92.

83 Alys Weinbaum, "Marx, Irigaray, and the Politics of Reproduction," *differences* 6: 1, 1994, 101.

84 Bini Adamczak, "On Circlusion," trans., Sophie Lewis, *Mask* magazine, 2017, maskmagazine.com.

85 This phrase comes from Julie Bindel's *Guardian* column of April 30, 2018: "Prostitution is not a job. The inside of a woman's body is not a workplace."

86 Shane, "Men Consume, Women Are Consumed."

87 Seth Mydans, "Surrogate Denied Custody of Child," *The New York Times*, October 23, 1990.

88 Luna Dolezal, "Phenomenology and Intercorporeality in the Case of Commercial Surrogacy" in Luna Dolezal and Danielle Petherbridge, eds., *Body/Self/Other: The Phenomenology of Social Encounters*, Albany: SUNY Press, 2017, 311–36, 320.

4. Dr. Patel Leans In

1   *Google Baby*, dir. Zippi Brand Frank, HBO, 2009, 77 minutes.

2   Asha Nadkarni, *Eugenic Feminism: Reproductive Nationalism in the United States and India*, Minneapolis: University of Minnesota Press, 2014, 209.

3   Sheryl Sandberg, *Lean In: Women, Work, and the Will to Lead*, New York, NY: Alfred A. Knopf, 2013.

4   Dawn Foster eviscerates Sandberg in *Lean Out*, London, UK: Repeater Books, 2015.

5   *House of Surrogates*, dir. Matt Rudge, BBC Four, 2013, 90 minutes.

6   Sharmila Rudrappa, personal correspondence, August 6, 2016; Shweta Bhatt, "Waiting in the Wings for Political Debut in Gujarat," DNA India, October 7, 2012.

7   Banu Subramanian, "Molecular Entanglements: Onto-Epistemologies and the Politics of Matter," paper presented as part of the seminar panel "Onto-Epistemological Entanglements" at the Gender Research Institute at Dartmouth (Dartmouth University), May 9, 2016.

8   Nadkarni, *Eugenic Feminism*, 205.

9   Amrita Pande, "'It May Be Her Eggs But It's My Blood': Surrogates and Everyday Forms of Kinship in India," *Qualitative Sociology*, 32, 2009, 379–97.

10 Lindsay B. Gezinski, Sharvari Karandikar, Alexis Levitt, and Roxanne Ghaffarian, "'We Want to Offer You Peace of Mind': Marketing of

Transnational Commercial Surrogacy Services to Intended Parents," *Health Marketing Quarterly* 34: 4, 2017, 302–14.

11 *House of Surrogate*s.

12 Sharmila Rudrappa, personal correspondence, February 7, 2016.

13 *House of Surrogates*.

14 Sharmila Rudrappa, "Reproducing Dystopia: The Politics of Transnational Surrogacy in India, 2002–2015," *Critical Sociology*, online first, 2017.

15 McCormick, quoted in Paul B. Preciado, *Testo Junkie: Sex, Drugs, and Biopolitics in the Pharmacopornographic Era*, trans., Bruce Benderson, New York: Feminist Press, 2013, 180.

16 Katherine McCormick, quoted in Lara Mark, "A 'Cage of Ovulating Females.' The History of the Early Oral Contraceptive Pill Clinical Trials, 1950–1959," in Soraya de Chadarevian and Harmke Kamminga, eds., *Molecularizing Biology and Medicine: New Practices and Alliances, 1910s–1970s*, Amsterdam: Harwood Academic Publishers, 1998, 208.

17 Silvia Federici, "Reproduction and Feminist Struggle in the New International Division of Labor," in Mariaroa Dalla Costa and Giovanna Dalla Costa, eds., *Women, Development and Labor of Reproduction: Struggles and Movement*, Trenton, NJ: Africa World Press, 47–82.

18 Laura Briggs, *How All Politics Became Reproductive Politics: From Welfare Reform to Foreclosure to Trump*, Oakland: University of California Press, 2017, 77.

19 Quoted in Ibid., 78.

20 Sayantani DasGupta, "Consuming Fetuses, Commodifying Bumps: Western Intended Parent Blogs and the Surveillance of Transnational Indian Surrogacy," paper presented at the annual meeting of the National Women's Studies Association, November 25, 2014.

21 Hedva Eyal and Adi Moreno, "'Quiet, Dependent, Nice and Loyal': Surrogacy Agencies' Discourse of International Surrogacy," in Hagai Boas and Yael Hashiloni-Dolev, eds., *Bioethics and Biopolitics in Israel*, Cambridge, UK: Cambridge University Press, 2017, 147.

22 Adrienne Arieff, *The Sacred Thread*, New York, NY: Crown, 2012, 5.

23 Stephanie Lee, "Outsourcing a Life," *San Francisco Chronicle*, September 30, 2013.

24 Lizzie Paton, "An Appointment with Dr. Patel," *The Sunday Times*, May 9, 2010.

25 AFP in New Delhi, "India Bans Foreigners from Hiring Surrogate Mothers," *The Guardian*, October 28, 2015.

26 Ibid.

27 PC Vinoj Kumar, "Giving a New Life to Many a Childless Couple

and a Livelihood for Women Renting Their Womb," *The Weekend Leader*, October 19, 2015.

28 Ibid.

29 Ibid.

30 Lakshmi Ajay, "Surrogate Mothers of Anand to Make Chocolates, Snacks," *Indian Express*, May 21, 2013.

31 Ibid.

32 Ibid.

33 Nayna Patel, "Surrogacy in India," Ted Talk, available at youtu.be/p7kIWc7S8IQ.

34 Ibid.

35 Katharyne Mitchell, "Celebrity Humanitarianism, Transnational Emotion and the Rise of Neoliberal Citizenship," *Global Networks* 16: 2, 2016.

36 Patel, "Surrogacy in India."

37 Brian Hatcher, "Bourgeois Vedānta: The Colonial Roots of Middle-Class Hinduism," *Journal of the American Academy of Religion* 75: 2, 2007, 1–26.

38 Amrita Pande, "Transnational Commercial Surrogacy in India: Gifts for Global Sisters?" *Reproductive Biomedicine Online* 23: 5, 2011, 618–25.

39 Heléna Ragoné, "Incontestable Motivations" in Sarah Franklin and Heléna Ragoné, eds., *Reproducing Reproduction: Kinship, Power, and Technology*, Philadelphia: University of Pennsylvania Press, 1998.

40 *Wombs for Rent in India*, Russia Today, 2015, available at youtube.com/watch?v=PSXZSdMmRdg.

41 Ibid.

42 Prospective clients and commissioning parents of the Akanksha form a "community" at dr-patel-surrogacy.com and at the Akanksha Facebook page facebook.com/AkankshaHospitalAnand.

43 Vidi Doshi, "'We Pray that the Clinic Stays Open'," *The Observer*, January 2, 2016.

44 *Ma Na Sapna*, dir. Valerie Gudenus, ZhDK, 2013.

45 Charis Thompson, *Making Parents: The Ontological Choreography of Reproductive Technologies*, Boston, MA: MIT Press, 2005.

46 *Google Baby*.

47 *Wombs for Rent in India*.

48 Poona Taneja, "India's Surrogate Mother Industry," BBC News, October 12, 2008.

49 Akanksha website, cached version dated May 21, 2016: ivf-surrogate.com.

50 Sharmila Rudrappa and Caitlyn Collins, "Altruistic Agencies and Compassionate Consumers," *Gender & Society* 29, 2015, 937–59.

51 Matthew Bishop and Michael Green, *Philanthrocapitalism: How the Rich Can Save the World*, London, UK: Bloomsbury, 2008.

52 Ananya Roy, *Poverty Capital: Microfinance and the Making Development*, New York, NY: Routledge, 2010.

53 Nadkarni, *Eugenic Feminism*, 204.

54 Kumkum Sangari, *Solid: Liquid: A (Trans)national Reproductive Formation*, Delhi, India: Tulika, 2015.

55 Charlotte Krølkke and Saumya Pant, "'I Only Need Her Uterus': Neo-liberal Discourses on Transnational Surrogacy," *NORA—Nordic Journal of Feminist and Gender Research* 20: 4, 2012, 233–348.

56 "Harjit Sarang Interviews Dr Nayna Patel of House of Surrogates," October 4, 2013, available at youtube.com/watch?v=RjbZTk-Pxso.

57 *Wombs for Rent in India*.

58 *House of Surrogates*.

59 *Commercial Surrogacy in India*, VPRO Metropolis, 2014, available at youtube.com/watch?v=qYVRovXEdn8.

60 Margot Cohen, "Birth of a Genre," *The Wall Street Journal*, October 9, 2009.

61 Daisy Deomampo, "Transnational Surrogacy in India: Interrogating Power and Women's Agency," *Frontiers* 34: 3, 2013, 167–88.

62 Lisa Ikemoto, "Reproductive Tourism: Equality Concerns in the Global Market for Fertility Services," in Osagie K. Obasogie and Marcy Darnovsky, eds., *Beyond Bioethics: Toward a New Biopolitics*, Berkeley: University of California Press, 2018, 346.

63 Michelle Esther O'Brien, "To Abolish the Family: Periodizing Gender Liberation in Capitalist Development," *Endnotes* 5, forthcoming.

64 *Wombs for Rent in India*.

65 Patel, "Surrogacy in India."

66 Michael Day and David Orr, "I'm Proud to Bear My Daughter's Twins," *The Telegraph*, February 1, 2004.

67 BBC News, "Twins for Surrogate Grandmother," January 30, 2004.

68 "Outsourcing Surrogacy."

69 Akanksha website, cached version (May 21, 2016): ivf-surrogate .com. Pande writes that this figure, "Divya" "plays a critical role in the production of a dual mother-worker subject"; Amrita Pande, *Wombs in Labor: Transnational Commercial Surrogacy in India*, New York, NY: Columbia University Press, 2014, 68.

70 Patel, "Surrogacy in India."

71 *Ma Na Sapna*.

72 Pande, *Wombs in Labor*, 70.

73 Doshi, "'We Pray that the Clinic Stays Open.'"

74 *House of Surrogates*.

5. "She Did It for the Money"

1 Roxane Dunbar, "Female Liberation as the Basis for Social Revolution," Robin Morgan, ed., *Sisterhood is Powerful*, New York, NY: Random House, 1970, 499.

2 *Something Like a War*, dir. Deepa Dhanraj, D & N Productions, 1991, 52 minutes.

3 Johnnie Tillmon, "Women on Welfare," quoted in Laura Briggs, *How All Politics Became Reproductive Politics: From Welfare Reform to Foreclosure to Trump*, Oakland: University of California Press, 2017, 62. On the overlooked anti-work politics of the NWRO, see Wilson Sherwin, "Rich in Needs: Revisiting the Radical Politics of the Welfare Rights Movement," PhD thesis, CUNY.

4 Mark Greif, "Octomom: A Year Later," *n+1*, no. 9, Spring 2010.

5 Kevin Rawlinson, "Interpol Investigates 'Baby Factory' as Man Fathers 16 Surrogate Children," *The Guardian*, August 23, 2014.

6 Natalie Fixmer-Oraiz, "(In)Conceivable: Risky Reproduction and the Rhetorical Labors of 'Octomom'," *Communication and Critical/Cultural Studies* 11: 3, 2014, 231–49, 242.

7 *The Florida Project*, dir. Sean Baker, Cre Film, 2017, 111 minutes.

8 Assata Shakur, *Assata: An Autobiography*, London, UK: Zed Books, 2014.

9 *Mammas*, dir. Isabella Rossellini, Sundance Channel, 2013.

10 Maggie Nelson, *The Argonauts*, Minneapolis, MN: Graywolf Press, 2015, 94.

11 Elizabeth Grosz, "What's Sex Got to Do with Family?" Keynote, the Graduate Center, City University of New York, October 5, 2009.

12 Alison Jolly, "Mother Love: Evolution and the Maternal Instinct," review of *Mother Nature* by Sarah Blaffer Hrdy, *The Guardian*, August 3, 2000.

13 Janelle Taylor, "A Fetish Is Born: Sonographers and the Making of the Public Fetus," in Janelle Taylor, Linda Layne, and Danielle Wozniak, eds., *Consuming Motherhood*, New Brunswick, NJ: Rutgers University Press, 2004, 187–210, 209.

14 Shulamith Firestone, *The Dialectic of Sex*, London, UK: Verso, 2015 [1970], 232.

15 Kate Griffiths and Jules Gleeson, "Kinderkommunismus: A Feminist Analysis of the 21st Century Family and a Communist Proposal for its Abolition," *Ritual* 0, 2015.

16 José Gabilondo, "Irrational Exuberance About Babies: The Taste for Heterosexuality and Its Conspicuous Reproduction," *B.C. Third World L.J.*, 28: 1, 2008, 1–74.

17 Friedrich Nietzsche, "Thus Spake Zarathustra," *The Portable Nietzsche*, ed. and trans. Walter Kaufmann, New York, NY: Penguin Books, 434.

18 Elizabeth Freeman, "Queer Belongings: Queer Theory and Kinship Theory," in George Haggert and Molly McGarry, eds., *A Companion to Lesbian, Gay, Bisexual, Transgender and Queer Studies*, London, UK: Blackwell, 2007, 308.

19 Rebekah Sheldon, *The Child to Come: Life After the Human Catastrophe*, Minneapolis: University of Minnesota Press, 2016.

20 José Esteban Muñoz, *Cruising Utopia: The Then and There of Queer Futurity*, New York: New York University Press, 2009, 92. See also *Out of the Woods*, "The Future is Kid's Stuff," *LibCom*, May 17, 2015. Inspired by Muñoz, *Out of the Woods*—a collective of which I am a part—argues in this piece that "the fetishism of the child and the mother in the abstract is inseparable from the actual and total violence perpetrated against children and their kin." In a related piece, *Out of the Woods* regrets that Naomi Klein's otherwise powerful call for a "Right to Regenerate" ultimately devolves into a "politics of the baby's face"; see "Klein vs. Klein," *The New Inquiry*, January 7, 2015.

21 Shelley Park, "Is Queer Parenting Possible?" in Rachel Epstein, ed., *Who's Your Daddy? And Other Writings on Queer Parenting*, Toronto, Canada: Sumach Press, 2009, 316–27.

22 Helen Hester, *Xenofeminism*, Cambridge, UK: Polity Press, 2018, 64.

23 Ibid., 298.

24 Ibid., 65.

25 Donna Haraway, "Making Oddkin: Storytelling for Earthly Survival," Yale University, Women's, Gender and Sexuality Studies symposium on Donna Haraway, October 23, 2017.

26 Briggs, *How All Politics Became Reproductive Politics*, 109.

27 Ibid., 110.

28 Janet Carsten, *After Kinship*, Cambridge, UK: Cambridge University Press, 2004, 167.

29 Paul B. Preciado, *Testo Junkie: Sex, Drugs, and Biopolitics in the Pharmacopornographic Era*, trans. Bruce Benderson, New York, NY: Feminist Press, 2013, 47.

30 Freeman, "Queer Belongings," 301.

31 Madeline Lane-McKinley and Marija Cetinic, "Theses on Postpartum," *GUTS* magazine, May 22, 2015, gutsmagazine.ca.

32 Griffiths and Gleeson, "Kinderkommunismus." The authors echo Cetinic and Lane-McKinley when they call for an "undoing of [the] distinction between parent and non-parent."

33 Gleeson and Griffiths are trenchant in their critique of what they call "queer rejectionism" and adamant that family abolition must go beyond it. This prevalent rejectionism, in their view, presents "either the vaguest vision of 'queer insurrection' against social norms, or in fact present no vision at all (focusing instead on the politics of 'survival'). While our rejectionist comrades have made a decisive case for rejecting liberal-subsumed LGBT NGOs, they do not make any advancement toward the family's end. Their politics is one of celebrating tension, not collapsing the material foundations of straight identities. Their nostalgic-historiographical poetics have failed to provide an emancipatory path that will destroy the heterosexualizing coercion of the family. They have failed even to speculate clearly as to what such a path might look like" (ibid.).

34 Michelle O'Brien, "Queer in the Eras of Capital," review of Peter Drucker, *Warped: Gay Normality and Queer Anti-Capitalism*, H-Net *Reviews in the Humanities and Social Sciences*, h-net.org.

35 "Judith Orr: Marxism, the Family, and Social Reproduction Theory," youtube.com, uploaded July 25, 2014.

36 Michelle O'Brien specifies that it is not the family per se but "the housewife-based family form" that has been abolished today, namely, by capital itself ("and with it the precision and clarity of previous eras of the demand to abolish the family"). Rising family abolition as a "demand and horizon" remains "urgent and necessary" because it offers "a means of combating the rise of the new gender conservatism, a mode of attack on the isolating role of current atomized reproduction, and a vision of gender and sexual liberation" whose roots date back at least to Engels's society of free love. Michelle Esther O'Brien, "To Abolish the Family: Periodizing Gender Liberation in Capitalist Development," *Endnotes* 5, forthcoming.

37 Sarah Brouillette, "Couple Up" (review of Melinda Cooper's *Family Values*), *Boundary* 2, June 2, 2017.

38 Melinda Cooper, *Family Values: Between Neoliberalism and the New Social Conservatism*, New York, NY: Zone Books, 2017.

39 Griffiths and Gleeson, "Kinderkommunismus."

40 Marge Piercy, *Woman on the Edge of Time*, New York: Fawcett Crest, 1983 [1976], 75.

41 Ibid., 76.

42 Ursula Le Guin, *The Left Hand of Darkness*, ed., Neil Gaiman, New York, NY: Penguin Books, 2016.

43 This phrase is Jo Freeman's: "When I think back on Shulie's contribution to the movement, I think of her as a shooting star. She flashed brightly across the midnight sky, and then she disappeared." Quoted

in Susan Faludi, "Death of a Revolutionary," *The New Yorker*, April 15, 2013.

44 Firestone, *The Dialectic of Sex*, 239.

45 Ibid., 233.

46 Ibid.

47 Madeline Lane-McKinley, "The Idea of Children," *Blind Field: A Journal of Cultural Inquiry*, 2018.

48 Sharmila Rudrappa, "Reproducing Dystopia: The Politics of Transnational Surrogacy in India, 2002–2015," *Critical Sociology*, online first, 2017.

49 Firestone, *The Dialectic of Sex*, 232.

50 Anindita Majumdar, "The Feminist Debates on Reproductive Choice in the Commercial Surrogacy Arrangement in India," *Gender, Technology and Development* 18: 2, 2014, 275–301, 297.

51 "India's Surrogate Mother Business Raises Questions of Global Ethics," *NY Daily News*, December 30, 2007.

52 See surromomsonline.com. In the Indian context, remarks of this nature are recorded, from unnamed surrogates, in the documentary *Made in India*, dir. Vaishali Sinha and Rebecca Haimowitz, PBS, 2014, 93 minutes.

53 Daisy Deomampo, *Transnational Reproduction: Race, Kinship and Commercial Surrogacy in India*, New York: New York University Press, 2016 (see Chapters 5 and 6).

54 Nilanjana Roy, "Protecting the Rights of Surrogate Mothers in India," *The New York Times*, October 4, 2011.

55 Orna Donath, *Regretting Motherhood*, Berkeley, CA: North Atlantic Books, 2017.

56 Nelson, *The Argonauts*.

57 Sara Ahmed, *The Promise of Happiness*, Durham, NC: Duke University Press, 2010.

58 Sigrid Vertommen, "Anticolonial Resistance Is Fertile: Sperm Smuggling and Birth Strikes in Israel/Palestine," 2018, unpublished manuscript.

59 W. B. Yeats, "Among School Children," *The Collected Poems*, ed. Richard Finneran, New York, NY: Simon and Schuster, 2008, 222. Hans Christian Andersen, *The Stories of Hans Christian Andersen*, ed. and trans., Diana Crone Frank and Jeffrey Frank, Durham, NC: Duke University Press, 2005.

60 "Milton produced his Paradise Lost for the same reason that a silkworm produces silk. It was an activity of his nature." *Theories of Surplus-Value*, 1, 1963 [1862], London: Lawrence and Wishart, 401.

61 For a discussion of "labors of love," see my "'Fuck Off To Back Where

You Came From': Notes on The Phantom Thread" and "Towards a Future Genealogy of the Date," *Blind Field: A Journal of Cultural Inquiry*, 2018 and 2016, blindfieldjournal.com.

62 Nat Raha, "Against the Day: Transfeminine Brokenness, Radical Transfeminism," *South Altantic Quarterly* 116: 3, 2017, 263–46; Siân Bradley, "Queer Work: Productivity, Reproduction and Change," masters thesis, Linköping University, 2016; Kathi Weeks, *The Problem with Work: Feminism, Marxism, Antiwork Politics, and Postwork Imaginaries*, Durham, NC: Duke University Press, 2011.

63 Nelson, *The Argonauts*, 134.

64 Ibid.

65 Donna Haraway, "Making Oddkin: Storytelling for Earthly Survival," presentation recorded on October 23, 2017 at Yale University, youtube.com/watch?v=z-iEnSztKu8. This quotation comes from one of Haraway's remarks during the Q&A, prefaced by the statement "I am not a pro-life person," at about 1:31:55.

66 Nelson, *The Argonauts*, 94.

67 Quoted in Briggs, *How All Politics Became Reproductive Politics*, 153, from Minnie Bruce Pratt's poetry collection *Crime Against Nature*.

68 Samantha Hunt, "A Love Story," *The New Yorker*, May 22, 2017.

69 Rebecca Yoshizawa, "Fetal-Maternal Intra-action: Politics of New Placental Biologies," *Body & Society* 22: 3, 2016, 79–105.

70 Philip Larkin, "This Be the Verse," in *High Windows*, London, UK: Faber & Faber, 1974.

71 Christine Battersby, *The Phenomenal Woman*, Cambridge, UK: Polity Press, 1998, 18. Quoted in Imogen Tyler, "Reframing Pregnant Embodiment," in Sara Ahmed, Jane Kilby, Celia Lury, Maureen McNeil, and Beverley Skeggs, eds., *Transformations: Thinking Through Feminism*, London, UK: Routledge, 2005, 288.

72 Iris Marion Young, "Pregnant Embodiment: Subjectivity and Alienation," *The Journal of Medicine and Philosophy: A Forum for Bioethics and Philosophy of Medicine* 9: 1, 1984, 45–62, 49.

73 Nelson, *The Argonauts*, 14.

74 Laboria Cuboniks, "Xenofeminism: A Politics for Alienation," 2015, laboriacuboniks.net.

75 Hester, *Xenofeminism*, 18.

76 Hunt, "A Love Story."

77 Nelson, *The Argonauts*, xx.

78 Rhacel Salazar Parreñas, "The Care Crisis in the Philippines: Children and Transnational Families in the New Global Economy," in Barbara Ehrenreich and Arlie Russell Hochschild, eds., *Global Woman:*

Nannies, Maids, and Sex Workers in the New Economy, London, UK: Palgrave, 2004, 39–54.

79 Briggs, *How All Politics Became Reproductive Politics*, 95–98.

80 Suzanne Moore, "The Case of Gammy Shows Surrogacy for the Repulsive Trade It Is," *The Guardian*, August 4, 2014.

81 Sophie Lewis, "Gestational Labors: Care Politics and Surrogates' Struggle," in Susanne Hofmann and Adi Moreno, eds., *Intimate Economies: Bodies, Emotions and Sexualities on the Global Market*, New York, NY: Palgrave, 2016. As I outline in this article, it is worth deconstructing how the Baby Gammy scandal, like all scandals of its type, is framed so as to become the basis for myriad calls for "regulation" of the surrogacy industry. Rarely was it noticed in the international media that Gammy was the beneficiary of lack of regulation in the sense that, contracts having been easily voided, he could straightforwardly be integrated into the Chanbua family. While Gammy was the catalyst for regulatory crackdowns across the region which, in turn, created unpleasant scenarios well into the following year, the more substantial controversy "ought" really to have surrounded the part of the surrogacy transaction that went smoothly, namely, Baby Pipah.

82 This is in fact the title of Chapter 2 in Jennifer Nelson, *Women of Color and the Reproductive Rights Movement*, New York: New York University Press, 2003.

83 Elizabeth Ziff, "'The Mommy Deployment': Military Spouses and Surrogacy in the United States," *Sociological Forum* 32: 2, 2017, 406.

84 Zsusza Berend, "'We Are All Carrying Someone Else's Child!': Relatedness and Relationships in Third-Party Reproduction," *American Anthropologist* 118: 1, 2016, 33.

85 Claudia Card, "Against Marriage and Motherhood," *Hypatia* 11: 3, 1996, 1–23.

86 Joshua Gamson, "The Belly Mommy and the Fetus Sitter: The Reproductive Marketplace and Family Intimacies," in A. Frank, P. T. Clough, and S. Seidman, eds., *Intimacies: A New World of Relational Life*, New York, NY: Routledge, 2014, 146–62.

87 Berend, "'We Are All Carrying Someone Else's Child!'" 29.

88 Ibid.

89 See for instance Sarah Jobe, *Creating with God: The Holy Confusing Blessedness of Pregnancy*, Brewster, MA: Paraclete Press, 2011, and Pam England, *Birthing from Within: An Ancient Map for Modern Birth*, Albuquerque, NM: Seven Gates Media, 2017.

90 Mai'a Williams, "Introduction," in Alexis Pauline Gumbs, Mai'a Williams, and China Martens, eds., *Revolutionary Mothering: Love on the Front Lines*, Oakland, CA: PM Press, 2016.

91 Sylvia Plath, "May 7th diary entry" [1962], in Moyra Davey, ed., *The Motherhood Reader: Essential Writings on Motherhood*, New York, NY: Seven Stories Press, 2001, 25.

92 Richard Yates, *Revolutionary Road*, New York, NY: Little & Brown, 1961.

93 Lionel Shriver, *We Need to Talk About Kevin*, New York, NY: Harper Perennial, 2003; *We Need to Talk About Kevin*, dir. Lynne Ramsay, BBC Films, 2011, 112 minutes

94 Laura Briggs, "Reproductive Technology: Of Labor and Markets," *Feminist Studies* 36:2, 359–374, 2010, 370.

95 Ann Lamott, "Maternal Anger: Theory and Practice," in Camille Peri and Kate Moses, eds., *Mothers Who Think*, New York, NY: Washington Square Press, 2000, 89–96.

96 Necropolitical tactics as means of resisting patriarchy are perhaps more widely accepted in Melanesia, as Marilyn Strathern suggests: "[A pregnant woman] was angry with her husband … and the two came to blows. So she hired a woman expert in abortion, and went down to a river where the expert pummelled her abdomen. The grateful wife gave her a fine quality netbag and some salt in payment. She lied to her husband, saying the child had died in her womb, and she did not know why—was it her own ancestors or the husband's ancestors who killed it?" Marilyn Strathern, *Women In Between: Female Roles in a Male World*, Lanham, MD: Rowman and Littlefield, 1972, 44.

97 In *Kindred*, the protagonist "Dana" props up the (named) institution of American chattel slavery by going back in time to overrule her enslaved grandmother's suicidal rebellion against her master in order to ensure that she, Dana, will one day be born. Octavia Butler, *Kindred*, New York, NY: Doubleday, 1979.

98 Toni Morrison, *Beloved*, New York, NY: Knopf, 1987.

99 Barbara Bush, "Hard Labor: Women, Childbirth, and Resistance in British Caribbean Slave Societies," in Londa Schiebinger, ed., *Feminism and the Body*, Oxford, UK: Oxford University Press, 2000, 234–62.

100 Yoko Ono and John Lennon expressed essentially this same view in the song "Woman is the Nigger of the World" in 1969. Their unfortunate and ignorant phrase was revived verbatim on a 2011 SlutWalk placard in New York, and then loosely echoed in a tweet by celebrity actress Rose McGowan on the subject of jokes about #MeToo and serial sex-predator Harvey Weinstein in 2017: "Replace the word 'women' w/ the 'N' word. How does it feel?" Indeed, the anti-intersectional, anti-solidaritous treatment of

women's interests and black people's interests as being in conflict or in competition with one another has been an unfortunate hallmark of Anglo-American feminism, ever since it began. The American suffragist Susan B. Anthony had, after all, infamously declared in 1848: "I will cut off this right arm of mine before I will ask for the ballot for the Negro and not for the woman." See Louise Michele Newman, *White Women's Rights: The Racial Origins of Feminism in the United States*, Oxford, UK: Oxford University Press, 1999.

101 Adrienne Rich, *Of Woman Born: Motherhood as Experience and Institution*, London, UK: Norton, 1977, 163.

102 Documentary produced by RedPix 24x7, 6 minutes, 11 seconds; footage includes interviews with the director of the small charity G-SMART, VK Karthirvan, and unnamed surrogacy workers (translated for the author by Dr Velaitham Umachandran).

103 Suzanne Sadedin, "War in the Womb," *Aeon*, August 4, 2014, aeon.co.

104 The trans-hostile group in question was Fair Play For Women (twitter.com/fairplaywomen) and the following two sample tweets, sent on 5 and 7 November 2017 respectively, linked to Suzanne Sadedin's article by way of commenting on the news that trans women might receive access to pregnancy through the NHS: "Won't happen. Any potential foetus would invade the host's body & proliferate like 1,000 cancers"; "Hahahahahahahahahahaha! Good luck to 'em. The foetus will invade their body like a virus." Nick Duffy, "Group Behind Metro Newspaper Ad Sent 'Chilling' Tweets about Trans Women Getting '1,000 Cancers,'" *Pink News*, October 12, 2018.

105 Ibid.

106 Emily Martin, *The Woman in the Body: A Cultural Analysis of Reproduction*, Boston, MA: Beacon Press, 2001.

107 Charlotte Krøløkke and Saumya Pant, "'I Only Need Her Uterus': Neo-liberal Discourses on Transnational Surrogacy," *NORA— Nordic Journal of Feminist and Gender Research* 20: 4, 2012, 233–348.

108 Berend, "'We Are All Carrying Someone Else's Child!'" 27.

109 Octavia Orchard quoted in Helen Roberts and Frances Hardy, "Our Rent-a-Womb child from an Indian Baby Farm," *The Daily Mail*, August 31, 2012.

110 Vicki Kirby, *What If Nature was Culture All Along?* Edinburgh, Scotland: Edinburgh University Press, 2017.

111 Erin Mahoney and Jenny Brown, "Abortion Without Apology," *Jacobin*, December 31, 2015.

6. Another Surrogacy Is Possible

1 Amrita Pande writes: "The few existing studies on infertility in India indicate that the incidence of total infertility in the country is around 8 to 10 percent, and for the vast majority of Indian women it is preventable, as it is caused by poor health, a lack of maternity services, and high levels of infection. Only about 2 percent of Indian women suffer from the kind of infertility that is amenable to ART alone." *Wombs in Labor: Transnational Commercial Surrogacy in India*, New York, NY: Columbia University Press, 2014, 215. In recent years there has been much coverage of the "desperation" of couples amid a decline in Indian fertility, quoting a finding of the Indian Society for Assisted Reproduction (hardly a neutral source) that the infertility rate is now closer to 14 percent. Neeta Lal, "India's Hidden Fertility Struggles," *The Diplomat*, May 30, 2018.

2 Amit Sengupta, "Medical Tourism: Reverse Subsidy for the Elite," *Signs* 36: 2, 2011, 312–19, 314.

3 Sharmila Rudrappa, *Discounted Life: The Price of Global Surrogacy in India*, New York: New York University Press, 2015, 96.

4 Ibid., 85.

5 *Ma Na Sapna*, dir. Valerie Gudenus, ZhDK, 2013.

6 Rudrappa, *Discounted Life*, 25. Rudrappa neatly encapsulates the intertwinement of reproductive "assistance" and "desistance" in the US context: "sterilization abuse of women of color was rampant … Yet, white U.S. women had no access to fertility control, until in 1965 when the U.S. Supreme Court awarded married women the right to use birth control as a constitutional right to privacy. Five years later President Nixon passed Title X of the Public Health Service Act, which made contraceptives available to all American women. Very quietly, however, along the heels of minimally invasive contraception, came another kind of reproductive intervention—fertility assistance."

7 Patel, quoted in Doshi, 2016.

8 Sama Resource Group for Women and Health, *Birthing A Market: A Study On Commercial Surrogacy*, New Delhi: Sama, 2012; Loretta Ross et al., ed., *Radical Reproductive Justice: Foundation, Theory, Practice, Critique*, New York: The Feminist Press, 2017.

9 Rudrappa, *Discounted Life*, 23.

10 Natalie Fixmer-Oraiz, "Speaking of Solidarity: Transnational Gestational Surrogacy and the Rhetorics of Reproductive (In)Justice," *Frontiers* 34: 3, 2013, 127, 141–61.

11 Juno Mac and Molly Smith, *Revolting Prostitutes: The Fight for Sex Workers' Rights*, London, UK: Verso, 2018; Sylvia Rivera, *Street*

Transvestite Action Revolutionaries, New York, NY: Untorelli Press, 2011; Shelley Park, "Adoptive Maternal Bodies: A Queer Paradigm for Rethinking Mothering?" *Hypatia* 21: 1, 2006, 201–26.

12 Shulamith Firestone, *The Dialectic of Sex*, London, UK: Verso, 2015 [1970], 77.

13 Dorothy Roberts, *Killing the Black Body: Race, Reproduction, and the Meaning of Liberty*, New York, NY: Pantheon, 1997.

14 D. Memee Lavell-Harvard and Kim Anderson, eds., *Mothers of the Nations: Indigenous Mothering as Global Resistance, Reclaiming and Recovery*, Ontario, Canada: Demeter Press, 2014, 5.

15 Elizabeth Freeman, "Queer Belongings: Queer Theory and Kinship Theory," in George Haggert and Molly McGarry, eds., *A Companion to Lesbian, Gay, Bisexual, Transgender and Queer Studies*, London, UK: Blackwell, 2007, 303.

16 Ibid.

17 Hartman, quoted by Christina Sharpe, "Lose Your Kin," *The New Inquiry*, 2016, thenewinquiry.com.

18 Hortense Spillers, "Mama's Baby, Papa's Maybe: An American Grammar Book," *diacritics* 17: 2, 1987, 65–81.

19 Catherine Waldby, "Oocyte Markets: Women's Reproductive Work in Embryonic Stem Cell Research," *New Genetics and Society* 27: 1, 2008, 19–31, 26.

20 Generations Ahead, "A Reproductive Justice Analysis of Genetic Technologies: Report of a National Convening of Women of Colour and Indigenous Women," in Miranda Davies, ed., *Babies for Sale?: Transnational Surrogacy and the Politics of Reproduction*, London, UK: Zed, 2017, 282.

21 Mai'a Williams, "Introduction," in Alexis Pauline Gumbs, China Martens, and Mai'a Williams, eds., *Revolutionary Mothering: Love on the Front Lines*, Toronto, Ontario: Between the Lines, 2016, 148.

22 Laura Kessler, "Transgressive Caregiving," *Florida State University Law Review* 33: 1, 2005.

23 Ibid., 86.

24 Alexis Pauline Gumbs, "m/other ourselves: A Black queer feminist genealogy for radical mothering," in Alexis Pauline Gumbs, China Martens, and Mai'a Williams, eds., *Revolutionary Mothering: Love on the Front Lines*, Oakland, CA: PM Press, 2016, 21.

25 In her discussion of the so-called "heathen mothers" and "bad mothers" of the British colonial imagination, Margaret Jolly describes how, across the Asia-Pacific region—particularly before missionary efforts were engineered to quash such communalism—"many become mothers not through pregnancy but through processes of adoption

and the labour of nurture." A maternal bond was conceptualized by colonists as a proprietary biogenetic tie sanctioned by God between no more than two people in each case (a mother and a baby). Because they had not learned this, "in several British colonies across the Pacific, mothers were ... singled out as a major cause of degeneration," racial decline, and population suicide. Margaret Jolly and Kalpana Ram, eds., *Maternities and Modernities*, Cambridge: Cambridge University Press, 1998, 2, 178.

26 Sandra Bamford and James Leach, eds., *Kinship and Beyond: The Genealogical Model Reconsidered*, New York, NY: Berghahn, 2009.

27 Marilyn Strathern, *The Gender of the Gift: Problems with Women and Problems with Society in Melanesia*, Berkeley: University of California Press, 1988, 316.

28 Heidi Verhoef, "'A Child Has Many Mothers': Views of Child Fostering in North-West Cameroon," *Childhood* 12: 3, 2005, 369–90.

29 Paul Bohannan, "Dyadic Dominance and Household Maintenance," in Francis Hsu, ed., *Kinship and Culture*, London, UK: Transaction, 2009 [1971], 59.

30 Out of the Woods, "Disaster Communism," *The Occupied Times*, October 23, 2014, theoccupiedtimes.org.

31 Initially in Ohio, prosecutors threatened Bresha Meadows with adult sentencing laws. Eventually Bresha submitted to a plea deal resulting in her incarceration for a year and a half, first in a juvenile facility, then a "treatment facility." See #FreeBresha.

32 Nancy Scheper-Hughes, *Death Without Weeping: The Violence of Everyday Life in Brazil*, Berkeley: University of California Press, 1992.

33 The doulas of the Ancient Song Doula collective in Brooklyn, New York, provide free and affordable care to pregnant people who are having abortions, miscarriages, surrogacy issues, or hospital- or home-births, whether they be citizens, undocumented, or in prison.

34 Gumbs et al., *Revolutionary Mothering*, 23.

35 Audre Lorde, "Eye to Eye: Black Women, Anger and Hatred," in *Sister Outsider: Essays and Speeches by Audre Lorde*, Berkeley, CA: The Crossing Press, 1984. Quoted by Alexis Pauline Gumbs as the title of her thesis.

36 Gumbs et al., *Revolutionary Mothering*, 79.

37 Alexis Gumbs, "Forget Hallmark: Why Mother's Day Is A Queer Left Black Left Feminist Thing," in *Revolutionary Mothering*, 120.

38 Ibid., 22.

39 Angela Davis, "Surrogates and Outcast Mothers: Racism and Reproductive Politics in the Nineties," in Joy James, ed., *The Angela Y. Davis Reader*, Malden, MA: Blackwell, 1998, 210–21.

40 Ibid, 212; Anita Allen, "The Black Surrogate Mother," *Harvard Black-letter*, no. 8, Spring 1991, 17–31.

41 Jeffner Allen, "Motherhood: The Annihilation of Women," in Rita Manning and Rene Trujillo, eds., *Social and Political Philosophy*, City, CA: Mayfield Press, 1993, 383.

42 Kahlil Gibran, *The Prophet*, ed., Suheil Bushrui, London, UK: One-world, 2012 [1923], 17.

43 Diane Ehrensaft, *Mommies, Daddies, Donors, Surrogates: Answering Tough Questions and Building Strong Families*, London, UK: Guilford Press, 2011.

44 It is Laura Briggs who alerts me to this (as with so many things), in *How All Politics Became Reproductive Politics*, 156.

45 Quoted by Alexis Pauline Gumbs in *Revolutionary Mothering*, 22.

46 Sigrid Vertommen, "Resistance Is Fertile: Sperm Smuggling and Birth Strikes for Reproductive Justice in Israel/Palestine," presentation at "Remaking Reproduction" conference, University of Cambridge, 27–29 June 2018.

47 Deboleena Roy, "Germline Ruptures: Methyl Isocyanate Gas and Transpositions of Life, Death and Matter in Bhopal," paper presented as part of the seminar panel Onto-Epistemological Entanglements at the Gender Research Institute at Dartmouth (Dartmouth University), May 9, 2016.

48 Yoshizawa, Rebecca, "Fetal-Maternal Intra-action: Politics of new Placental Biologies," *Body & Society* 22:3, 2016, 79–105.

49 Kajsa Ekman, "Being and Being Bought: An Interview with Kajsa Ekis Ekman," interview by Meghan Murphy, *Feminist Current*, January 20, 2014.

50 Kathleen Biddick, *The Shock of Medievalism*, Durham, NC: Duke University Press, 1998, 71.

51 Gilbert Meilaender, "The Fetus as Parasite and Mushroom: Judith Jarvis Thomson's Defense of Abortion," *The Linacre Quarterly*, 46: 2, 1979, 129, 133.

52 Mitchell Cowen Verter, "Undoing Patriarchy, Subverting Politics: Anarchism as a Practice of Care," in Chiara Bottici, Jacob Blumenfeld, and Simon Critchley, eds., *The Anarchist Turn*, London, UK: Pluto, 2013, 101–10, 104.

53 Patricia Piccinini, "Surrogate" (2005), "The Big Mother" (2005), and "Undivided" (2004), patriciapiccinini.net.

54 Donna Haraway, "Speculative Fabulations for Technoculture's Generations," *Australian Humanities Review* 50, 2011, 95–118, 116.

55 Ibid., 98. Quoted in The Laboratory for Aesthetics and Ecology (Labae) "M/OTHERS AND FUTURE HUMANS: A Traveling

Exhibition," The Multispecies Salon, multispecies-salon.org, March 26, 2018. Curators Ida Bencke, Eben Kirksey, Marnia Johnston, Nina Nichols, Karin Bolender, and Krista Dragomer write: "Fertility rates of black and brown bodies continue to be conceptualized as a threat within feminism, Sophie Lewis reminds us, even as critical geographers note ongoing genocidal patterns of mortality. At the cellular level, the maternal body challenges notions of individuality as feto-maternal microchimerism reveals the presence of cells from the fetus in the mother's body even decades after giving birth."

56 Kalindi Vora and Neda Atanasoski, *Surrogate Humanity: Race, Technology, Revolution*, Durham, NC: Duke University Press, forthcoming (2019).

57 Haraway, "Speculative Fabulations for Technoculture's Generations."

58 Ibid. (the phrase "multispecies reproductive justice").

59 Ibid.

60 Claire Horner, "My Child, Your Womb, Our Contract: The Failure of Contract Law to Protect Parties in Gestational Surrogacy," in Lisa Campo-Engelstein and Paul Burcher, eds., *Reproductive Ethics: New Challenges and Conversations*, Cham, Switzerland: Springer, 2017, 137–49, 141.

61 Shelley Park, *Mothering Queerly, Queering Motherhood: Resisting Monomaternalism in Adoptive, Lesbian, Blended, and Polygamous Families*, Albany: State University of New York Press, 2013.

62 Nancy Scheper-Hughes, "The Ends of the Body: Commodity Fetishism and the Global Traffic in Organs," *SAIS Review* 22: 1, 2002, 61–80, 77.

7. Amniotechnics

1 Democracy Now!, "Midwives at Dakota Access Resistance Camps: We Can Decolonize, Respect Women & Mother Earth," democracynow.org, October 18, 2016.

2 Changing Woman Initiative Blog, "Mni Wiconi Yaktan K'a Ni: Drink the Water of Life, and Live—Water Is Holy To Midwives," changingwomaninitiative.com, June 9, 2016.

3 Jason Robinson, Barbara Cosens, Sue Jackson, Kelsey Leonard, and Daniel McCool, "Indigenous Water Justice," *Lewis & Clark Law Review* 22:3, 2018, 873–953.

4 Astrida Neimanis, *Bodies of Water: Posthuman Feminist Phenomenology*, London, UK: Bloomsbury, 2017, 68–69.

5 Ibid., 39.

6 Ibid.

7 Lynn Margulis, *Symbiotic Planet: A New Look At Evolution*, New York: Basic Books, 1998.

8 "Amnion," Merriam-Webster.com, 2018, accessed October 14, 2018.

9 A. Al-Malt, "Premature Rupture of the Fetal Membranes," in Hung Winn and John Hobbins, eds., *Clinical Maternal-Fetal Medicine*, Boca Raton: CRC Press, 93.

10 Sylvia Plath, *The Unabridged Journals of Sylvia Plath (1957–1962)*, London, UK: Anchor, 2000, 495 (entry for Saturday, June 13, 1959).

11 See Hester's critique of Maria Mies: Helen Hester, *Xenofeminism*, London: Polity Press, 2017, 37–40.

12 Changing Woman Initiative Blog, "Mni Wiconi Yaktan K'a Ni: Drink the Water of Life, and Live—Water Is Holy To Midwives," unnumbered.

13 John Urry, *Global Complexity*, London: Polity Press, 2002.

14 Changing Woman Initiative Blog, "Mni Wiconi Yaktan K'a Ni: Drink the Water of Life, and Live—Water Is Holy To Midwives," unnumbered.

15 Frances Stonor Saunders, "Where on Earth Are You?" *London Review of Books* 38: 5, 2016.

16 For a discussion of an intervention made at a theater festival by Sally Hines of CRIBS International (Care for Refugee Interim Baby Shelter) see my article, "Less Population Talk, More Kin-making: On Manchester's B!RTH Festival," *Feminist Review*, 117, 2017, 193–199.

17 Kalindi Vora, "Re-imagining Reproduction: Unsettling Metaphors in the History of Imperial Science and Commercial Surrogacy in India," *Somatechnics* 5: 1, 2015, 88–103, 96.

18 Sonja von Wichelen, "Postgenomics and Biolegitimacy: Legitimation Work in Transnational Surrogacy," *Australian Feminist Studies* 31: 88, 2016, 172–86.

Index